# AILA Review

## Applied Cognitive Linguistics in Second Language Learning and Teaching

VOLUME 23    2010

John Benjamins Publishing Company
Amsterdam/Philadelphia

# Table of contents

# Introduction to the interplay between cognitive linguistics and second language learning and teaching

Jeannette Littlemore and Constanze Juchem-Grundmann
University of Birmingham / University of Koblenz-Landau

Cognitive linguistics is a relatively new discipline comprising a number of related theories, all of which assume that:

-   language is not an autonomous cognitive faculty
-   knowledge of language emerges from language use
-   language is a product of physical interaction with the world

Cognitive linguists believe that there is no special-purpose device in the mind that is responsible for language, but instead that the cognitive processes governing the learning and processing of language are identical to those involved in the learning and processing of information more generally.

The basic idea in cognitive linguistics, concerning both first and second language learning, is that knowledge of language is acquired through *use*. That is to say, through exposure to language in context, people are able to identify patterns, correspondences and relationships within the language system. They then use this knowledge to develop hypotheses about the language system which can be tested in authentic communicative contexts. Through this testing process, knowledge of the language system is broadened and deepened. In this respect, cognitive linguistic views of first and second language learning are not dissimilar to traditional theories concerning the roles of input, interaction and output (Gallaway & Richards 1994; Gass 1997; Gass & Mackey 2006). What cognitive linguistics adds is a detailed description of the cognitive processes that are at work in language and thought enabling people to extract language knowledge from language use. Cognitive linguistics also accords with current thinking in the SLA literature in that it treats both language and language learning as emergent dynamic systems (Ellis 2006a).

Although cognitive linguistics has the potential to make a significant contribution to our understanding of the second language learning process, it is a very new area and its implications are only just beginning to be explored. Some findings from cognitive linguistics lend further support to existing language teaching methodologies, whereas others have led to intriguing suggestions for alternative ways of presenting aspects of the lexis-grammar continuum in the language classroom. Moreover, cognitive linguistics offers some compelling explanations for the frequently perceived mismatch between what teachers have 'taught' and what learners have 'learned'. It may therefore be useful for language teaching practicioners and researchers to have some knowledge of cognitive linguistics, as its findings impact upon current theories of second language teaching and learning. In this introduction, we briefly assess how work in cognitive linguistics relates to current ideas on

*AILA Review* 23 (2010), 1–6.  DOI 10.1075/aila.23.01lit
ISSN 1461–0213 / E-ISSN 1570–5595 © John Benjamins Publishing Company

second language learning and teaching, and consider the impact that it might have on the way languages can be taught. We consider five key processes that are thought by cognitive linguists to be involved in extracting language knowledge from language use. We briefly discuss some of the implications they have for second language learning and teaching. These themes are then developed in more depth in the remaining papers in the volume.

The first process, **construal**, refers to the fact that we can perceive objects from different angles and in different ways. Language parallels this process in that it can be used to highlight different aspects of the same phenomenon. We can only witness phenomena through human eyes and from a human perspective. While there may be default ways of describing situations, there is no completely neutral way of describing them. As perspective is never neutral, the language we use is never neutral; rather, it reflects certain ways of viewing things. For example, in order to get to Austria from Belgium, we might drive *across* Germany or we might drive *through* Germany. Both describe the same event, but driving *through* Germany focuses attention on the journey itself, whereas driving *across* Germany focuses attention on the final destination. Language, therefore, is never 'objective'. Even if we try to present a piece of information as objectively as possible, the particular language that we speak will encode particular ways of conventionally construing events, which may differ from the way in which they are construed in other languages. In this respect one language can be no more or less 'logical' than another. Languages are simply different.

For instance, languages have been found to vary in terms of how they describe manner of motion (Talmy 1985; Slobin 1996). In 'satellite-framed' languages, such as English, the manner is encoded in the verb, so we can *crawl* along a tunnel, *slide* out of a hole, or *creep* round a haunted house. In 'verb-framed' languages, such as Spanish, the focus is more on the direction of movement and the manner is mentioned later. So a Spanish person would be more likely to 'move along the tunnel in a crawling manner' or 'leave the hole in a sliding manner'. Slobin (2000) found that, when asked to recount a story that they have recently heard, speakers of satellite-framed languages tend to be more interested in the manner of movement, whereas speakers of verb-framed languages are more interested in the direction. This has implications for language teaching. It may explain why Spanish-speaking students of English experience considerable difficulty with manner of movement verbs in English, particularly in the early stages of learning when the second language is still kind of 'piggy-backing' on the first (Ramirez 2006; Littlemore 2009). The reason for this may be that they are used to the Spanish way of 'construing' the event and that they find it difficult to overcome this L1 construal pattern. In other words, different world views are embedded in different languages, which means that learners may develop 'cognitive habits' (Hunt & Agnoli 1991) as a result of having acquired their first language, which may need to be broken, or at least brought to the learner's attention, in order to facilitate the learning of a second language. When they want to express thoughts in a new language they may need to repackage them in a slightly different way. This phenomenon is encapsulated by Slobin's (1997) 'thinking for speaking' hypothesis, which is discussed by Alejo Gonzalez in this volume.

The second process, **the construction of categories**, relates to how we divide up our knowledge of the world around us. As children acquire language conceptual knowledge through use, they form flexible categories in order to explain relationships between the different phenomena that they encounter. Languages vary in terms of the way they categorise things and the categorisation patterns that we learn in our first language can become **entrenched**, and as such are often very hard to overcome. This can make categorisation a significant area of difficulty for second language learners.

Categories tend to be **radial** and subject to **prototype effects**. In other words, they tend to have more or less prototypical members and the borders between them tend to be 'fuzzy'. For example, in the category of 'building', 'a house' might be seen by many as being the most representative (or 'prototypical'). Other types of building such as sheds and bridges are somewhat less prototypical and may even be seen as belonging to different categories (such as 'garden furniture' or 'infrastructure'), a fact which illustrates the fuzzy nature of the boundaries between categories.

Our knowledge of word senses is also thought to operate within radial categories, which are referred to as **radial semantic networks**. These networks are associated with particular words, and are structured around 'core' or 'basic' senses. For example, the word *over* in 'I looked over the fence and it was amazing' (BofE) is more 'core' than the word *over* in 'Audrey and Richard's friendship is raked over by gossip mongerers' (BofE). According to cognitive linguists, radial semantic networks underlie a great deal of polysemy. In cognitive linguistics, the senses of individual words constitute radial categories, with the most basic senses in the centre, and more figurative senses radiating out towards the margins. Knowledge of the radial nature of categories tends to be implicit and cannot easily be captured by explicit grammar rules: a fact that is of potential importance in second language teaching. The role of radial categories and implicit knowledge in second language learning is explored in depth by Roehr in this volume.

The fact that abstract senses of words are related to their more literal uses is sometimes referred to by cognitive linguists as **linguistic motivation**. Indeed, one of the most significant contributions that cognitive linguistics has made to second language teaching is that it offers explanations for certain form-form, form-meaning, meaning-meaning relationships in language (Boers & Lindstromberg 2006). Discussing the reasons why certain words are used in certain situations has the potential to remove the arbitrariness from language teaching and is potentially more effective than a reliance on rote memorisation, or simply being told by a teacher that 'that's just the way it is'. The pedagogical effectiveness of such an approach is discussed and measured in three of the papers in this volume (Deconinck et al., Llopis-García, Tyler et al.).

Extending the processes of motivation language and category formation still further, the third process involved in language learning is the identification of **constructions** and the relationships between them. In her work on **Construction Grammar**, Goldberg (1995, 2006) has shown how individual words group together to form 'constructions' that have meanings of their own. These meanings relate to everyday experience and exist in radial categories. For example, the 'resultative construction' has core exemplars (she was shaking her hands dry when the ring flew off) (BofE). and more peripheral examples ('he drank himself to death') (BofE). These sentences have an overarching meaning which is conveyed as much by the grammar as by the lexis. Cognitive linguistics thus accords with corpus linguistics regarding the inseparability of grammar and lexis. In first language learning, knowledge of constructions is acquired through pattern-finding and intention-reading skills. In other words, by predicting what it is that the other person is likely to be telling or asking them, and then mapping the language that they hear onto this prediction, children learn to associate particular expressions with particular meanings (Tomasello 2003). For example, if, when offering a child something to eat, a carer always uses the words 'Would you like a ....?', the child will eventually start to associate this expression with the fact that they are being offered something. Through a process of **contingency learning** (Ellis 2006b) from an early age onwards children gradually learn to associate certain words with certain constructions, and the use of a particular word will automatically trigger their expectations for a certain construction, and vice versa. In the context of second language learning, students are often given opportunities to use these skills but it is important to note that the kind of linguistic input received by children learning their first language is very different from that received by adults learning their second language. Two of the papers in this volume (Holme and Roehr) examine the types of input that second language learners are exposed to, and try to assess whether or not input provides sufficient opportunities for learners to acquire target language constructions.

The fourth process involved in language learning, **metaphor**, refers to our ability to see one thing in terms of another. We use it to understand new or novel phenomena in terms of what we already know and understand, which is why many abstract concepts are described in terms of more concrete, tangible phenomena. Metaphoric thinking can be viewed as an online dynamic cognitive process, which leaves its traces in language. Languages vary in terms of the metaphors that have become conventional. For example, Boers & Demecheleer (1995) found that English contains more metaphorical idioms based on the domains of hats and shipping, whereas French contains more metaphorical idioms based on food. These differences may be accounted for, at least in part, by historical and cultural factors. The fifth process, **metonymy**, refers to our use of one thing to refer to another closely related concept. Like metaphor we use metonymic thinking to make links between what we can see directly (or what is being directly referred to in language), and a broader scene or set of events. In non-linguistic metonymy, a photograph of a part of a building with which we are familiar may trigger a mental picture of the whole building or indeed of the whole street. Linguistic metonymy is exemplified by expressions such as 'Number Ten has declared there will be no whitewash' (BofE), where 'number ten' refers metonymically to the Prime Minister and his or her associates. Metonymy provides a mental shorthand, which like metaphor leaves strong traces in language. Although languages vary in the ways in which they employ both metaphor and metonymy, there is a considerable amount of overlap too. Metaphoric and metonymic thinking are likely to constitute important second language learning processes allowing learners to understand metaphors and metonymies that are novel to them, as well as allowing them to use the target language creatively (Littlemore & Low 2006; Juchem-Grundmann 2009). Two of the papers in this volume (Barcelona and MacArthur) deal with metaphor and metonymy in second language learning.

The papers in this volume discuss the various ways in which these processes relate to second language learning and teaching. Some of the papers have a more theoretical focus but provide valuable examples from student data; others describe empirical studies of the effectiveness of cognitive linguistics-inspired approaches to language teaching.

The first paper in the volume, by Roehr, focuses on language representation in the mind, applying a cognitive linguistics categories approach. She argues that cognitive linguistic work on categorisation provides a better description of the way in which implicit linguistic knowledge is stored in the mind than more conventional views of categorization. Implicit knowledge of target language grammar and vocabulary is likely to involve categories that are more flexible and radial than explicit knowledge of grammar rules. Roehr looks at the implications of these two ways of constructing knowledge for the teaching and learning of grammar in a second language.

The next five papers all focus in one way or another on motivated language in SLA. Tyler et al. present experimental work on the use of cognitive linguistic ideas on linguistic motivation and metaphoric thinking to teach modal verbs in English. Alejo provides a comprehensive review of the work on the motivated form-meaning connections in the teaching of phrasal verbs and in this context takes a critical look at the role of construal and the thinking-for-speaking hypothesis in second language learning. In a similar vein, Llopis-García draws on the idea that language is a symbolic representation of the speaker's mental model of the world and applies this to the teaching of mood-selection in Spanish. She also presents empirical data elicited in the foreign language classroom. Deconinck, Boers and Eyckmans study the benefits of asking learners to reflect on the potentially motivated nature of the connections between word form and word meaning and find mixed, yet positive results. Remaining in the area of motivated language, Holme discusses implications that recent work on motivation and construction grammars has for the way we teach the lexis-grammar continuum. He argues that some approaches to grammar teaching need to be further developed in order to benefit from cognitive linguistic findings, whereas other pedagogical methods already appear to correspond to insights arising from research in cognitive linguistics.

The final two papers focus on metonymy and metaphor. Barcelona takes a theoretical perspective in his discussion of the role of metonymy in pragmatic inferencing and the implications that this has for second language teaching. MacArthur takes a more practical approach, investigating metaphoric competence in Spanish learners of English. She discusses how explicit guidance, focusing on key notions such as 'metaphor', 'figurative use' and 'figurative extension', can lead to rapid development in vocabulary use in the course of an academic year.

The papers in this volume all examine potential benefits of applying cognitive linguistic theories to second language teaching. What emerges from all of these papers is a growing awareness of the complex dynamic systems that are at work on every level in second language teaching and learning. Approaches to language teaching that are inspired by cognitive linguistic theories often have significant and positive impacts on the language learning process, but they need to be considered within the wider process of learning in general, and the social settings within which it occurs.

## References

Boers, F. & Demecheleer, M. 1995. Travellers, patients and warriors in English, Dutch and French economic discourse. *Revue Belge de Philosophie et d'Histore* 73: 673–691.

Boers, F. & Lindstromberg, S. 2006. Cognitive linguistic applications in second or foreign language instruction: Rationale, proposals and evaluation. In *Cognitive Linguistics: Current Applications and Future Perspectives*, G. Kristiansen, M. Achard, R. Dirven & F.J Ruiz de Mendoza (eds), 305–55. Berlin: Mouton de Gruyter.

Ellis, N. 2006a. Cognitive perspectives on SLA: The associative-cognitive creed. *AILA Review* 19: 100–121.

Ellis, N. 2006b. Language acquisition as rational contingency learning. *Applied Linguistics* 27(1): 1–24

Evans, V. & Green, M. 2006. *Cognitive Linguistics: An Introduction*. Edinburgh: EUP.

Gallaway, C. & Richards, B.J. 1994. *Input and Interaction in Language Acquisition*. Cambridge: CUP.

Gass, S. 1997. *Input, Interaction, and the Second Language Learner: Second Language Acquisition Research: Theoretical & Methodological Issues*. London: Routledge.

Gass, S. & Mackey, A. 2006. Input, interaction and output: An overview. *AILA Review* 19: 3–17.

Goldberg, A. 1995. *A Construction Grammar Approach to Argument Structure*. Chicago IL: University of Chicago Press.

Goldberg, A. 2006. *Constructions at Work: The Nature of Generalization in Language*. Oxford: OUP.

Hunt, E. & Agnoli, F. 1991. The Whorfian hypothesis: A cognitive psychology perspective. *Psychological Review* 98: 377–89.

Juchem-Grundmann, C. 2009. "Dip into your saving!" Applying Cognitive Metaphor Theory in the Business English Classroom. An Empirical Study. PhD dissertation, University of Koblenz-Landau. Online: OPUS-Server University of Koblenz: "urn:nbn:de:hbz:kob7–4749".

Lazar, G. 2003. *Meanings and Metaphors*. Cambridge: CUP.

Lee, D. 2001. *Cognitive Linguistics: An Introduction*. Oxford: OUP.

Littlemore, J. 2009. *Applying Cognitive Linguistics to Second Language Learning and Teaching*. Basingstoke: Palgrave MacMillan.

Littlemore, J. & Low, G. 2006. *Figurative Thinking and Foreign Language Learning*. Basingstoke: Palgrave MacMillan.

Ramirez, L. 2006. Manner of Movement Verb. MA dissertation, University of Birmingham.

Slobin, D.I. 1996. Two ways to travel: Verbs of motion in English and Spanish. In *Grammatical Constructions: Their Form and Meaning*, M. Shibatani & S. A. Thompson (eds), 195–220. Oxford: Clarendon Press.

Slobin, D.I. 1997. Mind, code, and text. In *Essays on Language Function and Language Type: Dedicated to T. Givón*. J. Bybee, J. Haiman & S.A. Thompson (eds), 437–467. Amsterdam: John Benjamins.

Slobin, D.I. 2000. Verbalized events. A dynamic approach to linguistic relativity and determinism. In *Evidence for Linguistic Relativity*, S. Niemeier & R. Dirven (eds), 108–38. Amsterdam: John Benjamins.

Talmy, L. 1985. Lexicalization patterns: semantic structure in lexical forms. In *Language Typology and Syntactic Description*. T. Shopen (ed.), 36–149. Cambridge: CUP.

Tomasello, M. 2003. *Constructing a Language. A Usage-based Theory of Language Acquisition*. Cambridge MA: Harvard University Press.

*Authors' addresses*

Jeannette Littlemore
Centre for English Language Studies
Westmere
School of English, Drama, American and Canadian
Studies
University of Birmingham
Birmingham, UK

j.m.littlemore@bham.ac.uk

Constanze Juchem-Grundmann
English Department
University of Koblenz-Landau
Campus Koblenz
Universitätsstraße 1
56070 Koblenz, Germany

cjuchem@uni-koblenz.de

# Explicit knowledge and learning in SLA

## A cognitive linguistics perspective

Karen Roehr
University of Essex

SLA researchers agree that explicit knowledge and learning play an important role in adult L2 development. In the field of cognitive linguistics, it has been proposed that implicit and explicit knowledge differ in terms of their internal category structure and the processing mechanisms that operate on their representation in the human mind. It has been hypothesized that linguistic constructions which are captured easily by metalinguistic descriptions can be learned successfully through explicit processes, resulting in accurate use. However, increased accuracy of use arising from greater reliance on explicit processing may lead to decreased fluency. Taking these hypotheses as a starting point, I present a case study of an adult L2 learner whose development of oral proficiency was tracked over 17 months. Findings indicate that explicit knowledge and learning have benefits as well as limitations. Use of metalinguistic tools was associated with increased accuracy; moreover, there was no obvious trade-off between accuracy and fluency. At the same time, resource-intensive explicit processing may impose too great a cognitive load in certain circumstances, apparently resulting in implicit processes taking over. I conclude that explicit and implicit knowledge and learning should be considered together in order to gain a full understanding of L2 development.

## Introduction

The first decade of the 21st century has seen a number of publications concerned with applications of cognitive linguistics to second language (L2) learning and teaching (e.g. Achard & Niemeier 2004; Boers & Lindstromberg 2006; Robinson & N. Ellis 2008), thus establishing this theoretical approach as a framework for second language acquisition (SLA) research. In the field of SLA, the role of explicit knowledge and learning is an important area of investigation that has received much attention from researchers and practitioners alike (DeKeyser 2003; Dörnyei 2009; Doughty 2003; Norris & Ortega 2001). Up to now, the role of explicit knowledge in L2 learning and teaching has scarcely been considered from a cognitive linguistics perspective, however. In order to address this gap, I put forward a theoretically informed research agenda (Roehr 2008). The present paper begins with a brief up-to-date review of the theoretical analysis detailed in that article. I then offer two hypotheses arising out of the theoretical argumentation. The remainder of the present paper deals with an empirical study whose findings speak to these hypotheses.

*AILA Review* 23 (2010), 7–29. DOI 10.1075/aila.23.02roe
ISSN 1461–0213 / E-ISSN 1570–5595 © John Benjamins Publishing Company

## Theoretical background: Explicit and implicit knowledge and learning from a cognitive linguistics perspective

Explicit knowledge is defined as knowledge that is represented declaratively, can be brought into awareness and can be verbalized, while implicit knowledge is defined as knowledge that cannot be brought into awareness and cannot be articulated (Anderson 2005; R. Ellis 2004; Hulstijn 2005). Accordingly, explicit learning refers to situations "when the learner has online awareness, formulating and testing conscious hypotheses in the course of learning". Conversely, implicit learning "describes when learning takes place without these processes; it is an unconscious process of induction resulting in intuitive knowledge that exceeds what can be expressed by learners" (N. Ellis 1994: 38–39).

Explicit and implicit knowledge and learning are separable and distinct; at the same time, they are thought to be engaged in interplay, so one can influence the other (N. Ellis 1993; R. Ellis 2005; Segalowitz 2003). This point is crucial when considering explicit knowledge and learning in the context of SLA. During fluent language use, we draw on implicit processes, and our attention is focused on meaning rather than form. When comprehension or production difficulties arise, however, explicit processes take over (N. Ellis 2005). We then deliberately focus our attention on language form, and we make conscious efforts to analyze input or to construct or monitor output, utilizing internal or external resources.

Considered from a cognitive linguistics perspective, language can be understood as essentially functional and usage-based (e.g., Bybee & McClelland 2005; Evans & Green 2006; Goldberg 2003). The key assumptions which are common to most if not all approaches under the umbrella term of cognitive linguistics are that interpersonal communication is the main purpose of language, that language is shaped by our experience with the real world, that language ability is an integral part of general cognition, and that linguistic phenomena can be explained by a unitary account embracing the traditional domains of morphology, syntax, semantics, and pragmatics.

Language as represented in the human mind can be understood as "a structured inventory of conventional linguistic units" (Langacker 2000: 8). Conventional linguistic units, or constructions, are seen as inherently symbolic (Kemmer & Barlow 2000; Taylor 2002), so all constructions are pairings or associations of form and meaning (Goldberg 2003). These key assumptions about language refer to implicit linguistic knowledge and are complemented by a usage-based approach to language learning which refers to implicit processes of acquisition and use.

Cognitive linguists explain language learning and use in terms of entrenchment and categorization. Entrenchment can be understood as the strengthening of memory traces through repeated activation. Categorization refers to seeing sameness in diversity (Taylor 1998, 2003) or, more technically, to a comparison between an established structural unit functioning as a standard and an initially novel target structure (Langacker 2000).

In view of strong evidence from the field of cognitive psychology (Murphy 2004; Rosch 1978; Rosch & Mervis 1975), it is widely accepted that cognitive categories are subject to prototype effects. Categorization is influenced by the frequency of exemplars in the input as well as the recency and context of encounters with specific exemplars (N. Ellis 2002a, 2002b); memory traces can be more or less entrenched and thus more or less available for retrieval (Murphy 2004). By the same token, category members are potentially more or less prototypical, category membership may be a matter of degree, and category boundaries may be fuzzy (Langacker 2000).

In a usage-based approach, all learning is initially exemplar-based (Abbot-Smith & Tomasello 2006; Langacker 2000). In other words, learning begins with the entrenchment of specific instances encountered in the input. After prolonged experience and a proportionately greater number of repeated encounters with certain exemplars, our mental representations gradually change: Abstractions over instances are derived, that is, schemas are formed (Kemmer & Barlow 2000; Taylor

2002; Tomasello 2003). Schema formation can be defined as "the emergence of a structure through reinforcement of the commonality inherent in multiple experiences", so a schema is "the commonality that emerges from distinct structures when one abstracts away from their points of difference by portraying them with lesser precision and specificity" (Langacker 2000: 4). Schemas can facilitate further learning, since they allow for more efficient categorization of newly encountered exemplars.

In a usage-based account, representations of specific exemplars may be retained alongside more general schemas, so the same linguistic construction may be represented at different levels of abstraction. This results in a complex, hierarchical, redundantly organized network of form-meaning associations which represent our implicit knowledge of linguistic constructions.

Implicit knowledge is subject to similarity-based processing, which is flexible, dynamic, open, and susceptible to contextual variation (Diesendruck 2005; Markman et al. 2005). In similarity-based processing, a large number of an entity's properties can be taken into account; moreover, a partial match with the properties of existing representations is sufficient to allow for successful categorization (Pothos 2005).

To exemplify the theoretical line of argument, consider the acquisition of verbs in L1 English. The learner begins by learning specific exemplars of verbs they encounter in the input, e.g., *eat, sleep, put*. These early, frequent verbs are represented as specific constructions. At the same time, the learner implicitly tracks the distributional properties of words like *eat, sleep,* and *put* (Tomasello 2003, 2005). Gradually, commonalities in both form and function become apparent, e.g., position in the sentence, combination with certain inflectional morphemes (e.g., *-s*), predicative syntactic role, profiling of a process or, expressed more formally, "a relationship mentally scanned sequentially — instant by instant — in its evolution through time" (Langacker 1998: 19). This allows the learner to eventually abstract away from specific exemplars and form the schema VERB. Once this schema is available, new members can be assigned to the category. Importantly, however, frequency and context are taken into account, and prototype effects are in evidence. For instance, *eat* and *put* are likely to be central members of the category VERB, while *quarry* and *constitute* are likely to be more marginal members. Not only are they less frequent, but they can also be used as nouns (*quarry*) or are distant from the prototypical meaning of a verb as a process (*constitute*).

To summarize, implicit knowledge is characterized by flexible and context-dependent category structure which is subject to prototype effects. By the same token, implicit processing is similarity-based, flexible, and susceptible to contextual variation. Implicit learning is primarily exemplar-based or bottom-up.

Explicit language knowledge and learning can be contrasted with implicit language knowledge and learning in terms of both representation and processing. Explicit knowledge appears to be characterized by stable, discrete, and context-independent categories with clear boundaries, i.e., by what has been labelled Aristotelian category structure (Anderson 2005; Taylor 2003; Ungerer & Schmid 1996). Aristotelian categories do not take prototype effects into account; instead, all category members have equal status, regardless of frequency, recency of encounter, or context.

Explicit knowledge is subject to rule-based processing. Rule-based processing is conscious (Cleeremans & Destrebecqz 2005; Hampton 2005; Smith 2005), and it is characterized by compositionality, systematicity, commitment, and consistency (Diesendruck 2005; Pothos 2005; Sloman 2005). Compositionality refers to the fact that simpler components can be combined to form more complex representations without changing the meaning of the component parts. Systematicity means that a process or operation is applied in the same way to different classes of entities (Pothos 2005). Rule-based processing entails commitment to specific kinds of information, while contextual variations are neglected. A strict match between the properties of an exemplar and the properties specified in the rule that is being applied has to be achieved (Diesendruck 2005; Pothos 2005). Accordingly, rule-based, explicit learning is always top-down.

Explicit knowledge consists of either a schematic category or a relation between two categories, specific or schematic. Such a relation is expressed by means of a proposition, i.e., a rule. In SLA, explicit knowledge is typically drawn on when classroom instruction or self-study activities rely on metalinguistic descriptions which appear in the form of pedagogical grammar rules in language textbooks.

To exemplify with reference to L2 German, a metalinguistic description may state that 'in a subordinate clause, the verb needs to be placed at the end'. This rule takes the form of a proposition which expresses a relationship between two schematic categories, 'subordinate clause' and 'verb'. In order to apply this rule, the learner needs to make clear-cut decisions as to whether a certain multi-word construction is a subordinate clause and as to whether a certain word is a verb. Unless such a decision is taken, the rule is of little use. Accordingly, the explicit category 'verb' needs to be Aristotelian. In the simplest terms of pedagogical grammar, 'a verb is a doing-word'.

This rule captures the more prototypical members of the cognitive category VERB such as *essen* (*eat*) and *gehen* (*go*). In order to capture more marginal members such as *darstellen* (*constitute*), more detailed rules are required, e.g., 'a verb is a content word that denotes an action, occurrence, or state of existence' and 'a verb is the word class that serves as the predicate of a sentence' (http://wordnetweb.princeton.edu/perl/webwn?s=verb, retrieved 19/02/10). These rules consist of further propositions specifying categories and relations between categories; they capture the cognitive category VERB more fully, but at the same time are more complex than the initial simple rule.

As rule-based processing is controlled, conscious processing (Cleeremans & Destrebecqz 2005; Hampton 2005; Smith 2005) which draws on limited working memory capacity (Baddeley 2000; Baddeley & Logie 1999; Just & Carpenter 1992), it is costly in terms of resources. Put differently, the more complex the rule, the more difficult it is for the learner to process and utilize it.

At least two hypotheses about explicit knowledge and learning in SLA arise out of the theoretical line of argument which I have briefly reviewed above.

*Hypothesis 1*
A linguistic construction which can be captured relatively easily by an Aristotelian rule will be acquired faster and used more accurately if the learner draws on explicit knowledge than a linguistic construction which cannot easily be captured by an Aristotelian rule. Given the costliness of explicit processing, a rule that is high in schematicity, low in conceptual complexity, low in technicality of metalanguage, and high in truth value will be most favourable (DeKeyser 2005; R. Ellis 2006; Roehr & Gánem-Gutiérrez 2009). Schematicity refers to whether a rule concerns a schematic or a specific linguistic construction. A rule is low in conceptual complexity if it consists of few Aristotelian categories and relations between categories. Technicality of metalanguage refers to the relative familiarity and abstractness of the metalanguage used to formulate the rule. A rule is high in truth value if it applies without exception.

*Hypothesis 2*
A language learner's overall performance will be affected by reliance on explicit knowledge and learning. On the one hand, explicit knowledge and learning will help the learner use linguistic constructions captured by Aristotelian rules successfully. On the other hand, the costliness of explicit processing will slow down their language use. Thus, explicit knowledge and learning will be associated with increased accuracy and/or complexity of language on the one hand and decreased fluency on the other hand.

**Empirical evidence: A case study of an adult L2 learner**
In what follows, I present empirical evidence from a case study of an adult L2 learner which speaks to the hypotheses above.

*Research design*
The evidence presented is based on a case study of an individual adult learner of L2 German. The study had a longitudinal design, with data collected on 56 occasions over a period of 17 months. The resulting data set consisted of 56 recordings of learner-tutor interactions, which were subsequently transcribed and analyzed using the CHILDES tools (see next section for details). The tutor is the researcher; the learner is an L1 English male in his forties who will be referred to as H.

From 1977 to 1980, the participant learned German at school. In 1978, he additionally learned some French. Moreover, when his family was residing in Saudi Arabia from 1974 to 1976, H acquired basic Arabic in an immersion setting. He used neither of these languages after exposure had ended. H recommenced his learning of German in July 2006, i.e., about 25 years after encountering the language at school. Learning took place in the context of one-to-one classes. Normally, a class was held once a week and lasted from 60 to 120 minutes. Teaching and learning activities targeted all four skills, with a particular emphasis on oral communication, grammar, and reading. Focus on form was a regular feature both in class and in self-study activities.

From July 2006 to March 2007, the learner's core textbook was *Willkommen!* (Coggle & Schenke 1998), a general-purpose beginners' course for adult learners often used in evening classes and other non-specialist language courses. From March 2007 onwards, the *Passwort Deutsch* series (Albrecht et al. 2001; Albrecht et al. 2002) was used, starting with volume 2. This is a more academically oriented course which is normally employed in language classes at university level. All textbooks are accompanied by CDs and offer practice in all four skills; moreover, they contain form-focused exercises and metalinguistic descriptions in the form of pedagogical grammar rules.

In addition to exercises from the core textbooks, H used self-study material such as listening exercises from the *Hören Sie mal!* series (Hümmler-Hille & von Jan 1993, 1999) and stories from the *Easy Reader* series of edited and/or shortened works of literature for L2 learners (European Schoolbooks Publishing Ltd). According to H's own estimate, he spent an average of about two hours per week on self-study. In the course of the data collection period, H had naturalistic exposure to the L2 on two occasions during holidays in German-speaking countries lasting about ten days each.

Data collection began in February 2007 and ended in June 2008. During this period, a specific section of each of H's German classes was audio-recorded. This section always dealt with the same task, that is, the participant was asked to recount what he did the day before. This resulted in a learner-tutor dialogue in which the learner was expected to take a leading role and the tutor a supporting role, prompting with questions or comments, responding to learner requests for input, and offering implicit or explicit feedback on the learner's oral L2 performance, as required. Based on the resulting 56 audio-recordings of learner-tutor interactions, four research questions were addressed:

RQ1: How does the learner's oral L2 proficiency develop over time in terms of accuracy, complexity, and fluency?

RQ2: How does the learner's overt use of metalinguistic tools develop over time?

RQ3: What is the relationship between measures of oral L2 proficiency and overt use of metalinguistic tools?

RQ4: How does the learner's accuracy develop over time with regard to a selected linguistic construction which can be captured by a rule that is high in schematicity, low in conceptual complexity, low in technicality of metalanguage, and high in truth value?

The answer to RQ4 provides evidence that is relevant to the first hypothesis put forward above.[1] The answer to RQ3 speaks to the second hypothesis. RQ1 and RQ2 are included to prepare the ground for RQ3, since, to the best of my knowledge, there is no existing research which has tracked the development of oral L2 proficiency in conjunction with overt use of metalinguistic tools in an L2 learner over as long a period of time as covered in the present study.

*Construct definitions, operationalization, and data analysis*
The 56 audio-recordings which constitute the data set had a mean length of approximately 14 minutes each; the entire data set comprised 13 hours and 25 minutes of dialogue. All recordings were transcribed into CHAT format, the transcription system which allows for use of the CHILDES analysis programme CLAN (see http://childes.psy.cmu.edu/ for details). The resulting corpus of 56 transcripts was coded to facilitate quantitative analysis as well as qualitative analysis of selected sections. The constructs of interest were oral L2 proficiency, overt use of metalinguistic tools, and use of a selected linguistic construction which can be captured b ' an Aristotelian rule.

**Oral L2 proficiency**. Oral L2 proficiency was defined as the accuracy, complexity, and fluency[2] of the participant's productions.

Accuracy refers to "the ability to produce error-free speech" (Housen & Kuiken 2009: 461). Error-free speech was measured by calculating the number of errors per 100 words (R. Ellis & Barkhuizen 2005). A target-like use (TLU) measure was employed; this measure takes into account learner errors produced in both non-obligatory and obligatory contexts (Gass & Selinker 2008; Iwashita et al. 2008), so both overgeneralization errors and errors of omission are included. Lexical, morphosyntactic, and pragmatic errors were counted in order to arrive at a global accuracy measure. Lexical errors were operationalized as the semantically inappropriate choice of a word/words or a missing word/words at sentence level. Morphosyntactic errors were operationalized as sentence-level errors relating to morphology or syntax. Pragmatic errors were operationalized as discourse-level errors or use of constructions that were semantically and morphosyntactically correct at sentence level, but clearly indicative of non-nativelike selection. Examples can be found in the Appendix.

Complexity refers to the extent to which language is elaborate and varied (Housen & Kuiken 2009). Measures of lexical and morphosyntactic complexity were computed. Lexical complexity was operationalized as type-token ratio (Eskildsen 2009) of the first 50 utterances in a transcript. The number of utterances was held constant in order to avoid any effect of sample length (R. Ellis & Barkhuizen 2005; Larsen-Freeman 2006). Morphosyntactic complexity was defined as amount of subordination, which was operationalized as the total number of separate clauses divided by the total number of c-units; c-units are any utterances providing referential or pragmatic meaning (R. Ellis & Barkhuizen 2005: 155).

Fluency refers to the speed and ease with which linguistic representations are accessed in order to communicate meanings in real time (Housen & Kuiken 2009). In the present study, fluency was operationalized as the participant's contribution to the L2 interaction, measured in number of L2 words produced per minute of a recorded session.

**Overt use of metalinguistic tools**. Use of metalinguistic tools refers to the use of explicit knowledge about language and occurs during explicit learning. Explicit knowledge about language is characterized by conscious awareness, and it includes knowledge of pedagogical grammar rules (R. Ellis 2004; Roehr 2008). In the present study, overt use of metalinguistic tools was operationalized as episodes of learner requests for input per 100 words and episodes of learner acknowledgement of tutor input per 100 words.

Learner requests for input were a combined measure of requests for L2 input and requests for metalinguistic input. Learner requests for L2 input included explicit questions about how to express a meaning in the L2, the coining of words which was interpreted as an implicit question about how to a express a meaning in the L2, and explicit requests for repetition of tutor utterances. Requests for metalinguistic input included learner requests for explanation or clarification of L2 lexis or morphosyntax as well as explicit or implicit requests for feedback. Explicit requests for feedback were direct questions such as "Is this right?", while implicit requests for feedback were utterances in statement form, including incomplete utterances, which ended with a rising intonation.

Learner acknowledgement of tutor input was a combined measure of general acknowledgements of tutor input ("right", "yes", "mmhm", etc.) and specific acknowledgements which took the form of verbatim repetition or rehearsal of tutor input. In order to contextualize learner acknowledgements, episodes of tutor input per 100 words were taken into account. Tutor input was a combined measure of input of L2 utterances in response to a learner request, implicit feedback on learner performance in the form of recasts (Egi 2007), and explicit feedback on learner performance or responses to learner questions in the form of metalinguistic comments or explanations.

**Selected linguistic construction: Subject-verb agreement.** The linguistic construction selected as a focus point is subject-verb agreement. This construction was chosen because it can be captured easily by an Aristotelian rule that is high in schematicity, low in conceptual complexity, low in technicality of metalanguage, and high in truth value. Moreover, this construction was very frequent in the learner's speech, enabling robust and meaningful quantitative analysis.

German language textbooks make learners aware that German verb "endings change according to the subject used" (Coggle & Schenke 1998: 20), thus providing a pedagogical grammar rule. The inflectional paradigm of German verbs is typically presented in table format rather than in the form of rule-like propositions. Nonetheless, it is of course possible to formulate rules describing these inflectional paradigms. Such rules would consist of a number of simple propositions, e.g., 'In the first person singular present tense, the verb ends in -e. In the second person singular present tense, the verb ends in -st. In the third person singular present tense, the verb ends in -t.' etc.

Subject-verb agreement is presented early on in textbooks, typically via the introduction of personal pronouns together with present tense verb endings. In the case of the participant's first textbook, *Willkommen!*, the present tense inflectional paradigm is introduced step-by-step over the first three units. In subsequent units, the inflectional paradigms of modal verbs and of verbs which frequently appear in the *Präteritum* (simple past) and the perfect tense are added; these are typically the verbs *haben* (*have*) and *sein* (*be*), which are listed as exceptions to the regular 'verb stem plus ending' pattern. The inflectional paradigm for other verbs in the *Präteritum* is introduced in the participant's second textbook, *Passwort Deutsch 2*.

The core rule that German verb endings change according to the subject used is high in schematicity since it applies to all verbs and all nominal and pronominal subjects, i.e., schematic constructions. It is low in conceptual complexity since the learner needs to relate only two categories to each other, subject and verb. Technicality of metalanguage is likewise low because the only notions referred to are the basic concepts of subject and verb. Finally, the rule has very high truth value; subject-verb agreement is compulsory and there are no exceptions.

**Analysis procedures.** The data set was analyzed quantitatively using CLAN. Measures of the variables defined and operationalized above were obtained and entered into SPSS version 14.0 for statistical analysis. Moreover, selected episodes involving subject-verb agreement were analyzed qualitatively.

## Results and discussion

In order to answer research questions 1 and 2, non-parametric correlation coefficients (Spearman's rho) were calculated. Moreover, scatterplots for variables of interest were created and scrutinized with the aim of identifying any relationships which are not captured by bivariate correlations. To facilitate this, an interpolation line was superimposed and a Loess line was fitted to each scatterplot. The Loess line is based on a locally weighted polynomial regression and shows the underlying trend that is in evidence in the data set (Phil Scholfield, personal communication, 09/02/10).

*RQ1:  How does the learner's oral L2 proficiency develop over time in terms of accuracy, complexity, and fluency?*

This research question was addressed by considering measures of accuracy, complexity, and fluency in relation to time (data collection session). The correlation between global accuracy and time approached significance (rho = $-0.26$, $p = 0.05$; recall that accuracy was operationalized as number of errors per 100 words, so the coefficient is negative). The interpolation line superimposed on the scatterplot in Figure 1 tracks H's development from session to session; clearly, there is considerable variation between data points. However, the Loess line which indicates the underlying trend in the data shows with equal clarity that the learner's error rate gradually decreases after an initial slight rise. This suggests that H's speech is slowly improving in terms of global accuracy.

Calculations based on separate measures of lexical, morphosyntactic, and pragmatic accuracy yielded a weak significant correlation for morphosyntactic accuracy (rho = $-0.34$, $p = 0.01$). Thus, H's speech improved slightly but significantly in morphosyntactic accuracy over time. There was no significant improvement or backsliding with regard to either lexical or pragmatic accuracy.

Measures of lexical and morphosyntactic complexity did not result in significant correlations either, indicating that H's speech did not show any significant improvement or backsliding in terms of complexity. Figures 2 and 3 suggest that there are trends in evidence, however.

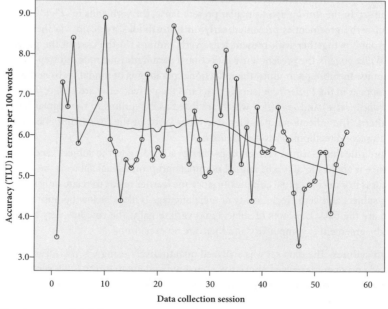

**Figure 1.** Development of global accuracy over time

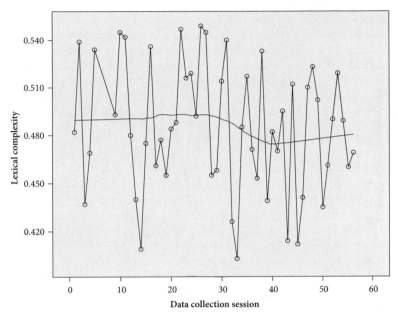

**Figure 2.** Development of lexical complexity over time

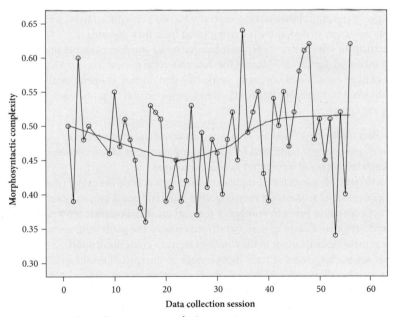

**Figure 3.** Development of morphosyntactic complexity over time

Apart from considerable variation between sessions as shown by the interpolation lines in both Figure 2 and Figure 3, the Loess line in Figure 2 implies that there was a decrease in lexical complexity after an initial period of very gradual increase. Two thirds into the data collection period, the trend appears to change, with utterances becoming more lexically complex again. The Loess line in

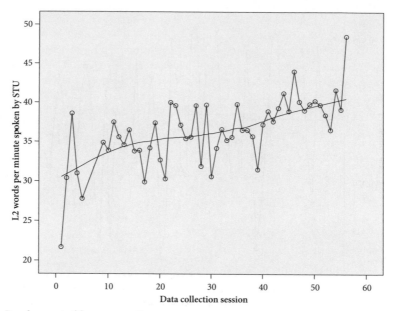

**Figure 4.** Development of fluency over time

Figure 3 suggests that morphosyntactic complexity was on a downward trend until roughly halfway into the data collection period; there is a rising trend from then onwards.

The participant's fluency of speech as measured by L2 words spoken per minute of a recorded interaction increased significantly during the data collection period (rho = 0.67, $p < 0.01$). The relationship is of quite considerable strength, suggesting that fluency as operationalized in the present study was the main factor accounting for H's development in oral L2 proficiency. Figure 4 illustrates the participant's progress.

*RQ2:  How does the learner's overt use of metalinguistic tools develop over time?*
This research question was addressed by considering measures of learner requests for input and learner acknowledgement of tutor input in relation to time.

The participant's requests for L2 input decreased significantly over time (rho = −0.40, $p < 0.01$); crucially, the number of requests for metalinguistic input did not decrease, however. While there is no significant correlation between number of requests for metalinguistic input and time, the Loess line in Figure 5 suggests a slight upward trend: interestingly, the participant seems to very gradually request more metalinguistic input in the course of the data collection period.

Learner acknowledgement of tutor input cannot be interpreted meaningfully without measuring tutor input. Overall, tutor input decreased significantly over time (rho = −0.44, $p < 0.01$); learner acknowledgement likewise decreased significantly over time (rho = −0.60, $p < 0.01$). If the different types of tutor input are scrutinized individually, it becomes clear that the decrease is due to a reduction in L2 input (rho = −0.50, $p < 0.01$) and a more moderate reduction in recasts (rho = −0.27, $p < 0.05$). These results are consistent with learner development in terms of accuracy of speech and requests for tutor input. As H's global accuracy shows a trend for improvement and as his morphosyntactic accuracy improves significantly during the data collection period, it is not unexpected that the tutor will supply less corrective feedback in the form of recasts. Moreover, the number of H's requests for L2 input also decreases significantly, so less L2 input provided by the tutor is a plausible reaction.

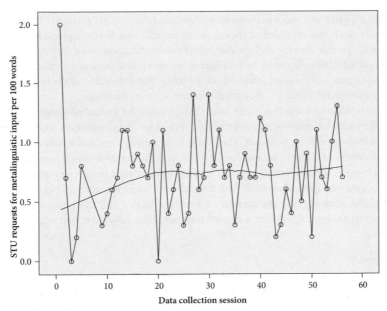

**Figure 5.** Requests for metalinguistic input over time

It has also been noted that the number of learner requests for metalinguistic input does not change significantly over time, with the trend line indicating a slight increase. Accordingly, it does not come as a surprise that the quantity of metalinguistic input offered by the tutor does not change significantly either.

Acknowledgement of tutor input appears to be one of H's preferred metalinguistic tools. There is a strong correlation between overall tutor input and overall learner acknowledgement (rho = 0.82, $p < 0.01$). If individual measures are considered separately, it becomes clear that the relationship remains significant for all three types of tutor input, i.e., L2 input (rho = 0.60, $p < 0.01$), metalinguistic input (rho = 0.51, $p < 0.01$), and recasts (rho = 0.47, $p < 0.01$).

### RQ3: What is the relationship between measures of oral L2 proficiency and overt use of metalinguistic tools?

In order to address research question 3, non-parametric correlation coefficients for measures of oral L2 proficiency and overt use of metalinguistic tools were calculated. With regard to measures of oral L2 proficiency, results show two significant relationships: there is a positive correlation of moderate strength between fluency and morphosyntactic complexity (rho = 0.36, $p < 0.01$) and a weak negative correlation between lexical and morphosyntactic complexity (rho = −0.29, $p < 0.05$). The latter finding suggests an apparent trade-off between lexical and morphosyntactic complexity, i.e., one increases at the expense of the other. Apart from this, however, there seem to be no trade-off effects. In particular, it is noteworthy that there is no significant negative relationship between accuracy and either complexity or fluency. Most interestingly perhaps, fluency and morphosyntactic complexity are positively correlated, so the greater the learner's contribution to the L2 interaction, the greater the amount of subordination in his utterances and vice versa. In other words, fluency and morphosyntactic complexity grow together.

Two significant relationships between measures of oral L2 proficiency and overt use of metalinguistic tools were found. First, learner requests for L2 input correlate negatively with both fluency (rho = −0.36, $p < 0.01$) and morphosyntactic complexity (rho = −0.31, $p < 0.05$). These correlations are admittedly weak, but nonetheless they seem to indicate that fewer requests for L2 input were associated with greater fluency and greater morphosyntactic complexity in the learner's speech. Second, a significant, though moderate correlation between global accuracy and learner requests for metalinguistic input was revealed (rho = −0.39, $p < 0.01$). Put differently, as the number of requests for metalinguistic input increases, the overall number of errors decreases.

In order to ascertain whether these relationships could be explained simply by the fact that several of the variables involved were correlated with time (data collection session), partial correlations controlling for time were run. The results indicate that time was a factor in two cases: the negative correlation of learner requests for L2 input with fluency and morphosyntactic complexity and the negative correlation between lexical and morphosyntactic complexity arose because these variables changed with time. Conversely, the correlation between learner requests for metalinguistic input and global accuracy and the correlation between fluency and morphosyntactic complexity remained significant even when time was partialled out. Thus, only these two relationships are discussed further.

*Interim summary*
The results so far can now be summarized and interpreted with reference to the second of my initial two hypotheses. I hypothesized that a language learner's overall performance will be affected by reliance on explicit knowledge and learning. More specifically, I predicted that explicit knowledge and learning will be associated with increased accuracy and/or complexity of language on the one hand and decreased fluency on the other hand. The empirical findings partly confirm and partly disconfirm this hypothesis.

The participant used overt metalinguistic tools throughout the data collection period, including requests for L2 input, requests for metalinguistic input, and acknowledgement of tutor input. Thus, there is evidence of explicit knowledge and learning. Furthermore, the learner's use of metalinguistic tools changes over time. While requests for L2 input decrease significantly, acknowledgement of tutor input remains a preferred tool, as demonstrated by the strong positive correlation between measures of tutor input and measures of learner acknowledgement. In addition, there is a trend towards a slight increase in requests for metalinguistic input.

My prediction that explicit knowledge and learning will be associated with increased accuracy and/or complexity was borne out with regard to accuracy. A significant correlation of moderate strength between number of requests for metalinguistic input and global accuracy was identified, indicating that error rates fell with increasing use of a metalinguistic tool.

Conversely, the prediction that there would be a trade-off between accuracy and/or complexity on the one hand and fluency on the other hand was not borne out. Over time, the participant improved significantly in terms of both fluency and morphosyntactic accuracy; moreover, global accuracy showed an upward trend. What is more, fluency and morphosyntactic complexity were significantly correlated, indicating not only the absence of a trade-off effect, but a mutually supportive association: greater fluency and greater morphosyntactic complexity went hand in hand.

Taken together, the findings suggest that the participant may be on the way to an overall more fluent and at the same time more controlled performance. Importantly, the learner generally appears to benefit from explicit knowledge and learning, with little trade-off in evidence.

*RQ4:  How does the learner's accuracy develop over time with regard to a selected linguistic construction which can be captured by a rule that is high in schematicity, low in conceptual complexity, low in technicality of metalanguage, and high in truth value?*

The linguistic construction selected as a focus point is subject-verb agreement. As argued above, the core pedagogical grammar rule capturing this construction is highly schematic, low in conceptual complexity and technicality of metalanguage, and high in truth value. According to the first of my two hypotheses put forward above, subject-verb agreement represents the kind of linguistic construction that should be particularly amenable to being learned explicitly.

As the use of subjects and verbs is obligatory in German sentences, subject-verb agreement is ubiquitous. Unsurprisingly, the construction is likewise very frequent in the participant's speech, with a total of 2,572 occurrences in the corpus. At 2.2%, the mean error rate for this construction is low;[3] it ranges from 0 to 8.5%.

The learner requests metalinguistic input relating to subject-verb agreement in only four of the 56 sessions; unsurprisingly, there is no significant relationship between his error rate and requests for input. Nonetheless, there is other evidence of explicit learning opportunities in connection with subject-verb agreement: the tutor provides fairly consistent feedback on H's performance, resulting in a significant positive correlation of medium strength between error rate and tutor input (rho = 0.55, $p < 0.01$). What is more, the participant almost always acknowledges tutor input with regard to this linguistic construction (rho = 0.87, $p < 0.01$).

Regarding the development of H's accuracy on subject-verb agreement, correlational analysis shows that there is no significant improvement or backsliding over time. Perhaps this is not entirely surprising; accuracy was high from the start, so there is arguably little room for improvement. The developmental trend is shown in Figure 6.

The Loess line in Figure 6 indicates a steady downward trend in terms of errors for a substantial period of time; towards the end of the data collection period, the trend appears to reverse, showing a

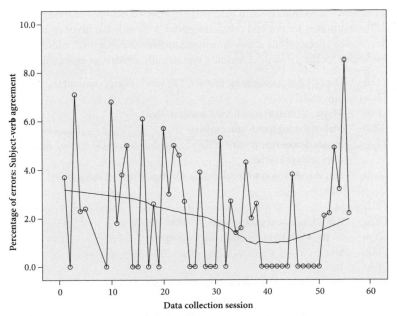

**Figure 6.**  Development of accuracy on subject-verb agreement over time

gradual rise in error rate. This suggests that although the participant's use of subject-verb agreement is often highly accurate, it is not perfect and, more interestingly perhaps, it is not stable (yet). Whilst the generally favourable properties of the core pedagogical grammar rule describing subject-verb agreement can help explain high levels of accuracy achieved through explicit learning, they cannot easily explain the observable fluctuation in the participant's performance. Therefore, it appears that there are other factors at play. In what follows, a qualitative analysis aimed at identifying these factors is presented. In summary, the qualitative analysis shows that a range of variables renders accurate use of subject-verb agreement more challenging than anticipated.

Scrutiny of instances of inaccurate subject-verb agreement suggests that H's errors fall into three main categories. The first group accounts for around 35% of all subject-verb agreement errors and comprises mistakes with nominal or pronominal subjects in the third person. Some of the errors in this category may be attributable to inappropriate transfer from the L1, e.g., in the case of collective nouns that behave differently from English cognates (*Familie* = singular; *family* = singular or plural); other errors may be attributable to the fact that the forms of the nouns involved are the same in the singular and the plural, e.g., *Fahrer* (driver/drivers), *Gebäude* (building/buildings), or *Schuppen* (shed/sheds). Moreover, indefinite pronouns seem to be problematic, e.g., *alle* (all), *beide* (both), or *einige* (some, several). Finally, it is noteworthy that the verbs most frequently appearing in this category are *sein* (be) and *haben* (have), both of which, though highly frequent, are listed as exceptions with irregular inflectional paradigms in H's textbooks.

The second group accounts for another 35% of all subject-verb agreement errors and comprises mistakes with pronominal subjects and verbs in the *Präteritum* (simple past). The inflectional paradigm of verbs in the *Präteritum* is slightly less transparent than in the present tense, which may be a possible source of errors. For instance, verbs in the first and third person singular have the same ending in the *Präteritum*, whilst they are clearly distinguished in the present tense.

The third group accounts for about 20% of all subject-verb agreement errors; it exclusively consists of errors involving the verb *gefallen* (be pleasing to). Before discussing this category in detail, it is worth noting that the remaining small percentage of errors comprises mistakes involving perfect tense verbs. These mistakes are rare and counterbalanced by literally hundreds of instances of correct usage. Their common characteristic seems to be their appearance in linguistic contexts which are particularly challenging for the participant, lexically, syntactically, or both, as exemplified in (1) and (2).[4]

(1)  STU:     Die [//] der Spaziergang [pause]. I'm sorry, I can't think of the words.
     Gloss:   The walk.
     STU:     Mach [//] macht durch zwei anderen Dorf.
     Gloss:   Makes through two other village.
     TEA:     Ja, der Spaziergang war ein Rundgang durch drei Dörfer, ja? Also M. und noch zwei andere Dörfer.
     Gloss:   Yes, the walk was a circular walk through three villages, right? M. and two other villages.
     STU:     Ja.
     TEA:     Also der Spaziergang ging durch drei Dörfer.
     Gloss:   So the walk went through three villages.
     STU:     Okay.
     TEA:     Ja.
     **STU:     So bald hat wir nach nächste [//] nächstes Dorf gekommen.**
     Gloss:   So soon we came to the next village.
     TEA:     Ja, bald sind wir zum nächsten Dorf gekommen.

Gloss:    Yes, soon we came to the next village.
STU:      Can you say that again?
TEA:      Bald sind wir zum nächsten Dorf gekommen.
STU:      Bald sind wir zum nächsten Dorf gekommen. (Session 22)

(2)  STU:    Ich [/] ich wollte noch [/] noch eine Paar Schuhe.
             **Die gleiche, das [//] die ich letztes Mal gekauft hat.**
     Gloss:  I wanted another pair of shoes. The same ones that I bought last time.
     TEA:    Habe.
     STU:    Habe. (Session 55)

In (1), it is clear that the participant is struggling to express intended meanings in the L2. After hesitating, stating that he does not have the means to say what he would like to say, and then making an unsuccessful attempt, the tutor provides L2 input. The participant then takes up the thread of the narrative, producing the utterance in bold. The tutor recasts the inaccurate sentence, correcting several errors simultaneously, including subject-verb agreement. The participant asks the tutor to repeat the recast and subsequently rehearses it accurately.

With regard to the targeted utterance shown in bold, H's self-correction indicates that he was monitoring the use of adjectival inflection which depends on number, gender, and case of the noun that is being qualified. The gender of the noun *Dorf* (*village*) is neuter, so the self-corrected inflection *nächstes* (*next*) is closer to the target than the original form of the adjective (*nächste*), but the learner fails to take dative case into account, which would yield the correct form *nächsten*. Furthermore, *nach* (*to*) is the incorrect preposition, since it is only used with proper names of geographical locations; *zu* (*to*) is required for locations such as *Dorf* (*village*). In addition, the verb *kommen* (*come*) requires the auxiliary *sein* (*be*) in the perfect tense rather than *haben* (*have*). Finally, subject and verb are correctly inverted; if a sentence begins with an adverbial such as *bald* (*soon*), the finite verb appears in second position and the subject is moved to third position.

The last four sentences in the preceding paragraph recite pedagogical grammar rules which H had encountered in his textbooks and his classes. Thus, together with subject-verb agreement, no fewer than five rules would have to be retrieved and applied in order to formulate the targeted utterance accurately with the help of explicit knowledge. In addition, the correct lexical items had to be called up as well. All in all, this represents a considerable cognitive load — too great a load in this case, as the relatively large number of errors and the participant's deliberate repetition of the tutor's recast indicate.

In (2), H constructs a relative clause. This structure was introduced fairly late in the learner's third textbook *Passwort Deutsch 3* and is correspondingly infrequent in the participant's speech as recorded in the corpus. The pedagogical grammar rule pertaining to relative clauses is conceptually far more complex than the rule covering subject-verb agreement, with a number of categories and relations between categories to be taken into account. The rule in H's textbook states that the relative pronoun has the same gender as the noun in the main clause, while the case of the relative pronoun is determined by the verb and/or preposition in the relative clause (translated from Albrecht et al. 2002:67). As H's self-correction indicates, it is likely that the participant tried to draw on this conceptually complex metalinguistic description when constructing the relative clause in the targeted sentence. At the same time, explicit monitoring of subject-verb agreement was neglected, resulting in the inaccurate production of *hat* as opposed to the correct form *habe*.

In summary, it seems that in challenging linguistic contexts as exemplified in (1) and (2), successful explicit processing is not always possible. Online processing of a large number of pedagogical grammar rules and/or of a conceptually complex rule can constitute too great a cognitive load.

The final group of subject-verb agreement errors comprises mistakes involving the verb *gefallen* (*be pleasing to*). As *gefallen* constructions alone account for about 20% of all subject-verb agreement errors, they arguably merit more detailed consideration, both with regard to incorrect and correct patterns of usage. Scrutiny of errors with *gefallen* suggests that the source of difficulty may be found outside what is covered by the core pedagogical grammar rule describing subject-verb agreement. In fact, all errors display the same pattern: a subject in the third person plural is combined with a verb marked for the third person singular, as exemplified in (3) and (4).

(3)    TEA:     Aber leider hast du keine Schuhe gefunden für dich?
        Gloss:    But unfortunately you didn't find any shoes for you?
        STU:     **Nein, die Schuhe gefällt mir nicht.**
        Gloss:    No, I don't like the shoes. (Literally: No, the shoes is not pleasing to me.)
                  (Session 5)

(4)    STU:     Ich habe zwei Paar Hosen anprobiert.
        Gloss:    I tried on two pairs of trousers.
        TEA:     Mmhm.
        STU:     **Aber die gefällt mir nicht.**
        Gloss:    But I don't like them. (Literally: But they is not pleasing to me.) (Session 33)

Differences between L1 and L2 might be a potential source of difficulty surrounding subject-verb agreement in the *gefallen* construction and others like it. The constructional schema in L2 is SUBJECT-*gefallen*-DATIVE OBJECT(-NEGATION). Conversely, the most common L1 translation equivalent is the constructional schema SUBJECT(-NEGATION)-*like*-DIRECT OBJECT. In the English construction, the human agent is in subject position; in the corresponding German construction, however, the human agent is in object position whereas the entity that is pleasing to the human agent is in subject position. This contrast in the two constructional schemas could have played a role: instead of inflecting the verb in accordance with person and number of the subject, H's errors in (3) and (4) are consistent with inflection according to the number, though not the person, of the human agent in object position.

Whilst this explanation is plausible, further analysis indicates that L1-L2 contrast is probably not the main factor impacting on the participant's performance. Instead, H's developing use of the *gefallen* construction in the course of the data collection period suggests that exemplar-based, bottom-up learning rather than explicit, top-down learning may be the key explanatory variable in this case. As detailed in what follows, the participant seems to have acquired the item-based schema X *gefällt mir (nicht)* (X is (not) pleasing to me) first. From this, X *gefällt* Y *(nicht)* (X is (not) pleasing to Y) is quickly abstracted. Then a second item-based schema for past reference is acquired, that is, X *hat* Y *(nicht) gefallen* (X was (not) pleasing to Y). The fact that these item-based schemas are structured around singular verbs means that subject-verb agreement errors occur whenever the subject is in the plural.

The first step in H's developmental sequence is illustrated in (5) and (6).

(5)    TEA:     Es war sehr scharf.
        Gloss:    It was very spicy.
        STU:     Sehr scharf, mmhm. **Es gefällt mir, aber nicht dir [//] dich?**
        Gloss:    Very spicy, mmhm. I like it, but you don't?
        TEA:     Dir.
        STU:     Dir. (Session 27)

(6) TEA:    Und denkst du, dass das eine gute Überraschung war für S., eine gelungene
            Überraschung?
    Gloss:  And do you think it was a good surprise for S., a welcome surprise?
    TEA:    Oder denkst du ⟨er war ein bisschen⟩ [///] ja, er war nicht so begeistert?
    Gloss:  Or do you think he was a bit, well, that he wasn't so enthusiastic about it?
    STU:    **Nein, ich [/] ich denke, dass es [/] es gefällt ihm.**
    Gloss:  No, I think he likes it. (Session 28)

Excerpts (5) and (6) exemplify instances of use of the *gefallen* construction initiated by the partici-pant, i.e., there was no prior input or modelling from the tutor. Both instances are representative of correct subject-verb agreement, with both the subject and the verb in the third person singular. Note that H uses the schema X *gefällt mir (nicht)*, with the more abstract schema X *gefällt Y (nicht)* emerg-ing. In both (5) and (6), the perfect tense would have been required, but the participant's apparent reliance on a schema based around the present tense verb form *gefällt* does not yet allow for use of the appropriate tense. In (6), moreover, the finite verb should appear at the end of the subordinate clause (*dass es ihm gefällt*). Apart from application of a pedagogical grammar rule, such compliance with conventional word order would require a wholly abstract constructional schema, however. The item-based schema X *gefällt Y (nicht)* cannot accommodate changes in word order; accordingly, the finite verb remains in second position.

The item-based schema for *gefallen* constructions with past reference is used from session 21 onwards. Excerpt (7) shows the participant's first unprompted use of the construction; excerpt (8) exemplifies a later occurrence.

(7) TEA:    Ja, es gab nur drei Filme, nicht?
    Gloss:  Yes, there were only three films, weren't there?
            (...)
    STU:    **Ja, die [/] die hat uns nicht gefallen.**
    Gloss:  Yes, we didn't like them.
            (Literally: Yes, they was not pleasing to us.) (Session 21)

(8) STU:    Die Kneipe heißt H.
    Gloss:  The pub is called H.
    TEA:    Ja.
    STU:    **Aber sie hat uns nicht gefallen.**
    Gloss:  But we didn't like it. (Session 45)

In (8), the subject is in the singular, so the singular verb is appropriate and no subject-verb agree-ment error occurs. In (7), however, subject and verb do not agree, with the previously identified error pattern of third person plural subject plus third person singular verb in evidence, as illustrated in (3) and (4) above. All other subject-verb agreement errors occurring in the *gefallen* construction with past reference display the same pattern. At the same time, the object seems to have as little impact on the verb form as the subject: the plural object *uns* (*to us*) in (7) and (8) does not prompt any change in verb inflection. This circumstance weakens the argument that L1-L2 contrast may be responsible for subject-verb agreement errors with the *gefallen* construction. It is, however, fully consonant with the use of an item-based schema of the form X *hat Y (nicht) gefallen*.

Up to now, the discussion of the *gefallen* construction has focused on instances of use which were initiated by the participant himself. Scrutiny of H's use of the *gefallen* construction in tutor-initiated discourse provides further corroborating evidence for the argument of exemplar-driven

**Table 1.** The *gefallen* construction in tutor-initiated discourse

| TEA | STU | Item-based schema | Session |
|---|---|---|---|
| Hat es dir gefallen? | Ja, es gefällt mir. | X gefällt mir (nicht) | 1 |
| Hat es dir geschmeckt? | Ja, es gefällt mir. | " | 5 |
| Hat dir der Film gefallen? | Ja, es [//] er gefällt mir. | " | 10 |
| Hat es dir gefallen? | Ja, es gefällt mir. | " | 14 |
| Das hat dir nicht geschmeckt? | Nein, es gefällt mir nicht. | " | 18 |
| Und hat dir der Film gefallen? | Ja, der Film gefällt mir. | " | 32 |
| Hat dir der Film gefallen? | Ja, der Film hat mir gefallen. | X hat mir (nicht) gefallen | 36 |
| Hat es dir gefallen? | Ja, ⟨es gefällt mir⟩ [//] es [/] es hat mir gefallen. | " | 39 |
| Hat dir der Film gefallen? | Ja, der Film hat mir gefallen, aber das Ende ⟨hat mir⟩ [/] hat mir nicht gefallen. | " | 42 |
| Hat dir der Film gefallen? | Ja, der Film gefällt mir. | X gefällt mir (nicht) | 53 |
| Hat dir das Haus gefallen? | Ja, es gefällt mir. | " | 56 |

learning resulting in the use of item-based schemas. Table 1 displays the participant's responses to direct tutor questions regarding his likes or dislikes of certain attitude objects.

Even though all tutor questions refer to past events and are thus formulated in the perfect tense, it is not until session 36 that the learner responds in the same tense. As mentioned above, the corresponding X *hat* Y *(nicht) gefallen* schema emerges in session 21 after initially being modelled by the tutor in session 18, but Table 1 indicates that the use of this schema remains unstable throughout, with the earlier X *gefällt* Y *(nicht)* schema still dominant. Tutor questions employing the verb *schmecken* (*taste*) further substantiate the argument that H's item-based schemas are anchored around forms of the verb *gefallen*. The verb *schmecken* behaves in the same way as *gefallen*, with the tutor's questions explicitly modelling the required constructional pattern (sessions 5 and 18); however, H continues to employ the *gefallen* construction in his answers, apparently as yet unable to abandon the item around which the schema is structured in his mental representation.

*Interim summary*
The findings concerning H's use of subject-verb agreement can now be summarized and interpreted with reference to the first of my initial two hypotheses. I hypothesized that a linguistic construction which can be captured relatively easily by an Aristotelian rule will be acquired faster and more accurately if the learner draws on explicit knowledge than a linguistic construction which cannot easily be captured by an Aristotelian rule. Given the costliness of explicit processing, a rule that is high in schematicity, low in conceptual complexity, low in technicality of metalanguage, and high in truth value will be most favourable.

The analysis focused on a selected linguistic construction, subject-verb agreement, which is captured by a core pedagogical grammar rule that should be highly amenable to explicit processing. In view of the constraints of the present paper, the participant's performance on subject-verb agreement was not compared directly with his performance on other linguistic constructions, so the available evidence is indirect and cannot be regarded as final. The findings so far provide some interesting indications, however.

Overall, the participant's generally high accuracy with regard to subject-verb agreement — an ubiquitous construction appearing in many different linguistic contexts — was noted. Likewise, overt use of metalinguistic tools in conjunction with subject-verb agreement was in evidence, as exemplified by occasional learner requests for metalinguistic input, quite regular tutor feedback in response to learner errors, and above all highly consistent learner acknowledgement of tutor input with respect to the selected linguistic construction.

The apparent amenability of subject-verb agreement to explicit, top-down processing and the apparent use of metalinguistic tools neither explain the fluctuations in H's performance from session to session nor the overall developmental trend, however. Indeed, qualitative analysis of the learner's usage patterns revealed that a range of factors appears to influence accuracy with subject-verb agreement.

First, situational context is likely to impact on performance. Subject-verb agreement errors occurred when the participant's cognitive resources were taxed either by the need to simultaneously apply a number of pedagogical grammar rules or by the need to use a conceptually complex metalinguistic description in conjunction with the subject-verb agreement rule.

Second, the error patterns identified suggest that both the nature of the verbal inflectional paradigm and the form of nominal subjects have a role to play. Specifically, exceptions to regular inflectional patterns and non-transparent form-function mappings may lead to inaccuracies. Previous research has reported that transparent one-to-one form-function mappings are easier to acquire than more opaque mappings of one form marking many functions or one function being marked by many forms (Collins et al. 2009; DeKeyser 2005; Kempe & MacWhinney 1998). In German subject-verb agreement, non-transparent mappings occur more often with regard to verbs in the *Präteritum* than verbs in the present tense, with the form -*e* marking both the first person and the third person singular *Präteritum*. Moreover, non-transparent mappings occur with regard to certain nouns such as *Fahrer* and *Gebäude* where singular and plural are expressed by the same form. While transparency of mapping has been discussed in connection with implicit learning (DeKeyser 2005; Roehr & Gánem-Gutiérrez 2009), it nonetheless seems to have an impact in this case. This implies that implicit and explicit processes occur alongside one another and, ultimately, may only be fully understood if they are considered together.

Indeed, detailed analysis of H's productions involving the *gefallen* construction yielded considerable evidence for exemplar learning resulting in the use of item-based schemas. This type of bottom-up learning has been identified as a key acquisition process in both L1 (Abbot-Smith & Tomasello 2006; Tomasello 2003) and L2 learning (N. Ellis 2002a, 2003; Eskildsen 2009). The present findings strongly suggest that in addition to using explicit knowledge and learning, the participant also relied on fast and cognitively efficient bottom-up processes.

While this is perhaps unsurprising in itself, the analysis showed that these bottom-up processes can apparently override comparatively slower and more costly top-down processes. Interestingly, this seems to happen even in a learner such as H whose performance is otherwise strongly indicative of explicit learning. Hence, it is likely that implicit processes not only subserve fluent and effortless language use (N. Ellis 2005), but may also take over again by default when the cognitive resources available for explicit processing are pushed to their limits — because of the time pressures inherent in meaning-focused oral communication (R. Ellis 2005, 2006) and/or because of cognitive overload, as argued above.

## Conclusion
In this paper, I put forward two hypotheses concerning the potential role of explicit knowledge and learning in SLA; these hypotheses were informed by a cognitive linguistics perspective on language

representation and processing. I then presented empirical evidence from a longitudinal case study of an adult L2 learner which spoke to these hypotheses.

Linking the bird's eye view of theoretical argumentation with the fine-grained detail of an individual learner's oral L2 performance led to a number of instructive insights. Evidence of explicit learning was found throughout the data set: direct evidence in the form of overt use of metalinguistic tools by the learner, including requests for and acknowledgement of tutor input, and indirect evidence in the form of performance patterns which showed the hallmarks of resource-intensive explicit processing.

Possible benefits of explicit knowledge and learning in SLA were uncovered: the number of learner requests for metalinguistic input and global accuracy of speech were significantly correlated, indicating that decreasing error rates were associated with increasing use of a metalinguistic tool. Claims about cause and effect in this relationship cannot be made, but other evidence points in the direction of a beneficial role for explicit knowledge and learning with regard to accurate language use: the absence of a trade-off between accuracy and fluency is an indicator; moreover, greater fluency and greater morphosyntactic complexity showed a mutually supportive association.

Potential limitations of explicit knowledge and learning in SLA emerged with equal clarity, though. The learner used a linguistic construction that was hypothesized to be particularly amenable to explicit processing with a high level of accuracy. Yet, analysis of specific usage situations suggested that the properties of pedagogical grammar rules describing linguistic constructions may be inadequate predictors in the context of communicative language use. If the cognitive load imposed by explicit processing becomes too onerous, even rules that are highly amenable to explicit learning may no longer be beneficial: with resources depleted, they are either not applied successfully, or they are not applied at all because implicit, exemplar-based processing takes their place.

Last but not least, the limitations of the present study should be acknowledged and avenues for future research highlighted. The key strength of a longitudinal case study is its amenability to detailed analysis at the level of specific linguistic constructions. This is offset by the main weakness of such a research design: comparisons across learners cannot be made, and generalizability is limited. Thus, future research should seek to address hypotheses about explicit knowledge and learning informed by a cognitive linguistics perspective in a group of participants in order to allow for direct comparison between different linguistic constructions and across different individuals. Findings would complement the present study and provide researchers, teachers, and learners with more robust evidence about the role of explicit knowledge and learning in SLA.

## Notes

1. Due to space limitations, only one linguistic construction is focused on in the present paper, so a comparison with other linguistic constructions is not provided.

2. Accuracy, complexity, and fluency have been defined and operationalized in different ways (R. Ellis & Barkhuizen 2005; Housen & Kuiken 2009). Thus, it is worth bearing in mind that the use of different measures could potentially lead to different results.

3. The error rate was calculated as the percentage of incorrect instances out of all instances of use of the construction. This approach was taken because the number of occurrences of subject-verb agreement varied between sessions. Percentage-based error rates were likewise calculated for other selected constructions which are not discussed in the present paper. The mean error rates were higher, e.g., use of correct auxiliary with the perfect tense 7.0%, form of the past participle 5.3%, case inflection 12.7%.

4. STU refers to the learner, TEA to the tutor. The constructions under discussion are shown in bold. Further details about CHAT transcription conventions can be found in the Appendix.

## References

Abbot-Smith, K. & Tomasello, M. 2006. Exemplar-learning and schematization in a usage-based account of syntactic acquisition. *The Linguistic Review* 23: 275–290.

Achard, M. & Niemeier, S. (eds). 2004. *Cognitive Linguistics, Second Language Acquisition, and Foreign Language Teaching*. Berlin: Mouton de Gruyter.

Albrecht, U., Dane, D., Fandrych, C., Grüßhaber, G., Henningsen, U., Kilimann, A., Knaus, H., Köhl-Kuhn, R., Papendieck, K. & Schäfer, S. 2001. *Passwort Deutsch 2*. Stuttgart: Klett.

Albrecht, U., Fandrych, C., Grüßhaber, G., Henningsen, U., Hesselmann, O., Kilimann, A., Knaus, H., Köhl-Kuhn, R. & Papendieck, K. 2002. *Passwort Deutsch 3*. Stuttgart: Klett.

Anderson, J.R. 2005. *Cognitive Psychology and its Implications,* 6th edn. New York NY: Worth Publishers.

Baddeley, A.D. 2000. The episodic buffer: A new component of working memory? *Trends in Cognitive Sciences* 4: 417–423.

Baddeley, A.D. & Logie, R.H. 1999. Working memory: The multiple-component model. In *Models of Working Memory: Mechanisms of Active Maintenance and Executive Control,* A. Miyake & P. Shah (eds), 28–61. Cambridge: CUP.

Boers, F. & Lindstromberg, S. 2006. Cognitive linguistic applications in second and foreign language instruction: Rationale, proposals, and evaluation. In *Cognitive Linguistics: Current Applications and Future Perspectives,* G. Kristiansen, M. Achard. R. Dirven & F. J. Ruiz de Mendoza (eds), 305–355. Berlin: Mouton de Gruyter.

Bybee, J.L. & McClelland, J.L. 2005. Alternatives to the combinatorial paradigm of linguistic theory based on domain general principles of human cognition. *The Linguistic Review* 22: 381–410.

Cleeremans, A. & Destrebecqz, A. 2005. Real rules are conscious. *Behavioral and Brain Sciences* 28: 19–20.

Coggle, P. & Schenke, H. 1998. *Willkommen! The New Course in German for Adult Beginners*. London: Hodder & Stoughton.

Collins, L., Trofimovich, P., White, J., Cardoso, W. & Horst, M. 2009. Some input on the easy/difficult grammar question: An empirical study. *Modern Language Journal* 93: 336–353.

DeKeyser, R.M. 2003. Implicit and explicit learning. In *The Handbook of Second Language Acquisition,* C.J. Doughty & M.H. Long (eds), 313–348. Malden MA: Blackwell.

DeKeyser, R.M. 2005. What makes learning second-language grammar difficult? A review of issues. *Language Learning* 55: 1–25.

Diesendruck, G. 2005. 'Commitment' distinguishes between rules and similarity: A developmental perspective. *Behavioral and Brain Sciences* 28: 21–22.

Dörnyei, Z. 2009. *The Psychology of Second Language Acquisition*. Oxford: OUP.

Egi, T. 2007. Interpreting recasts as linguistic evidence: The roles of linguistic target, length, and degree of change. *Studies in Second Language Acquisition* 29: 511–537.

Ellis, N.C. 1993. Rules and instances in foreign language learning: Interactions of explicit and implicit knowledge. *European Journal of Cognitive Psychology* 5: 289–318.

Ellis, N.C. 1994. Consciousness in second language learning: Psychological perspectives on the role of conscious processes in vocabulary acquisition. *AILA Review* 11: 37–56.

Ellis, N. C. 2002a. Frequency effects in language processing: A review with implications for theories of implicit and explicit language acquisition. *Studies in Second Language Acquisition* 24: 143–188.

Ellis, N.C. 2002b. Reflections on frequency effects in language processing. *Studies in Second Language Acquisition* 24: 297–340.

Ellis, N.C. 2003. Constructions, chunking, and connectionism: The emergence of second language structure. In *The Handbook of Second Language Acquisition,* C.J. Doughty & M.H. Long (eds), 63–103. Malden MA: Blackwell.

Ellis, N.C. 2005. At the interface: Dynamic interactions of explicit and implicit language knowledge. *Studies in Second Language Acquisition* 27: 305–352.

Ellis, R. 2004. The definition and measurement of L2 explicit knowledge. *Language Learning* 54: 227–275.

Ellis, R. 2005. Measuring implicit and explicit knowledge of a second language: A psychometric study. *Studies in Second Language Acquisition* 27: 141–172.

Ellis, R. 2006. Modelling learning difficulty and second language proficiency: The differential contributions of implicit and explicit knowledge. *Applied Linguistics* 27: 431–463.

Ellis, R. & Barkhuizen, G. 2005. *Analysing Learner Language.* Oxford: OUP.

Eskildsen, S.W. 2009. Constructing another language: Usage-based linguistics in second language acquisition. *Applied Linguistics* 30: 335–357.

Evans, V. & Green, M. 2006. *Cognitive Linguistics: An Introduction.* Mahwah NJ: Lawrence Lawrence Erlbaum Associates.

Gass, S.M. & Selinker, L. 2008. *Second Language Acquisition: An Introductory Course,* 3rd edn. London: Routledge.

Goldberg, A.E. 2003. Constructions: A new theoretical approach to language. *Trends in Cognitive Sciences* 7: 219–224.

Hampton, J.A. 2005. Rules and similarity — a false dichotomy. *Behavioral and Brain Sciences* 28: 26.

Housen, A. & Kuiken, F. 2009. Complexity, accuracy, and fluency in second language acquisition. *Applied Linguistics* 30: 461–473.

Hulstijn, J.H. 2005. Theoretical and empirical issues in the study of implicit and explicit second-language learning: Introduction. *Studies in Second Language Acquisition* 27: 129–140.

Hümmler-Hille, C. & von Jan, E. 1993. *Hören Sie mal! Übungen zum Hörverständnis.* Munich: Max Hueber.

Hümmler-Hille, C. & von Jan, E. 1999. *Hören Sie mal! 2: Übungen zum Hörverständnis.* Munich: Max Hueber.

Iwashita, N., Brown, A., McNamara, T. & O'Hagan, S. 2008. Assessed levels of second language speaking proficiency: How distinct? *Applied Linguistics* 29: 24–49.

Just, M.A. & Carpenter, P.A. 1992. A capacity theory of comprehension: Individual differences in working memory. *Psychological Review* 99: 122–149.

Kemmer, S. & Barlow, M. 2000. Introduction: A usage-based conception of language. In *Usage-based Models of Language,* M. Barlow & S. Kemmer (eds), vii–xxviii. Stanford CA: CSLI.

Kempe, V. & MacWhinney, B. 1998. The acquisition of case marking by adult learners of Russian and German. *Studies in Second Language Acquisition* 20: 543–587.

Langacker, R.W. 1998. Conceptualization, symbolization, and grammar. In *The New Psychology of Language: Cognitive and Functional Approaches to Language Structure,* Vol. 1, M. Tomasello (ed.), 1–40. Mahwah NJ: Lawrence Erlbaum Associates.

Langacker, R.W. 2000. A dynamic usage-based model. In *Usage-based Models of Language,* M. Barlow & S. Kemmer (eds), 1–64. Stanford CA: CSLI.

Larsen-Freeman, D. 2006. The emergence of complexity, fluency, and accuracy in the oral and written production of five Chinese learners of English. *Applied Linguistics* 27: 590–619.

Markman, A.B., Blok, S., Kom, K., Larkey, L., Narvaez, L.R., Stilwell, C.H. & Taylor, E. 2005. Digging beneath rules and similarity. *Behavioral and Brain Sciences* 28: 29–30.

Murphy, G.L. 2004. *The Big Book of Concepts.* Cambridge MA: The MIT Press.

Norris, J.M. & Ortega, L. 2001. Does type of instruction make a difference? Substantive findings from a meta-analytic review. *Language Learning* 51: 157–213.

Pothos, E.M. 2005. The rules versus similarity distinction. *Behavioral and Brain Sciences* 28: 1–49.

Robinson, P. & Ellis, N.C. (eds). 2008. *Handbook of Cognitive Linguistics and Second Language Acquisition.* London: Routledge.

Roehr, K. 2008. Linguistic and metalinguistic categories in second language learning. *Cognitive Linguistics* 19: 67–106.

Roehr, K. & Gánem-Gutiérrez, G.A. 2009. Metalinguistic knowledge: A stepping stone towards L2 proficiency? In *Issues in Second Language Proficiency,* A. Benati (ed.), 79–94. London: Continuum.

Rosch, E. 1978. Principles of categorization. In *Cognition and Categorization,* E. Rosch & B.B. Lloyd (eds), 27–48. Hillsdale NJ: Lawrence Erlbaum Associates.

Rosch, E. & Mervis, C.B. 1975. Family resemblances: Studies in the internal structure of categories. *Cognitive Psychology* 7: 573–605.

Segalowitz, N. 2003. Automaticity and second languages. In *The Handbook of Second Language Acquisition,* C.J. Doughty & M.H. Long (eds), 382–408. Malden MA: Blackwell.

Sloman, S. 2005. Avoiding foolish consistency. *Behavioral and Brain Sciences* 28: 33–34.

Smith, E.E. 2005. Rule and similarity as prototype concepts. *Behavioral and Brain Sciences* 28: 34–35.

Taylor, J.R. 1998. Syntactic constructions as prototype categories. In *The New Psychology of Language: Cognitive and Functional Approaches to Language Structure,* Vol. 1, M. Tomasello (ed.), 177–202. Mahwah NJ: Lawrence Erlbaum Associates.

Taylor, J.R. 2002. *Cognitive Grammar.* Oxford: OUP.

Taylor, J.R. 2003. *Linguistic Categorization,* 3rd edn. Oxford: OUP.

Tomasello, M. 2003. *Constructing a Language: A Usage-Based Theory of Language Acquisition.* Cambridge MA: Harvard University Press.

Tomasello, M. 2005. Beyond formalities: The case of language acquisition. *The Linguistic Review* 22: 183–197.

Ungerer, F. & Schmid, H.-J. 1996. *An Introduction to Cognitive Linguistics.* London: Longman.

## Appendix

Transcript excerpts are presented in edited format to ensure maximum readability. The symbol [/] is CHAT code for retracing; [//] refers to self-correction; [///] refers to reformulation. Angled brackets ⟨ ⟩ are placed around the retraced expression if it comprises more than one word.

Accuracy: Examples of lexical, morphosyntactic, and pragmatic errors

Wir sind *in Debenham's gegangen. (Session 41)
Gloss: We went to Debenham's.
Lexical error: A word that is incorrect at sentence level was chosen; the correct preposition is *zu* in this case.

Aber [/] aber wir konnten nicht im Garten Picknick *gemacht. (Session 9)
Gloss: But we could not have a picnic in the garden.
Morphosyntactic error: The learner uses the past participle of the verb (*gemacht*) when the infinitive form (*machen*) is required.

Und wir haben eine Tasse Tee *gekauft. (Session 52)
Gloss: And we bought a cup of tea.
Pragmatic error: Although *gekauft* is a semantically accurate description of the event H is referring to, the verb is inappropriate in the given German discourse. The pragmatically appropriate choice would be *getrunken.*

*Author's address*

Department of Language & Linguistics
University of Essex
Wivenhoe Park
Colchester CO4 3SQ

kroehr@essex.ac.uk

# Applying cognitive linguistics to instructed L2 learning

## The English modals

Andrea Tyler, Charles M. Mueller and Vu Ho

Georgetown University / George Washington University

This paper reports the results of a quasi-experimental effects-of-instruction study examining the efficacy of applying a Cognitive Linguistic (CL) approach to L2 learning of the semantics of English modals. In spite of their frequency in typical input, modal verbs present L2 learners with difficulties, party due to their inherent complexity — modals typically have two divergent senses — a root[1] sense and an epistemic sense. ELT textbooks and most grammar books aimed at L2 teachers present the two meanings as homophones, failing to address any systematic semantic patterning in the modal system as a whole. Additionally, ELT texts tend to present modals from a speech act perspective. In contrast, CL analyses (e. g., Langacker 1991; Nuyts 2001; Sweetser 1990; Talmy 1988) offer both a systematic, motivated representation of the relationship between the root and epistemic meanings and a rather precise representation of the semantics of each modal. To test the pedagogical effectiveness of a CL account of modals, an effects-of-instruction study was conducted with three groups of adult, high-intermediate ESL learners: a Cognitive treatment group, a Speech Acts[2] treatment group, and a Control group. Results of an ANCOVA indicated that the Cognitive treatment group demonstrated significantly more improvement than the Speech Acts treatment group. The experiment thus lends empirical support for the position that CL, in addition to offering a compelling analytical account of language, may also provide the basis for more effective grammar instruction than that found in most current ELT teaching materials.

## Introduction

For many years, practitioners in second language (L2) learning research and pedagogy have focused their attention on issues of methodology and psychology, such as the importance of interaction or short-term memory in L2 learning, with little regard for the underlying model of language being assumed. Larsen-Freeman (1996), among others, has argued that linguistic research outside of the areas of pragmatics and discourse analysis have seemed to offer L2 teachers and learners little in the way of useful presentations of grammar or lexis. Recently, L2 practitioners have begun to turn their attention to the potential insights of a relatively new approach to linguistics, Cognitive Linguistics[3] (CL), which offers both a usage-based analysis and a fresh view of the structure of language (e.g., Achard & Niemeier 2002; Boers & Lindstromberg 2008; De Knop & De Rycker 2009; Dirven 2001; Ellis & Cadierno 2009; Holme 2009; Pütz, Niemeier & Dirven 2001; Radden & Dirven 2007;

*AILA Review* 23 (2010), **30–49**. DOI 10.1075/aila.23.03tyl
ISSN 1461–0213 / E-ISSN 1570–5595 © John Benjamins Publishing Company

Robinson & Ellis 2008; Tyler & Evans 2002). The evidence is mounting that CL can provide motivated, precise explanations of linguistic phenomena, including some of the most difficult areas for L2 learners, such as prepositions, phrasal verbs, conditionals, and articles (e.g., Dirven 2001; Radden & Dirven 2007; Tyler & Evans 2003). Using English modal verbs as a lens, this paper considers the usefulness of a CL approach to instructed L2 learning. Two key goals are to provide an analysis of the English modal verbs that is accessible to ELT professionals and language learners, i.e., not overly burdened with jargon and theoretical discussion, and to offer experimental evidence, in the form of the results of a quasi-experimental effects-of-instruction study, that such applications of the theory can form the basis for L2 research and effective teaching materials.

The article first presents a comparative overview of the speech act approach to modals, which is the basis for most current ELT materials, versus a CL-based approach. In the course of the comparison, we present several key tenets of each approach and establish that a CL analysis of modal verbs (Sweetser 1990; Talmy 1988; 2000)[4] provides a more systematic, precise explanation than those offered by a speech act analysis. Next the article presents a quasi-experimental effects-of-instruction study that offers support for the effectiveness of using a CL approach to teaching the modals. Finally, we end with a few words about future directions.

## The English modal verbs

### A basic overview

English, like many languages, has a system to represent the speaker's attitude relating to permission, ability, and obligation within social situations when giving advice, suggestions, permission, orders, and so on, and commitment to surety in predictions and reasoning. In English these attitudinal colorings are expressed by the modal verbs (as well as adverbial phrases such as *is likely, is probable*, etc.). The modal verbs include *can, could, will, would, shall, should, may,* and *might.*

The semantics of modal verbs involves the strength of the speaker's position and aspects of status among the participants in a speech event.

(1)  a.  *You could get more exercise.*
     b.  *You must get more exercise.*
     c.  *You should get more exercise.*

Advice using *could* is interpreted as weaker than advice using *must*. Native speakers of English would likely interpret sentence (a) as a friendly suggestion rather than directive advice. In contrast, the use of *must* in sentence (b) carries a strong sense of directive force and could even be considered a command in certain contexts (e.g., *You must finish writing this contract before 5 o'clock or the firm will have to let you go*). The appropriateness of using the stronger form is generally tied to the speaker's status vis-à-vis the addressee, for instance in the case of a doctor speaking to a patient, or the intensity of the speaker's feelings. When *should* is used to give advice, as in (c), it introduces a moralistic dimension not found with *could* or *must*.

An additional complexity is that almost all English modals exhibit two meanings, one involving the external, physical-social world of ability, obligation, or permission, often called the *root* meaning, and a second meaning involving speaker-internal mental reasoning and logical conclusion, called the *epistemic* meaning. Root meaning is illustrated in:

(2)  *The doctor said I should get more exercise.*

Here the speaker is expressing the strong social obligation imposed by the doctor. Epistemic meaning is illustrated in:

(3)    Doorbell rings. Speaker: *That should be John now.*

Here the speaker is indicating the strong belief in the conclusion that the unseen person at the door is John.[5]

*Speech Act view*

An examination of 10 current ELT texts showed that modals tend to be presented from a speech act perspective. Since several modals can occur in the same speech act and each modal can occur in more than one speech act, under the speech act presentation their distribution and meaning appear to be largely idiosyncratic. As demonstrated above, native speakers of English have intuitions about the subtle differences in meaning among the modals as they occur in a particular speech act, however, precise definitions of the modals which would clarify these differences in meaning have been largely lacking in ELT textbooks and pedagogical grammars. Current speech act accounts leave both the teacher and the learner with the impression that the only approach to mastering modals is to memorize formulaic expressions for each speech act, and the particular modals which happen to occur in those expressions. Indeed, Celce-Murcia and Larsen-Freeman (1999) have noted that acquiring modals is one of the most difficult aspects of L2 English precisely because of their seemingly idiosyncratic nature.

A representative approach to the teaching of modals from a speech act perspective is provided in Werner and Nelson (1996) *Mosaics 2: A Content-based Grammar,* which is aimed at advanced-intermediate learners. For instance, *may/might/can/could* are represented as relating to expressing ability and possibility; *may/can* as relating to granting permission; *may/could/can* as relating to asking for permission; *would/could/will/can* as relating to asking for assistance. Even from this brief overview, we can see that *could* occurs in the categories of ability and permission, asking for permission and asking for assistance. *Can* appears in all four. No explanation is given for this distribution. Moreover, the relationship between the root uses and the epistemic uses is completely ignored. Hence, any systematic patterns of usage remain unexplored. This results in a fragmented picture of the lexical class in question, leaving the learner with the impression that the various uses are arbitrary.

Perhaps even more problematic is the lack of precision introduced by presenting the modals in this particular fashion. The subtle yet fundamental differences in speaker's attitude signaled by modal verbs such as *might* versus *should* are obscured as the presentations list several modals together as functional equivalents that are essentially interchangeable when giving advice (or performing other speech acts).

The informed teacher, of course, might be able to help her students come to an integrated, accurate account of the modals based on this limited speech act approach, but this presupposes that the teacher has been able to construct an accurate and systematic understanding of the modal system.

Unfortunately, most traditional and pedagogical grammars, even corpus-based ones (e.g., Biber et al. 1999), simply do not provide teachers with such an overview. For instance Biber et al. represent *can, could, may, might* as the modals of 'possibility' and *will/would/be going to* as the modals of 'prediction.' This presentation has a number of problems. First, the difference between 'possibility' and 'prediction' is blurry. Consider the following sentences:

(3)    a.    *That could/may/might be John.*
       b.    *That will/would be John.*

Both groups of modals would seem to convey the speaker's sense of the possibility of a particular situation or the speaker's prediction about a situation. How the two categories differ remains a mystery. It may also be noted that with the exception of *can,* all modals are used to indicate logical prediction or the speaker's assessment of logical possibility in their epistemic uses. So singling out a subset of the modals as indicating either possibility or prediction fails to address the epistemic uses of *must* and *should*, and so on. Conversely, placing *can* with *could, may*, and *might* as indicating possibility seems to suggest that *can* has an epistemic use, a conclusion that is not accurate. As with the ELT textbooks, speech act-based grammars offer no explanation as to the relationship between root and epistemic uses of the individual modals. Rather, they simply offer examples of utterances which fall into the two categories.

Finally, the typical speech act presentation notes that a limited set of modals (*can/could, may/ might, shall/should*, and *will/would*) have past tense forms. However, no discussion of the fact that *could, might, should*, and *would* are regularly used in non-past situations is included. For instance, the speech act approach offers no explanation as to why the past tense *should* can be used to make statements about the future, such as "Given my calculations, Karen should be here in an hour."

It is our estimation that most language teachers would be at a loss to discern systematic, motivated patterns from these accounts (see Tyler 2008 for a fuller review of the representation of modals from the 1999 corpus-based *Longman Grammar of Spoken and Written English* by Biber et al. (1999). This is a grammar specifically aimed at L2 teachers).

*A cognitive linguistic account*
Several cognitive linguists have developed alternative analyses of the semantics of modal verbs. For the purposes of our analysis, we draw primarily on Sweeter (1990) and Talmy (1988; 2000), who base their analysis on force dynamics. Specifically, they argue that the root meanings of modals have to do with physical forces, forward motion, and paths. Further, there is a systematic, metaphorical mapping between our understanding of these physical forces and our understanding of conceptual forces and paths, which is reflected in the epistemic uses. Here we primarily follow Sweetser's analysis, which emphasizes intentional, directed forces and paths and their metaphorical extensions.

A key tenet of CL is that our spatial-physical-social experiences structure much of our cognition and this structure is reflected in language. In other words, humans regularly think about events and experiences in one conceptual domain (e.g., reasoning and logical prediction) in terms of another domain (e.g., the spatial-physical-social); this is thinking metaphorically. A wealth of studies (e.g., Boroditsky 2000; Gibbs 1994, 2006; Spivey 2007) shows that metaphorical thinking is a ubiquitous cognitive process which shapes human cognition in many vital ways. Specifically, our observations of the external, spatial-physical world, such as basic force dynamics (e.g., motion of entities along a path and types of forces that cause forward motion), provide important event schemas that we use to reason and talk about the non-physical. This pattern is found in many uses of English, not just the modal verbs. One example of how language from the realm of physical perceptions is used to describe mental operations involves the use of verbs of perception to talk about the mental operation of understanding.

(4)  a.  *I see your point.*
     b.  *I hear what you're saying.*

Lakoff and Johnson (1980) have also pointed out that verbs of physical manipulation are used to talk about mental operations. So when English speakers want to convey their degree of understanding of an issue, they may say something like:

(5)  a.  *I have a good **grasp** of the issues.*
     b.  *I don't have a good **grip** on the theory.*

English speakers also use general language of physical compulsion, forward motion, and paths to talk about internal states of understanding and reasoning:

(6)  a.  *Her carefully developed argument **forced** me **to move from** my original **position**.*
     b.  *He **swayed** the crowd **to his side** with his passionate speech.*
     c.  *My thoughts were **racing ahead to the next point** in the argument.*
     d.  ***Part way through** his argument, he suddenly **changed direction**.*

As Sweetser (1990) argues, "a pervasive and coherently structured system of metaphors underlies our tendency to use vocabulary from the external domain in speaking of the internal domain" (p. 49).

Historically, the English modals developed from non-modal lexical items that first expressed physical strength or social obligation; for instance, *may/might* derive from *magan* 'be strong' (clearly physical strength) and *must* derives historically from *moste*, the past form of *mot*, meaning 'obliged' (clearly social obligation). The general pattern of historical development for modal verbs was that the semantics and usage of the non-modal forms gradually extended to root modal meaning and later broadened to epistemic meaning. Sweetser (1990) argues that these historical changes are systematically motivated by the ubiquitous cognitive pattern of using language from the external world to express aspects of the internal, mental world. She further notes, "Thus, we view our reasoning processes as being subject to compulsions, obligations, and barriers just as our real-world actions are subject to modalities of the same sort" (p. 50). Sweetser also emphasizes that physical forces are not objectively similar to our mental processes, but rather that humans' experience of the physical world and the domain of reasoning share a certain amount of common structure which allows metaphorical mappings between the two.

In her analysis, Sweetser (1990) offers distinct root meanings for each of the modals based on different kinds of forces emanating from different sources. Here we will consider her representations of *must, need to, may*, and *can*. The root meaning of *must* is represented as an irresistible force directing the subject or mover toward an act, an irresistible compulsion imposed by someone else, as in the following, from a high school policy statement:

(7)  *You **must** get your research paper in by the deadline or you will not be allowed to graduate with your class.*

Here the compelling force is the authority of the institution which is imposing the writing of a research paper on the student. In distinction from *must*, Sweetser represents *need to* as a compelling force imposed by something **internal** to the actor. For instance, in *I **need to** get a haircut*,[6] the internal force involves the speaker's desire to have a particular groomed appearance. Sweetser illustrates the semantic distinction in the following sentences:

(8)  a.  *I **need to** get this paper in, but I guess I'll go to the movies instead.*
     b.  *??I **must** get this paper in, but I guess I'll go to the movies instead.* (p. 54)

Here we can understand that an internal force, even if it is strong, can be rejected by the speaker/actor, thus accounting for the acceptability of a), while the compelling external force is irresistible, thus accounting for the oddity of b).

*May* is represented as a situation in which an authority figure takes away or keeps away a potential barrier that would prevent the doer from undertaking some action. In other words, keeping the barrier at bay has the result of allowing the doer to perform the action. Thus, the meaning focuses on the lack of restriction imposed on the doer by someone else who has the authority or power to impose the restriction, and hence the interpretation of permission granted by an authority who could potentially block the doer's action. In contrast, *can* is represented as a positive physical or social ability on the part of the doer, analogous to potential energy in physics. The energy or ability emanates from the doer. Sweetser (1990) argues that if we assume that the domain of reasoning is understood in terms of the social-physical world, we have an accurate, motivated explanation for the systematic polysemy of root and epistemic meanings found with virtually all the modals. Thus, each epistemic modal usage is metaphorically correlated with that real-world modality which is its closest parallel in force-dynamic structure. In terms of *may*,

> "we can see why general sociophysical potentiality, and specifically social permission, should be …chosen as analogous to possibility in the world of reasoning. *May* is an absent potential barrier in the sociophysical world, and the epistemic *may* is a metaphorically extended case to the world of reasoning. The meaning of epistemic *may* would thus be that there is no barrier to the speaker's process of reasoning from the available premises to the conclusion expressed in the sentence qualified by *may*…"                                                   (Sweetser, 1990:59)

Sweetser offers the following examples:

(9)  a.  *John may go* = John is not barred by authority from going.
     b.  *John may be at the party* = I am not barred by my premises from the conclusion that he is there. (p. 59)

The epistemic uses of *might, could, will, would, must, shall, should,* and so on all represent parallel extensions of the particular forces and barriers indicated by the modal in the social-physical world to the domain of reasoning and logical prediction.

As Sweetser points out, if root modals are understood as referring to speech acts, such as permission or advice, it is almost impossible to account for their epistemic uses. From a speech act perspective, the *may* of permission, as in *You may leave the table* seems to have little connection to epistemic *may* as in *That may be John now.* For the L2 learner, presentations of modals solely in terms of speech act uses have the result that, rather than creating a systematic schema to understand and learn modal usage, all the various uses of each modal must be memorized piecemeal.

So far we have seen how metaphoric extension of force dynamics into the domain of reasoning is a key conceptual metaphor for explaining the modal verbs. A second metaphor central in our analysis of modals is the proximal-distal metaphor, NOW IS HERE — THEN IS THERE. In general, this conceptual metaphor involves English speakers' use of tense to code non-temporal information and maps proximal and distal spatial phenomena and their real world consequences to temporal language. An important reflex of the proximal-distal metaphor involves the use of present tense to indicate a higher degree of surety, realis, and speaker force, in contrast to the use of past tense to indicate a lower degree of surety, irrealis, and an attenuation of speaker force or control. Experientially, humans are much surer of the reality that they can immediately perceive with their physical senses than they are of the reality that is out of range of their physical senses. This includes being surer of that which is experienced in the immediate moment than that which we remember. Thus, present tense is used to express higher degrees of surety, realis, and force than is past tense. The metaphor explains the systematic lessening of surety and realis indicated by the use of historically past tense modals. Thus in the present/past pairs *will/would, can/could,* and *shall/should,* we find the past tense forms consistently indicating less surety on the part of the speaker or less social and/or physical force. For example, in legal discourse *shall* indicates a legally binding circumstance while *should* indicates a preferred, but non-binding circumstance.

This metaphor also offers a coherent explanation for politeness phenomena. An important aspect of entities being physically proximal is that they are potentially under our physical control. If a parent wants to control an unruly two-year-old, physical constraint, and hence physical proximity, is often required. In many situations, humans have learned to use language to assert control in lieu of physical control. In situations of possible imposition (or face threat), English speakers tend to make requests, offer invitations, and so on, using the past tense, even when there is no implication of reference to past time. Following the logic of the conceptual metaphor THEN IS THERE, using the past tense implies that the speaker is physically distant from the addressee and therefore cannot exercise physical control over the addressee. The further implication is that the addressee is free to agree to or reject the imposition. It is always more pleasant to feel one has the choice to agree rather than feeling that one is being forced to agree. Hence, the metaphor accounts for otherwise puzzling uses of past tense to indicate politeness. Fleishman (1990) cites the following as a conventionally polite way to issue an invitation:

(10)   *Hi, are you busy? I **was** hoping you **were** free for lunch.*

The typical interpretation is that the hoping continues into the moment of speaking, not that it is in the past. Indeed, it would seem quite odd for a speaker to announce such a hope if it were no longer the case that she/he wanted to invite the addressee to lunch. This example is exploiting the implication of physical distance, cued by the use of past tense, which gives a nod to the polite fiction that the addressee is freer to accept or reject the request. The modal verbs reflect this systematic pattern of present and past tense in the uses of the historically past tense modals *could* and *would* as the polite forms of *can* and *will* to make requests, suggestions, etc.

A CL-based analysis of modals grounded in force dynamics and metaphorical extension allows for a principled explanatory representation of the semantics of these modals. Sweetser (1990) has provided precise, distinct definitions of each of the root meanings and their epistemic counterparts. Drawing on the notion of conceptual metaphor and embodied meaning, CL also offers a systematic account of the relations between the historically present and past modal forms.

Moreover, the emphasis on embodied experience and force dynamics within the spatial-physical world allows Tyler (2008) to represent the meaning of each modal with diagrams or depictions of scenes, rather than relying solely on linguistic propositions or dictionary definitions.[7] These diagrams rather straightforwardly capture the nuanced differences among the various modals. This allows for detailed, accurate specification of the meaning of the modals with a minimum of technical explanations or jargon, thus offering the possibility that the CL-based visual representations of the modals are more accessible to language learners.

Figure 1 attempts to represent Sweetser's analysis of *will, would must, should, could can,* and *may* with a minimum amount of jargon or explanation.

Some explanation is needed in order to interpret the diagrams. The first column represents the social/physical (or root) interpretation of the modal. The second column offers a metaphoric translation of the root use into the logical reasoning (or epistemic) use. The third column provides examples of logical reasoning uses.

The actor/mover is the figure walking forward. Internal force is represented by lines in the actor/mover's head, as in the representation of *will*. Double arms indicate greater force than single arms, as in the representations of the external authority in *must* versus the external authority in *should*. Historically present tense modals are represented in solid lines. Historically past tense modals are represented in dotted lines.

If we take the representation of *will* in the first column, the actor/mover is moving forward along a path. The extended, double arms are meant to represent strong forward momentum. The lines inside the actor's head indicate that the force is internally generated, coming from the actor's own desire or ability. The solid lines indicate this is the present tense form and thus the stronger form of the modal.

Physical/Social                    EXTENSION                    Predictive/Reasoning
                                                                **SITUATION: SOMEONE IS
                                                                KNOCKING AT THE DOOR.
                                                                THE SPEAKER CAN'T SEE WHO
                                                                IT IS**

WILL

Force comes from actor/mover.          *Just as I am sure about the state*    *That will be Liz at the door.*
Absolute certainty or commitment       *of the world and my commit-*          I have no question that Liz is
or desire → future implied             *ments, the evidence leads me*         knocking at the door. All the
                                        *to the absolute certainty of my*      information I have leads me to this
*You will finish the paper*             *conclusion.*                          conclusion.
*today*=strong command from
superior                                                                       Very strong certainty. Not used very
*Don't worry, you will finish this pa-*                                        often.
*per today and then you'll feel much*
*better*= strong encouragement

WOULD

Strong, but slightly weakened          *The evidence gives strong support*    *That would be Liz at the door.*
commitment or desire= *You would*      *for my conclusion, but there is a*    'I think there is a very good chance
*finish this paper today (if you work*  *little room for doubt or lessening*   that Liz is at the door. There is a
*all afternoon)*                        *of my desires.*                       small chance it is someone else, like
 Speaker is making a strong sug-                                               the next door neighbor who often
gestion.                                                                       drops by.

MUST

Outside authority
Irresistible force

*You must finish this paper today* (or you'll fail the course)
*You must be happy you took this course.* (After all, you earned an A+ and the professor has offered you an assistantship in his lab).

SHOULD

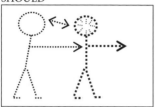

3 forces: strong outside authority; the actor/mover's recognition of the legitimacy of the outside authority; mover's internal force (somewhat weakened). Often signals a sense of obligation.

*You should finish this paper today. (You know it was due yesterday and the professor said he'll take points off for late homework)*
Speaker is indicating outside force and also appealing to the listener's sense of responsibility or obligation.

COULD

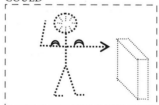

Weakened ability to under-take action. Implies possibility.

*You could finish the paper today.*
Speaker is indicating a possibility; making a suggestion that doesn't imply the speaker is attempting to put pressure on the mover.

*The evidence is so strong it forces me to the conclusion.*

*If all the evidence holds, or all the events follow according to the way they have in the past, or if everything follows the rules, then I can conclude X.* (Past experience acts like the external authority; mover recognizes the legitimacy of the outside authority)

The evidence provides weakened support to possibly conclude X, but other evidence suggests a different conclusion

*That must be Liz.*
The information is so strong that I am forced to conclude Liz is at the door.

Very high certainty. Often indicates the speaker has considered a couple options, then come to a very strong conclusion.

*That should be Liz.*

The information strongly suggests that it is Liz. Speaker was probably expecting Liz and no one else. If events are following their planned or expected course, Liz is knocking at the door.

*That could be Liz =*

Some of the facts suggest that there is a possibility that Liz is at the door. Other facts suggest someone else is at the door.

The speaker is not sure who is at the door. There is a possibility it is Liz.

CAN                                                                    *CAN

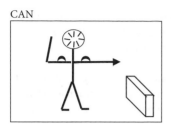

Indicates ability or know how.          This is the only modal that spe-
                                        cifically relates to ability. Doesn't
I know I can lift 100 pounds. Nancy     have an epistemic extension.
can multiply huge numbers in her
head.

MAY

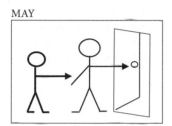

External authority allows action,    *Nothing bars me from concluding*   *That may be Liz.* =
takes away possible barrier to       *X* (but nothing compels me to      'The speaker is not sure who is at
action.                              conclude this)                      the door. There is no evidence bar-
                                                                         ring the speaker from concluding
You may leave whenever you are                                           it is Liz, but neither is there strong
finished.                                                                evidence indicating that it is Liz.

**Figure 1.** Considering the English Modal Verbs from a FORCE DYNAMIC PERSPECTIVE

The diagram for *must* involves an external authority, represented by the larger figure with double arms, which is directly placing pressure on the actor/mover's back. This represents irresistible
force. This contrasts with the representation for *should* which involves both internal and external
forces. In this diagram, the larger, external authority is pushing on the actor/mover's back. There are
also lines inside the actor/mover's head indicating internal motivation. The actor/mover's recognition of the external force's legitimate authority is represented by a double-headed arrow between the
external authority and the actor. It is this recognition of the legitimacy of the external authority on
the part of the actor/mover that gives *should* a moral dimension in certain contexts.

### Experimental support for the approach
To examine the efficacy of using a CL-based approach to teaching the modals, a quasi-experimental
effects-of-instruction experiment was conducted.

### Participants
The 64 participants were matriculated college students who had received at least a score of 80 on the
Internet-based TOEFL test or its equivalent. Institutional specific tests indicated that they needed
ELT support. They were judged to be at an advanced intermediate level. Nearly all were graduate stu-
dents. Most were majoring in science or finance-related fields. Participants spoke a wide assortment

of L1s, including Chinese, Arabic, Turkish, Farsi, Korean, Spanish, Portuguese, Russian, Kazakh, and French. Over half were native speakers of Chinese. Most had resided in the U.S. or another English-speaking country for less than a year. As part of their regular classroom instruction, the participants were presented a unit on the modals.

The participants were divided into three groups. 38 participants were in the Cognitive treatment group and 16 were in the Speech Act treatment group. Ten were in a control group which took the pre and posttest but received no instruction on the modals; the purpose of this testing was to ensure that learning did not take place simply by taking the test twice.

*Design*

Table 1 summarizes the overall design of the study: Both the cognitive treatment group and the Speech Act treatment group took a pretest on the first day. The second day of treatment, each group received teacher-fronted instruction on the modals followed by pair work that focused on appropriately using these modals in various scenarios. The third day, both groups participated in computer-delivered self-instruction, followed by a posttest. Care was taken to ensure that both groups spent equal amounts of time on task and both received equal amounts of exposure to the modals. The control group simply took the pretest and several days later the posttest. They received no classroom instruction on the modals. In order to provide adequate explanation for the Cognitive group, as well as practice using the forms appropriately, it was decided to target only four modals: *could, would, should, must.*

**Table 1.** Overview of Experimental Procedure

| Group | Session 1 | Session 2 | Session 3 |
|---|---|---|---|
| Cognitive | Pretest | (1) 50-minute teacher-fronted instruction<br>(2) 30 minutes of pairwork | (1) 50-minute instruction delivered via computer<br>(2) Posttest |
| Speech Act | Pretest | (1) 40-minute teacher-fronted instruction<br>(2) 40 minutes of pairwork | (1) 50-minute instruction delivered via computer<br>(2) Posttest |
| Control | Pretest | | Posttest |

*Pre- and posttests*

Two tests were developed, Version A and Version B. The tests had a forced-choice, fill-in-the-blank format. The tests consisted of 40 short dialogs or paragraphs, each of which was missing a modal. Subjects were asked to choose the most appropriate modal from among four possible choices. The dialogs and paragraphs were constructed so that only one choice was appropriate. The tests were piloted with native speakers of English and adjusted until each paragraph received 100% agreement on the appropriate modal choice. For each of the tests, 20 items targeted a social (or root) meaning and 20 targeted a logical prediction (or epistemic) meaning. For each of the four target modals, four social and four logical prediction items were constructed; thus, eight items were constructed for each targeted modal for a total of 32 target items. An additional eight filler items were constructed which targeted uses of the modal *might*. Subjects' scores on the filler items in which *might* was the targeted answer were not used in calculating scores. Below are examples of the test items:

a.    Logical prediction (Epistemic) — Appropriate answer is *must.*
      Instructions: Circle the most appropriate modal verb within the context.
      **might, must, should, would**

John: I can't believe he's 52! He doesn't look a day older than 20.

Tom: There's just no way a person that age can look like that without some special help. He _____ have had plastic surgery.

b.   Social/real world (root) — Appropriate answer is *should*.
Instructions: Circle the most appropriate modal verb within the context.
**could, must, should, would**

A:   I wonder why they haven't delivered the pizza. When did you order it?

B:   About an hour ago.

A:   That's strange. Usually they deliver in 30 minutes. It _____ be here by now! I wonder if the driver is having trouble finding the house.

B:   Why don't you try calling them and see what's happening?

The tests were blocked so that half the subjects in each group received Version A as the pretest and half received Version B. Those who received Version A as the pretest received Version B as the post-test and vice versa. To determine whether the test forms were equivalent, the scores on the two tests were compared. A two-way ANCOVA with both Treatment and Test Form Order as between subject variables and pretest scores as covariate was conducted. Mean scores for the Test Form A pretest group, with scores adjusted to account for pretest results, was 21.9, whereas the mean for the Test Form B pretest group was 22.0. The ANCOVA indicated no significant different between the Test Form orders, and the eta squared value indicated that no variance was due to the test form order, $F(1,53) = .013$, $p = .909$, $\eta_p^2 = .000$. The results of comparing the two test versions are represented in Table 2:

**Table 2.** Descriptive Statistics Comparing the Two Modals Test Forms.

|                | N  | M    | SD  | Range |
|----------------|----|------|-----|-------|
| Pretest Form A  | 27 | 20.5 | 3.5 | 12–27 |
| Pretest Form B  | 27 | 21.6 | 3.4 | 13–27 |
| Posttest Form A | 27 | 22.1 | 3.7 | 12–29 |
| Posttest Form B | 27 | 22.9 | 4.3 | 13–32 |

In sum, the level of difficulty of Version A and Version B were highly comparable.

*Cognitive treatment*
One of the researchers led a 50 minute teacher-fronted, interactive explanation of a force dynamic and metaphoric extension interpretation of the modals. The researcher began by mentioning some of the modal verbs (e.g., *will, would, can, could, should*, and *must*) and the fact that most second language learners found modal verbs confusing because they were difficult to define and because many had more than one meaning. Next the researcher explained that the class would be looking at the modals from a perspective that involved defining the modals in terms of physical forces and metaphorical extensions from the physical/social world to the world of reasoning (or making logical predictions). After the brief introduction, the students were given a worksheet which represented the force dynamics associated with each modal in terms of the diagrams illustrated in Figure 1 and discussed in the previous section. Students were allowed to quickly look over the handout. Next, the researcher explained the conventions used in the diagrams, such as double outstretched arms indi-

cating more force than single outstretched arm and external force or authority being represented by a larger figure applying various amounts of pressure on the actor's back, as with *must* and *should*.

Also, the researcher discussed the HERE IS NOW-THERE IS THEN metaphor and the notion that humans are more sure of events and situations happening in the present moment than in the past because the events and situations in the present are perceptually verifiable. The solid lines indicated a present tense form and thus the stronger form of the modal.

Using the worksheet as a basis for discussion, the researcher led a discussion of each modal. A variety of techniques to engage the participants were used. For instance, when *will* was introduced, the researcher acted out forward motion with arms outstretched and discussed the noun *will*, as in phrases such as '*My own free will*' or '*She has a lot of will power.*' Throughout the teacher-fronted portion, participants were encouraged to provide their own examples and ask questions. The discussion lasted approximately 50 minutes.

The teacher-fronted instruction was followed by an interactive task in which the participants worked in pairs. The participants were given a worksheet with one model scenario with accompanying questions and two additional scenarios. The researcher led the class through the model scenario and the accompanying questions. The model scenario appears in Figure 2.

After modeling the interactive task, the researcher asked the participants to consider two additional scenarios with their partners and to write their responses to the questions on their worksheets. The participants were encouraged to refer to their handout with the diagrams and to use force dynamic interpretations of the modals as they discussed the examples. All the pairs finished discussing the two scenarios within the allotted 20 minutes. Two of the researchers circulated among the groups, engaging them in discussion and answering questions.

---

Example 1: You **should** *go to the doctor.*
In what context do you use **should?**
Context sentence is underlined.
Case A: You've been coughing for two weeks. You **should** go to the doctor.

Do you think **should** works for this context? Why or why not?

Answer: Yes, **should** works. By using **should**, the speaker (who is acting as the outside authority) is giving a strong suggestion. The speaker is very concerned about his friend's health since he has been sick for so long. **Should** also shows the speaker thinks the listener has some responsibility to follow the suggestion. Anyone who has had a bad cough for two weeks knows going to the doctor is a good idea. The speaker thinks that it is clearly in the listener's best interest to follow this suggestion.

---

**Figure 2.** Cognitive group: sample pair work exercise.

Four days later, the participants met in a computer lab and worked through a computer-delivered, self-instruction module which reviewed the force dynamic explanation of the modals, provided multiple examples of the uses of the modals *should, would, could,* and *must,* and which also presented eight example scenarios of each targeted modal (4 root uses; 4 epistemic uses). Each scenario was accompanied by three questions which focused on a CL-based explanation for the use of the modal. A sample scenario and a question illustrating the physical/social use of *must* appears in Figure 3.

All the participants finished the computer-delivered self-instruction within the allotted 50 minutes. Immediately after finishing the self-instruction, particpants completed the posttest.

Consider the forces at play in this use of **MUST**:

Rachel: *Our professor is very strict about meeting deadlines. He said he would not accept any late home-work. That means I **must** get my homework in by 5pm today or not get any credit.*

Click on the source of the force shown by Rachel's use of **must**:

1. *Rachel's internal desire to do well in the course.*
2. *Rachel's respect for the professor and her internal acceptance of his authority.*
3. *Rachel's understanding of the professor's right to set strict deadlines and that she has no choice but to follow the rules if she wants to get credit for the homework.*

(Correct choice is 3).

**Figure 3.** Cognitive group: Self-instruction materials. Sample scenario and questions illustrating the physi-cal/social use of *must*

### Speech Act treatment

The lesson was taught by two of the researchers. It began with a short video clip from a popular U.S. sitcom. The two characters in the clip were discussing a small crafts business that character A was involved in. Character A knew very little about practical business matters, whereas B was a highly educated, but socially incompetent, math expert. A and B determined that A was losing money. B declared that he knew how to make the business viable. At this point, B began to leave.

(11)  A:  B, **could** you help me make this work?
      B:  Yes, of course, I **could.** (B again begins to leave.)
      A:  Wait B, **would** you help me?

The researchers led a discussion of the uses of *could* and *would* in the dialog. The key points are that the first use of *could* is technically ambiguous. The most likely interpretation is that A is requesting B's help. However, it is also possible to interpret this as a query about B's ability to help. B appears to be responding to the second, less likely interpretation. This emphasizes a rule found in most of the ELT materials that when a speaker makes a request for assistance using the form *could*, the appropri-ate affirmative response is to use *can*, not *could* (As in, *Yes, of course I can help.*). The second point was to contrast the meaning difference between B's use of *could* and A's use of *would*.

Next, the researchers distributed the 'Modal Verbs and their Functions' handout and led a dis-cussion over the major speech act functions and the modals that are used to express those speech acts. The worksheet was based on the presentation of modal verbs found in 10 current ELT texts. The worksheet presented nine major speech acts functions expressed by modal verbs, along with each modal verb that was claimed to be used to express that speech act. The speech acts included: (1) expressing physical ability, (2) seeking and granting permission, (3) making a request, (4) giving advice, (5) giving a suggestion, (6) stating a preference, (7) expressing necessity and obligation, (8) discussing future possibility, and (9) making assumptions. Figure 4 provides examples for two func-tions, giving advice and making assumptions.

As with the Cognitive treatment group, the researchers used a variety of techniques to engage the students. For instance, when introducing 'making assumptions', two students were asked to step outside the room, close the door, and then one knocked on the door. The participants who remained in the room were asked how sure they were that student X was knocking on the door. When they indicated they were sure it was one of the two students who had just left the room even though they could not see who was knocking, but were not able to say with certainty which of the two was knocking, the researcher directed their attention to the making assumptions (or logical prediction)

| Speech Act | Modal | Examples |
|---|---|---|
| *Give advice* | **should** | Anne seems to struggle with math and physics. She <u>should</u> get a good tutor. |
| | **ought to** | If you are having trouble making friends, you <u>ought to</u> spend more time with the rest of us. |
| | **had better** | Harry looks very tired. He'<u>d better</u> get some rest. The exam is tomorrow morning. |
| *Make assumption* | **may** | I have tried to call Mary several times but no one has answered. I <u>may</u> have the wrong number. |
| | **might** | She <u>might</u> be at the library. She always studies hard for her exams. |
| | **could** | I heard someone at the door. It <u>could</u> be my husband coming home from work. |

**Figure 4.** Traditional group: Sample excerpt from worksheet, Modal verbs and their Speech Act functions *can, could, may, might, must, ought to, should, will, would*

use of *might and could*. The researchers asked individual participants to read the example sentences out loud and explain the meaning of the modal in terms of the strength of the speaker's attitude. The researchers were careful to actively engage the participants by acting out sample sentences and making sure that each participant made at least one oral contribution. Participants were also asked to volunteer additional examples of their own for each of the speech acts. This discussion lasted approximately 40 minutes. The group discussion was followed by three interactive tasks.

The three interactive tasks were developed to encourage the participants to consider the various speech acts that had been identified with modals verbs and to practice using the appropriate modal verb in context. The tasks included controlled construction of a dialog (followed by a suggested model dialog using appropriate modals); this task was done in pairs. The second task was a dialog in which 6 errors with modals occurred and where the participants were asked to identify the errors and change them to appropriate modal choices; this task was done in pairs. In the final task, participants were put in groups of four. This was an open-ended task in which the participants were given a current TV schedule and asked to come to a determination of which specific program to watch at a particular time. This task emphasized the speech acts of requesting, giving advice, giving suggestions, and stating a preference. Completion of each task was followed by a large group discussion of the groups' results. Across the three tasks, care was taken to balance the number of opportunities to use each of the nine speech acts and each of the modal verbs, so that participants had the opportunity to use each of the modal verbs listed on the handout at least once for each of the speech act functions identified on the worksheet. Participants were encouraged to consult the worksheet as they completed the tasks.

Four days later, the participants were given a 50 minute, computer-delivered lesson on modals. The instruction consisted of nine passages based on current ELT teaching materials. Each passage highlighted one of the nine speech acts presented on the first day's handout. Care was taken to include visuals such as cartoons and pictures to make the materials engaging. Each passage was introduced with a brief review of the targeted speech act. The review section of the self-instruction was followed by a set of exercises. The exercises were of two types: (1) a passage in which three modals were bolded, where the participants were asked to determine the speech act each modal was expressing; (2) a passage containing several errors with modals, where the participants were asked to identify the errors and supply the appropriate modal. The length of the Speech Act computer delivered instruction was closely matched with that of the Cognitive computer delivered instruction. The Cognitive instruction involved more explanation of concepts, such as force dynamics and metaphorical extension. This was balanced by providing more examples of modals used in context in the Speech Act materials. All the participants completed the self-instruction module within the allotted 50 minutes. Immediately after completing the module, they took the posttest.

## Results

To determine whether the cognitive treatment group ($N = 38$) outscored the speech act treatment group ($N = 16$) when the effect of prior knowledge was taken into account, an Analysis of Covariance (ANCOVA) was conducted using SPSS. The between-subjects independent variable of treatment type had two levels (cognitive and speech act). The dependent variable consisted of modal posttest scores. The covariate consisted of modal pretest scores.

The assumptions for ANCOVA were met. The pretest and posttest scores of each group had a normal distribution, and all tests for skewedness and kurtosis were nonsignificant. As required by ANCOVA, the covariate (pretest scores) was independent of the effects of the treatment. Moreover, a Levene's Test of Equality of Error Variances was nonsignficant ($p = .902$), showing that the assumption of homogeneity of variance had not been violated.

The adjusted means for the posttest (adjusted to account for pretest results) were 23.3 and 20.6 respectively for the Cognitive and Speech Act groups. The ANCOVA revealed a main effect for treatment type: $F(1,53) = 7.31$, $p = .000$, $\eta_p^2 = .125$. The confidence interval at $p = .05$, using a Bonferroni adjustment for multiple comparisons, was between 0.7 and 4.6 for the mean difference between the Cognitive and Speech Act group. The Cognitive group thus significantly outperformed the Speech Act group, with treatment type able to account for 12.5% of the between-subject variance. These results are represented on Table 3.

**Table 3.** Scores of three instruction type groups on the 32-item modal test

| Instructional Type | N | Pretest | | Posttest | |
|---|---|---|---|---|---|
| | | M (SD) | Range | M (SD) | Range |
| Control | 9 | 22.4 (2.1) | 17–27 | 22.7 (3.5) | 18–24 |
| Speech Act | 16 | 20.3 (3.4) | 13–26 | 20.2 (4.4) | 12–28 |
| Cognitive | 38 | 21.3 (3.5) | 12–27 | 23.4* (3.5) | 17–32 |

* Significant at $p < .001$

The gain scores for the groups are represented in Figure 5.

In sum, the results show that the Cognitive group improved in their use of the modals, while the Speech Act group showed no gain.

## Discussion

The results of the statistical tests show that the Cognitive group experienced significant gains over the Speech Act group. It is important to note that the treatment effect was moderate (a 2.7-point gain). However, we argue the gain was considerable in light of the limited duration of the treatment. Both groups received approximately 2 hours of instruction on the modals. The Cognitive group had many new concepts to learn. For instance, they were asked to think about the modals in terms of force dynamics and consider the role of metaphor in structuring the grammatical system. These represent radically different ways of thinking about grammar. At the same time, they were asked to learn specific, new meanings for each of the modals presented and think about how the modals are

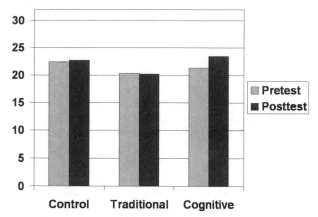

**Figure 5.** Modal pretest and posttest scores of three experimental groups.

used to make meaning in context. This represents a set of relatively heavy cognitive demands. In contrast, for the most part, the material presented to the Speech Act group was a review of an analysis they had been introduced to in the past. They were not asked to learn a new system for thinking about the modals; rather they were given many contextualized examples of the modals and a set of formal rules to guide their appropriate choice of the modals.

Although the approach to modals was not new, the treatment did allow considerable opportunity for the participants in the Speech Act group to learn (or memorize) contextualized uses of the modals that they had not yet mastered. In other words, the Speech Act group received considerable implicit input. During the teacher-fronted instruction, the researchers actively engaged the participants in the Speech Act group, encouraging them to consider how each of the modals functioned in context. The self-instruction component provided many contextualized uses of the target items. Thus, we feel that the gains demonstrated by the Cognitive group provide important support for the efficacy of using a CL approach to teaching the modals.

Nevertheless, some caveats must be issued. The target items in this study are not a full representation of the modal system. Several of the modals and periphrastic constructions were not addressed. Meaning shifts that occur when modals are negated or used in questions were also unaddressed. These are important, complicating aspects of the system. Tyler (2008) offers a fuller CL-based analysis of the modal system. An important direction for future research would be a longitudinal study which targets a fuller representation of the modal system.

Moreover, all the students had been introduced to the modals in previous classes. All of them knew a number of formulaic, speech act uses of the modals. In spite of our criticism of the speech act analysis, we must acknowledge that in order for students to gain full mastery of the modals, they are likely to need a great deal of contextualized exposure to how native speakers use the modals in order to perform various speech acts. This suggests that an approach that combines a CL approach with a contextualized speech act approach might be optimal. An important direction for future research would be a long-term study that uses such a combined approach.

Finally, the Cognitive treatment was presented by the lead researcher, who developed the analysis. The Speech Act treatment was presented by both the lead researcher and a second researcher, neither of who had been instrumental in developing the analysis. Although the researchers tried to present both approaches with enthusiasm and imagination, it is possible that the Cognitive group sensed more enthusiasm for the approach than did the Speech Act group.

## Conclusion

We believe that L2 researchers and teachers would be well served by reassessing their (often implicit) assumptions about the nature of language and the traditional models of language that forms the basis of most L2 texts and grammars.

We further argue that Cognitive Linguistics, which represents a radical departure from the models found in current ELT textbooks, is a theoretical approach that offers important new insights into grammar and lexis. The focus of the present experimental work has been on the English modals, but there are many other areas of grammar that have been analyzed by cognitive linguists, yielding insights that the interested language teacher would find informative. A major challenge to applied cognitive linguists is to demonstrate to L2 researchers and teachers that Cognitive Linguistics is not only a more complete and accurate theoretical approach to language, but also one that is of particular benefit to L2 learners. Key to this endeavor is creating and testing language teaching materials that maintain the precision offered by the theoretical model, but that are also accessible to L2 teachers and learners. The experimental examination of effectiveness of using CL-based teaching materials for the modals represents a promising step in this process.

## Notes

1. Within formal semantics, what we term root meaning is often referred to as deontic.

2. The speech act-based approach to modals found in the 10 current ELT textbooks we examined is sometimes also referred to as a Notional-Functional account. These texts did not strictly adhere to the taxonomies developed by Austin (1962) or later by Searle (1969). Rather these textbook authors developed their own unique taxonomies, using terms for speech acts such as (1) expressing physical ability, (2) seeking and granting permission, (3) making a request, (4) giving advice, (5) giving a suggestion, (6) stating a preference, (7) expressing necessity and obligation, (8) discussing future possibility, and (9) making assumptions. None of these texts discussed theoretical foundations for their analysis or presentation of language points. It is particularly important to note that our use of the term 'functional' does not refer to the broad set of research endeavors, such as Dik's functional model (1989) or Halliday's Functional Systemic Grammar. Indeed, several of these research endeavors have addressed English modals in far more sophisticated, systematic ways than found in the 'notional-functional' approaches used in typical ELT textbooks. However, since none of these analyses have been adopted into current ELT textbooks, consideration of their potential contribution to ELT pedagogy is beyond the scope of the present paper.

3. CL is best described as an approach to language, which shares a number of common assumptions, rather than a specific model of language. CL includes at least two versions of Cognitive Semantics (e.g. Lakoff 1987/1991; Talmy 2000), Cognitive Grammar (Langacker, 1987, 1991), Construction Grammar(s) (e.g., Goldberg 1995, 2006), and Blending Theory (Fauconnier & Turner 2002).

4. Other Cognitive Linguists, most notably Langacker (1991) and Nuyts (2001) have offered somewhat different accounts of English modals than those proposed by Sweetser (1990) and Talmy (1988; 2000). We chose to base our experimental materials on Sweetser (1990) because her account focuses on several basic tenets of CL (such as embodied meaning in the form of human understanding of force dynamics, metaphorical extension from the socio-physical to the more internal and abstract, and motivated polysemy) which we believe are particularly important for L2 practitioners and students to understand. The analyses offered by Langacker and Nuyts are more technically dense and less readily understandable by the non-expert. Their insights, such as Langacker's notion of subjectivity, may ultimately provide important additions to a presentation of the modals for L2 practitioners and learners. However, at this point, we felt attempting to incorporate these theoretical tenets into our presentation of the modals was beyond the scope of the current project.

5. The overview of modals presented in this paper represents a rudimentary outline of the system. There are additional modals, such as the so-called periphrastic modals, and a number of quirks having to do with

shifting meanings when modals are negated or used in questions which are not addressed. A review of all these properties represents a book length discussion.

**6.** It is possible to say something like *I must get my hair cut*. Following Sweetser's argument, this would indicate a subtle shift in the speaker's stance, perhaps indicating a sense of obligation to meet certain societal expectations about grooming.

**7.** Since their early work on CL, researchers like Langacker (1987), Lakoff (1987) and Talmy (2000) have conceptualized the semantics of verbs, prepositions, grammatical aspect and other linguistic elements in terms of spatial scenes. The use of diagrams to depict the meanings of linguistic forms is a well-established CL tradition.

## References

Austin, J. 1962. *How to Do Things with Words*, 2nd edn. Oxford: OUP.

Achard, M. & Niemeier, S. (eds). 2004. *Cognitive Linguistics, Second Language Acquisition, and Foreign Language Teaching*. Berlin: Mouton de Gruyter.

Biber, D., Johansson, S., Leech, G., Conrad, S. & Finegan, E. 1999. *Longman Grammar of Spoken and Written English*. London: Longman.

Boers, F. & Lindstromberg, S. (eds). 2008. *Cognitive Linguistic Approaches to Teaching Vocabulary and Phraseology*. Berlin: Mouton de Gruyter.

Celce-Murcia, M. & Larsen-Freeman, D. 1999. *The Grammar Book: An ESL/EFL Teacher's Course*, 2nd edn. Boston MA: Heinle & Heinle.

De Knop, S. & De Rycker, T. (eds). 2008 *Cognitive Approaches to Pedagogical Grammar*. Berlin: Mouton de Gruyter.

Dirven, R. 2001. English phrasal verbs: Theory and didactic application. In *Applied Cognitive Linguistics*, II: *Language Pedagogy*, M. Pütz,

S. Niemeier & R. Dirven (eds), 3–27. Berlin: Mouton de Gruyter.

Ellis, N.C. & Cadierno, T. 2009. Constructing a second language: Introduction to the special section. *Annual Review of Cognitive Linguistics* 7(1): 111–139.

Fauconnier, G. & Turner, M. 2002. *The Way We Think*. New York NY: Basic Books.

Fleischman, S. 1990. *Tense and Narrativity*. London: Routledge

Gibbs, R. 1994. *Poetics of the Mind*. Cambridge: CUP.

Gibbs, R. 2006. *Embodiment and Cognitive Science*. Cambridge: CUP.

Goldberg, A. 1995. *Constructions: A Construction Grammar Approach to Argument Structure*. Chicago IL: Chicago University Press.

Goldberg, A. 2006. *Constructions at Work*. Oxford: OUP.

Holme, R. 2008. *Cognitive Linguistics and Language Teaching*. Basingstoke: Palgrave Macmillian.

Lakoff, G. & Johnson, M. 1980. *Metaphors We Live By*. Chicago IL: University of Chicago Press.

Lakoff, G. 1989. *Women, Fire, and Dangerous Things*. Chicago IL: Chicago University Press.

Langacker, R.W. 1987/1991. *The Foundations of Cognitive Grammar*, Vol. I & II, Stanford CA: Stanford University Press.

Langacker, R.W. 1991. *Concept, Image, and Symbol: The Cognitive Basis of Grammar*. Berlin: Mouton de Gruyter.

Larsen-Freeman, D. 1996. The role of linguistics in language teacher education. In *Proceedings of the 1995 Georgetown Roundtable*, J. Alatis, C. Straehle, B. Gallenburger & M. Ronkin (eds). Washington DC: Georgetown University Press.

Nuyts, J. 2001. *Epistemic Modality, Language, and Conceptualization. A Cognitive-Pragmatic Perspective* [Human Cognitive Processing 5]. Amsterdam: John Benjamins

Pütz, M., Niemeier, S. & Dirven, R. (eds). 2001. *Applied Cognitive Linguistics*, I & II: *Language Pedagogy*. Berlin: Mouton de Gruyter.

Radden, G. & Dirven, R. 2007. *Cognitive English Grammar*. Amsterdam: John Benjamins.

Robinson, P. & Ellis, N.C. (eds). 2008. *Handbook of Cognitive Linguistics and Second Language Acquisition*. London: Routledge.

Searle, J. 1969. *Speech Acts: An Essay in the Philosophy of Language*. Cambridge: CUP.

Spivey, M. 2007. *The Continuity of Mind*. Oxford: OUP.

Sweetser, E. 1990. *From Etymology to Pragmatics: Metaphorical and Cultural Aspects of Semantic Structure*. Cambridge: CUP.

Talmy, L. 1988. Force dynamics in language and cognition. *Cognitive Science* 12: 49–100.

Talmy, L. 2000. *Towards a Cognitive Semantics*, Vol. 1 and 2. Cambridge MA: The MIT Press.

Tyler, A. 2008. Cognitive linguistics and second language instruction. In *Handbook of Cognitive Linguistics and Second Language Acquisition*, P. Robinson & N.C. Ellis (eds), 456–488. London: Routledge.

Tyler, A. & Evans, V. 2000. My first husband was Italian: Examining "exceptional" uses of English tense. In *Linguistic Agency of University of Duisburg (L.A.U.D,)* Series A: *General and Theoretical Papers*.

Tyler, A. & Evans, V 2001. The relation between experience, conceptual structure and meaning: Non-temporal uses of tense and language teaching. In *Applied Cognitive Linguistics. I: Theory and Language Acquisition*, M. Pütz, S. Niemeier & R. Dirven (eds), 63–105. Berlin: Mouton de Gruyter.

Tyler, A. & Evans, V. 2003. *The Semantics of English Prepositions: Spatial Scenes, Embodied Meaning and Cognition*. Cambridge: CUP.

Werner, P. & Nelson, J. 1996. *Mosaics Two: A Content-based Grammar*. New York NY: McGraw-Hill.

*Authors' address*

Department of Linguistics
454 ICC
Georgetown University
Washington, DC 20057

tyleran@georgetown.edu

# Making sense of phrasal verbs

## A cognitive linguistic account of L2 learning

Rafael Alejo González
University of Extremadura, Spain

Phrasal verbs (PVs) have recently been the object of interest by linguists given their status as phraseological units whose meaning is non-compositional and opaque. They constitute a perfect case for theories of language processing and language acquisition to be tested. Cognitive linguists have participated in this debate and shown a certain interest for PVs, although their research on this topic stems in most of the cases from their central interest on prepositions and the language of spatiality. In this paper, I aim to make a comprehensive and critical summary of the cognitive linguistics (CL) literature on PVs with particular attention to its connection with usage-based approaches, especially in Second Language Acquisition (SLA), and to the concept of (meaning) motivation, which has proven to be useful in teaching. I will also present a CL analysis of the *out*-PVs (i.e., those containing the particle *out*) used by 3 groups of non-native speakers of English whose L1 respectively belongs to a Germanic satellite-framed (S-) language (Swedish and Dutch), a non-Germanic S-language (Russian and Bulgarian) and a verb-framed (V-) language (Spanish and Italian). The results obtained from this analysis show: (1) that both Germanic and Non-Germanic S-language learners use a greater number of *out*-PVs than V-language learners, not only when these verbs have a motional meaning but also when they express other meanings; and (2) that S-language learners also use a greater elaboration of path (Slobin 1996) when non-motional *out*-PV meanings are involved. These findings suggest that 'the thinking for speaking hypothesis' (Slobin 1996, 1997; Cadierno 2004), which has been shown to work for the domain of manner and path of motion, may in part be extended to the acquisition of PVs by L2 learners.

## Introduction

Since one of the defining features of Cognitive Linguistics (CL) is the assumption that language reflects the general workings of the human mind (cf. Evans & Green 2006), it is reasonable to infer that SLA provides an ideal testing ground, where the validity of CL intuitions and explanations can be put to the test. However, the amount of CL-oriented research focusing on SLA can still be considered as scarce and there are still many ways in which these two fields can work together.

Phrasal verb (PV) acquisition is one of the research areas where the collaboration between these two fields may bring benefits. Indeed, L2 acquisition of PVs has attracted some attention in second language teaching research, but very little research has been conducted using a strict CL approach, which among other things can offer an approach that differs greatly from other linguistic schools. Moreover, as we saw in the introduction to this volume, CL provides SLA with a language

*AILA Review* 23 (2010), 50–71. DOI 10.1075/aila.23.04ale
ISSN 1461–0213 / E-ISSN 1570–5595 © John Benjamins Publishing Company

typology, i.e., one that distinguishes between satellite-framed and verb-framed languages (Slobin 1996; Talmy 1985, 2000), which may shed light on the influence of the L1 on L2 learning.

This article is an attempt to summarize the main insights that CL has provided to explain the acquisition of PVs by L2 learners while at the same time exploring some novel ways in which CL can help to account for L1 influence on their acquisition. To achieve these goals, the article is organized as follows. First, I will focus on issues such as the definition, the terminology and linguistic debate generated by these verbs, which in my view shape the way in which the applied research is carried out. Then I will outline the applied linguistic literature that has dealt with PVs in the context of language teaching and SLA. Finally, I will present the results of a study of how CL can also be used to analyze the influence of the L1 of the learners in the acquisition of PVs by extending the 'thinking for speaking hypothesis' to these verbs.

*Definitions and terminology*
Much attention has been devoted, by the linguistics literature, to the study of PVs. It is beyond the scope of the present article to give a full account of the intricacies and complexities of the analyses provided by the different linguistic schools, as my focus is on L2 acquisition. However, a short introduction to the terminology and the relevant linguistic debates is important given its impact on methodology. What the learners are acquiring has to be defined, delimited and understood in the context of linguistic theory, because there are obvious discrepancies among schools and most importantly because their differing definitions also involve diverse boundaries of the phenomenon.

Although in this article the term PV is used, as it is the one preferred by the CL literature, there are other terms used with a very close meaning to it. For example, the term *multi-word verb* (Quirk *et al.* 1985) refers to the combination of a verb and an adverbial particle or a preposition when they function as a single unit where the meaning of the whole is not predictable from the meaning of its parts. The problem with the Quirk *et al.* definition is that it only uses the term *phrasal verb* for one of the groups of *multi-word verbs*, the other two being *prepositional verbs* and *phrasal prepositional verbs*. This restrictive use of the term *phrasal verb* is not the one used in this article since it is not the one generally adopted by the CL literature and its criteria are not semantically relevant from a CL perspective.

Another term is *verb particle constructions*, which is used both by generativists (cf. Dehé *et al.* 2002) and in approaches that are closer to Construction Grammar (Jackendoff 1997, 2002, 2010; Cappelle 2004, 2005). This term roughly corresponds to Quirk *et al.*'s *phrasal verbs* as it is based on the distinction between *particles* and *prepositions*, the only difference being that, at least in constructionist approaches, there is no need to make the distinction between *particles* and free combining adverbs as they are both form-function pairings. The main discrepancy lies in the idiomatic meaning of the former. For these authors, a variety of syntactic tests can be used to establish the distinction between *particles* and *prepositions*, but the usefulness of these tests is limited as they do not always work adequately (see O'Dowd 1998 and Cappelle 2005 for a full account).

*Particles* are interpreted in a different light under the CL perspective (Lindner 1981; Tyler and Evans 2003), as they are linguistic elements whose basic meaning can be traced back to their prototypical use as spatio-temporal adverbs. From this origin, the rest of the meanings can be said to be derived in a radial web of senses, which are sometimes thought to be the result of metaphor and sometimes the result of experiential correlation (Brugman 1981; Lakoff 1987; Morgan 1997; Tyler & Evans 2003). This also means that a strict topological conception of prepositions is clearly inadequate and that a richer functional understanding becomes necessary (Vandeloise 1991, 1994, Svorou 1994, Coventry & Garrod 2004; Deane 1993, 2005; Navarro 2002).

CL establishes no separation between *particles* and *prepositions* (Lindstromberg 1998; Campoy 1996; Dirven 2001; Silvestre 2009; Evans & Tyler 2004). This is also the approach adopted by reference works such as Huddleston and Pullum (2002). As a consequence, in this article, no distinctions will be made within the group of *multi-word verbs*. I will use the term PV. This is the traditional practice in much language teaching material and, more importantly, in most CL-oriented research.

*PVs in the linguistic debate*

The definition of PVs that one chooses to adopt provides insights into the way one views language. Thus different linguistic schools of thought have tended to adopt different definitions. I will outline three of the most controversial areas that divide the different schools.

**PVs as an example of the lexis-grammar continuum.** PVs are a typical case of the difficulty of establishing the limits between grammar and lexis. On the one hand, they are not a 'construction' *per se*, since there is no rule whose application produces new instances of PVs. Rather, as with lexical items in general, conventionalisation plays a major role in the creation of new PVs in the language. On the other hand, they cannot simply be categorized as vocabulary items because they show some productivity or, as Jackendoff (2002) puts it, semi-productivity. In other words, new instances of PVs are generated on the basis of existing patterns (Jackendoff 1997, 2002).

In an added note to a new edition of his 2002 article, which advocates the separation between syntax and lexis, Jackendoff (2010) concludes the following:

> "There are six phenomena that make use of the syntactic structure V-NP-Prt…There seems absolutely no semantic unity among these various phenomena, despite sharing the same syntax. […] I take this to be a strong argument for the (partial) autonomy of syntax from semantics. A Construction Grammar approach that insists on matching every syntactic pattern directly to a meaning has to treat the syntactic identity among these six phenomena as fortuitous […]. The syntactic principles behind the verb-particle construction are to some degree independent of its varied semantics." (Jackendoff 2010: 249).

However, for Construction Grammar, which is closely associated with CL, language consists of form-meaning pairings and therefore there would be no problem in assuming a new meaning link to each of the constructions posited. In fact, following its usage-based approach, there would be no problem in positing six different constructions with different syntactic and semantic constraints, which would finally converge in a more abstract syntactic construction. As has been suggested (e.g., Goldberg 1995, 2006; Tomasello 2003), constructions work at many different levels of granularity and, in a particular construction, other constructions operating at different levels can be found.

**PVs and the compositionality continuum.** PVs also belong to that group of linguistic units which can be viewed from contrasting perspectives with respect to the way their meaning is conceived. On the one hand, they can be placed together with idioms and seen as categorically different from the rest of the units in the language in the sense that their meaning cannot be recovered bottom-up. This is the view of formalistic approaches to language (generativists and also structuralists), which consider PVs as linguistic anomalies whose meaning has to be stipulated. In strict terms, for this view, a verb like *go up* cannot be considered a PV since its meaning is obtained from the addition of its individual components. On the other hand, PVs can be viewed as units which, in spite of having an overall meaning, retain to a certain extent the meaning of their components. Like idioms (and indeed some consider PVs to be a type of idiom), they can be placed on a continuum that can be operationalized in different ways (see Wulff 2008).

CL assumes a certain degree of compositionality for all PVs, even for those with an opaque or idiomatic meaning. As the literature on idioms has repeatedly shown (Nunberg *et al.* 1994), the elements of idiomatic expressions can be assigned an individual or separate interpretation (Langlotz 2006: 27). This interpretation, which is reinforced by repeated use in similar meaningful contexts, is also facilitated by syntactic flexibility (Gibbs & Nayak 1989). Thus, the discontinuous construction of PVs (e.g., *Turn the volume down — BofE example*) can be seen as evidence that meaning of the particle is not completely undistinguishable from that of the PVs. More clearly, as Cappelle (2005: 118) points out, there are particles whose meaning does not depend on the presence of the verb: *lights out, on and on and on (BofE)*.

CL not only assumes that analyzability is possible but, more importantly, it has provided a detailed description of the meanings of prepositions and particles, as these linguistic elements are important in the construal of 'scenes', especially in the basic domain of space. These descriptions have tended to take the form of *semantic networks*, in which a basic or prototypical meaning gives rise to different semantic extensions, by metonymy, metaphorisation, or other mechanisms. Thus, for example, the particle *up*, whose basic meaning is associated with vertical position or movement, has been described as having different meaning extensions (cf. Lee 2001: 36): increase in size (*scale up, speed up*), heightened activity (*brighten up, cheer up*), 'approach' (*move up, walk up, run up*), decrease in size (*roll up, fold up*), or completion (*use up, cut up*).

However, the actual existence of semantic networks has been questioned by some authors (Sandra & Rice 1995; Cuyckens *et al.* 1997; Rice *et al.* 1999). They argue that the CL view, in which the different meanings of a word are extended from a basic spatial meaning, has no psycholinguistic support. On the other hand, as suggested by Zlatev (2007: 341), "this does not invalidate analyses of polysemy explications of the level of linguistic norms/conventions". The process of acquisition may indeed have been wrongly guessed by CL but the resulting schema of conventionalisation remains in place and is still a useful way to categorize the meanings. It may also serve as a useful pedagogical tool.

**PVs in the mental lexicon.** Closely linked to the above linguistic debate is the question of language processing. The lexicalist and non-compositionalist account provided by generativists and structuralists assumes that idiomatic PVs (e.g., *carry out*) must be retrieved from the long-term memory, whereas transparent PVs (e.g., *go out*), which as we have seen in a strict interpretation by some grammarians would not be considered as PVs (Fraser 1976; Quirk *et al.* 1985), must be built online. For these approaches, there is no possibility of redundant storage and either a PV is listed in the long-term memory or it is built online.

However, for a usage-based approach to language, there is no such clear-cut separation between listing and online construction. Other factors such as frequency are also to be taken into account. In a recent neurolinguistic study (Cappelle *et al.* 2009), the evidence showed that frequently used PVs are not built online but stored in the long-term memory.

### PVs in Applied Linguistics: teaching and acquisition
**Teaching PVs: CL insights.** Historically, insights from the main linguistic schools have been used to support different approaches to language teaching methodology (e.g., the audio-lingual method, or the cognitive code, etc.). CL, however, has not been consistently applied by a specific method, but has given rise to a host of potential applications to the teaching of languages.

As in the case of other linguistic approaches, what CL has to offer to language teaching is mostly a way of raising language awareness. One of its main contributions lies in helping learners to create what Boers & Lindstromberg (2008) call 'meaning-meaning connections'. That is, CL aims at making learners aware of connections between the different senses of a word and how these can be extended to be used in different contexts. In other words, using Pütz's (2007: 1145) words, "uncovering the iconic structure of language" is one of the main contributions of CL to Applied Linguistics in general and language teaching in particular.

The teaching of PVs has occupied a prominent place in the application of CL to language teaching. This is a natural result of cognitive linguists' interest in prepositions and more specifically in the radial networks they have developed to explain how meanings are derived. The meaning extensions of some of these prepositions can only be analyzed when they appear in the context of a verb, i.e., when they are used as *particles* (cf. subsection on terminology above).

The best-known application of this approach to PVs is the textbook by Rudzka-Ostyn (2003). In this book, learners with a post-intermediate level are systematically provided with practice on English PVs, organized not alphabetically or by topic, but following an explicit cognitive approach, by the individual prepositions and the meanings expressed by them. However, Rudzka-Ostyn's book is not the only attempt to promote this approach. *English Prepositions Explained* by Lindstromberg (1998) also employs this approach but is intended more as reference material than as a textbook.

The effectiveness of didactic applications of CL theory has been explored by Boers & Demecheleer (1998), who showed that teaching students the central or basic meaning of *beyond* using a CL-based explanation helped them to better understand figurative meanings in a reading text. Kövecses & Szabó (1996) and Boers (2000) also established that CL could be helpful in the teaching of PVs. They experimentally demonstrated that those students who were made aware of the conceptual metaphor behind English PVs (e.g., MORE IS UP, HAPPY IS UP, VISIBLE IS OUT, VISIBLE IS UP) outperformed, in a gap-filling exercise carried out immediately after the presentation, those in the control group who had been given other explanations such as L1 translations or synonyms.

Condon (2008) confirmed and extended the findings by Kövecses & Szabó (1996) as did Boers (2000) in an experiment that attempted to reproduce the condition and context of real class teaching, i.e., lasting for several weeks instead of one or two sessions, and including both a pre-test and a delayed post-test. In general, a CL approach appears to improve students' learning although some caveats are to be noted. First, as Boers (2000) states and Condon confirms, students do not easily transfer the CL motivations they have been taught to the new PVs they incidentally encounter. Second, the motivation of abstract meanings (e.g., *out* is changed from existence to non-existence' as in *black out*, cf. Condon 2008: 153) seems to be more difficult to grasp by learners than that of more basic and spatially related meanings. Finally, as Skoufaki (2008) points out, the findings made by Boers (2000) and Kövecses & Szabó (1996) cannot be considered conclusive. The former study includes PVs together with other lexical categories and it is not possible to establish whether these linguistic elements benefit from CL motivation at the same level as other elements, while the latter does not ensure that the advantage obtained by learners is the result of a CL motivation and not simply the result of categorisation in general.

**L2 acquisition of PVs.** While CL has devoted some attention to the teaching of PVs, the amount of CL-inspired research on the acquisition of PVs is very scarce. The cross-fertilization between SLA and CL is relatively recent and has mainly been spurred by constructionist approaches (Robinson & Ellis 2008; Ellis & Cadierno 2009), which have focused more on other constructions such as resultatives or caused motion (e.g., Ellis & Ferreira 2009).

However, it may be argued that the existing SLA research on the acquisition of PVs does not need to be complemented from CL as the former has always had a cognitive bent to it. However, a preliminary look at the major findings by the SLA literature on PV acquisition may be sufficient to show that, while it has touched on important aspects, it has left many others untouched.

Here is the list of the main factors that have been found to affect the acquisition of PVs:

1. **Nativeness**: A clear distinction between native (NS) and non-native speakers (NNS) of English in the use of PVs has been found (Siyanova & Schmitt 2007; Ishii & Sohmiya 2006).

2.  **Language distance effects**: L1 Dutch (Hulstijn & Marchena 1989) or Swedish (Sjöholm 1995) learners show less avoidance than L1 Hebrew learners (Dagut & Laufer 1985).
3.  **Developmental sequence** (from avoidance to non-avoidance): Advanced students show less avoidance than students at other levels (Liao & Fukuya 2004). However, this remains a controversial matter since a more recent study (Siyanova & Schmitt 2007) has found no difference in avoidance between proficiency levels.
4.  **Context of acquisition**: Both learners of English as a Foreign Language and as a Second Language have difficulty in acquiring PVs (Siyanova & Schmitt 2007). This of course may be another way of expressing the fact that proficiency levels have no determining influence on the final outcome.
5.  **Idiomaticity**: More opaque PVs will be susceptible to higher avoidance by L2 learners (Dagut & Laufer 1985; Liao & Fukuya 2004; however see Ishii & Sohmiya 2006 for different findings).
6.  **Task effects**: More controlled tasks, such as multiple choice tests, will produce a lower level of avoidance (Liao & Fukuya 2004).

Two main features stand out from the foregoing list. On the one hand, the linguistic approach used to identify PVs is on the whole structuralist, and assumes that there is a clear separation between *phrasal verbs* and *prepositional verbs* in the sense used by Quirk *et al.* (1985). On the other hand, most of these studies focus on avoidance (Laufer & Eliasson 1993), a term used by the literature on communicative strategies to state that learners do actually know the verbs but avoid using them as they do not feel they can use them accurately. Very few studies have actually measured underuse, i.e., the tendency to use on average fewer PVs than native speakers, (Alejo 2010; Cobb 2003) as a corpus linguistic methodology is needed for this kind of study.

Perhaps as a result of the methodology adopted, these SLA studies on PV acquisition do not touch on aspects that recent SLA research has highlighted. Thus, very little mention is made of frequency effects (see Alejo 2010; Alejo *et al.* 2010), Zipfian[1] tendencies (Alejo *et al.* 2010), and other aspects such as saliency and construal. More importantly, the underlying assumption that these studies adopt is one whereby PVs are still perceived as a unitary phenomenon and not as a family of constructions (see Gries 2003; Dirven 2001).

**Methodology in the study of PVs.** As has already been pointed out in the previous section, most of the literature dealing with L2 acquisition of PVs (see Liao & Fukuya 2004 for a revision) uses multiple-choice tests where learners are presented with a number of options to complete a sentence. Among these options, they will typically find, as well as the target PV, a one-word verb with an equivalent meaning. PV avoidance is then established when a pattern of preference for one-word verbs is found, most typically among L1 speakers of non-Germanic languages (Hulstijn & Marchena 1989; Dagut & Laufer 1985). Obviously, using this methodological approach amounts to considering PVs as complex lexical items, whose syntactic flexibility is not taken into account.

The availability of a corpus such as the International Corpus of Learner English (ICLE) has made it possible to use a corpus-linguistic methodology (Waibel 2007, 2008; Alejo 2010). The advantage of such an approach lies in that it analyzes natural occurring data and that a much greater number of PVs can be studied. What is measured in this case is not so much the avoidance of PVs by L2 learners but their pattern of underuse, which is established by taking native speaker use of PVs (using an equivalent corpus such as the LOCNESS) as the norm. However, while this type of analysis is more appropriate to gauge the actual use of PVs forms by L2 learners, it is also true that the study of meaning and construction represents a challenge (although see Alejo 2010).

Even though these are the two main methodological approaches used, the study of acquisition of PVs by L2 learners can also benefit from related areas of research. Thus, the study of meaning can greatly benefit from the methodology used in the study of radial networks of prepositional meanings by L1 speakers (Rice 1999, 2003) and by L2 learners (González-Alvarez & Doval-Suárez 2008). For its part, the study of language transfer can exploit the use of the so-called 'frog story' (Slobin 1996, 1997, 2000, 2003), whose design is appropriate to elicit both prepositions and PVs. Finally, although designed to study the importance of compositional and syntactic structure in native speaker use of PVs, Konopcka & Bock (2009) provide an excellent example of how a controlled experiment should be designed.

*The context for the present study: cross-linguistic influence in the acquisition of PVs*
Having seen an overview of the contribution of CL to the analysis and acquisition of PVs, in this section I deal with the specific focus of the present article, i.e., the influence of the L1 of the learners in the acquisition of PVs following the tenets of CL. In my view, the analysis carried out by the SLA literature on language transfer and more specifically on the avoidance of PVs by learners with a non-Germanic L1 background can greatly benefit from using a more CL-oriented language typology and from extending to PVs the 'thinking for speaking hypothesis', which the CL literature has repeatedly demonstrated to be at work for motion events.

Accordingly, the differences in avoidance or underuse of PVs by learners is not only to be found between those with a Germanic and non-Germanic L1 background, as suggested by Dagut & Laufer (1985) and Hulstijn & Marchena (1989), but, more accurately, between those with a satellite-framed L1 background (i.e., English, Dutch, German, but also Russian) and those with a verb-framed L1 background (i.e., Spanish, Portuguese, Catalan, Italian, etc.). I already proposed the same idea in a previous article (Alejo 2010) but the present research increases the number of L1 backgrounds analyzed and includes both Germanic and non-Germanic representatives of the satellite-framed group.

**Satellite-framed vs. verb-framed languages**. According to Talmy, (1985, 1991, 2000), languages can be divided into satellite-framed (S-languages) and verb-framed (V-languages)[2] on the grounds that they use distinct lexicalization patterns to encode motion events, i.e., those events which describe "a theme's change along a trajectory from a place at one time to another place at a later time" (Radden & Dirven 2007: 278). Thus, in the former group we find Germanic languages but also Slavic (e.g., Russian) and Finno-Ugric ones, whereas the latter mostly comprises Romance languages (e.g., Spanish, Italian, Portuguese), Semitic (e.g., Hebrew) and other languages such as Japanese.

As put forward by Verhagen (2007), Talmy's language typology foregrounds the idea of construal. The two different ways of linguistically encoding motion events arise from the relevance given to the different components of both the basic motion event (figure, ground, motion and path) and the typically co-occurring event (manner and cause). S-languages foreground path while conflating manner and motion (e.g., English: *He crawled* [motion/manner] *out* [path] *of the room*). For their part, V-languages conflate path and motion while expressing manner of motion separately (e.g., Spanish: *entró* [motion/path] *corriendo* [manner]; *he entered running*).

These patterns cannot be interpreted in absolute terms, as there is some degree of intra-linguistic variation. In both S-languages and V-languages, expressions lexicalising motion events in non-typologically appropriate ways can also be found. All in all, however, this trend has been found to hold true and has consistently been demonstrated to be useful in establishing differences in the way language is acquired, as will be shown in the next section on the 'thinking for speaking hypothesis'.

**The 'thinking for speaking hypothesis' in language acquisition**. One of the main consequences of Talmy's typology is the way it has been used by Slobin and his associates (Slobin 1996, 1997, 2000, 2003), in what is termed as the 'thinking for speaking hypothesis', to emphasize the impact that language has on thought at the time of speech (cf. Cardini 2010).

In this respect, this hypothesis can be said to have focused on the weak link between language and thought and has mostly paid attention to the acquisition and use of the language of spatiality by speakers of different languages. It is therefore related but should not be identified with other research more directly concerned with testing the Whorf hypothesis in its stronger formulation (e.g., Davidoff, et al. 1999; Gentner & Goldin-Meadow 2003; Boroditsky 2001; Phillips & Boroditsky 2003; Papafragou *et al.* 2007; Cardini 2010).

A summary of the present state of knowledge can be found in the following quotation:

> "Whereas crucial differences have been found in the way native speakers from typologically different languages attend to the various components of motion events in speech — oral and written — and gesture as well as in translation activities dealing with motion, the question of whether language typology has an effect on linguistic reception, that is, on native speakers' categorization and memory about motion events still remains unclear" (Cadierno 2008: 255).

From the point of view of SLA, the 'thinking for speaking hypothesis' has a clear impact on a key research area: cross-linguistic influence or language transfer (Jarvis & Pavlenko 2008; Odlin 1989). Stated in simple terms, the hypothesis would predict that learners whose L1 and L2 share the same lexicalization patterns for motion events will benefit from positive transfer and would therefore have less difficulty in learning those form-meaning pairings in the L2. By contrast, learners whose L1 belongs to a different typological group from the L2 they are learning will show signs of negative transfer and/or avoidance. However, as shown by Cadierno (2004) and Cadierno & Ruiz (2006), the results of the experiments carried out to test this prediction are mixed and hold only partly. Thus, while it is true that learners use more elaboration of path than native speakers, no difference in the use of manner of motion verbs and event conflation (that is, the combination of locative trajectories — path, ground, source, etc. — within a single clause) was found. These results are further complicated by empirical evidence available from studies analyzing the simultaneous use of language and gesture (Stam 2006; Kellerman & Van Hoof 2003), which shows that, even though the cross-linguistic influence may not be present on the surface, the analysis of gesture may be indicative of thinking for speaking patterns not perceivable at the level of language.

Given the connection between PVs and motion events the analysis presented below has benefitted from the methodology and conclusions of the research on L2 acquisition of motion events. Among other things, it has helped me to identify some of the relevant factors that could be taken into account in the analysis (e.g., elaboration of path, event conflation, etc.) and to formulate hypotheses in a way that is consistent with the findings of the 'thinking for speaking hypothesis' for motion events.

**Hypotheses.** Based on the foregoing, it is reasonable to pose the following questions:

1.  Does Talmy's distinction between S- and V-languages hold not only for the different linguistic means of encoding motion events but also for other linguistic units such as PVs? and
2.  Do S-languages typically have PVs or related constructions while V-languages do not?

One of the reasons why the answer to the first question may be affirmative can be stated in simple terms. There is a large group of PVs that can be labelled as 'motion events' in the broad sense of the expression (Talmy 1985, 1991) and therefore the analysis that holds for motion events as a whole also holds for PVs as a highly frequent way of encoding them. To this group of PVs belong many of those that make use of 'directional particles' (Cappelle 2005; Jackendoff 2002, 2010), or those used in the caused-motion constructions (Goldberg 1995, 2006). In other words, motion events feature among the meanings expressed by PVs.

**Table 2.** Results of the category-wise kappa for meaning categories

| Kappa | z | p.value |
|---|---|---|
| COMPLETION | 0.740 8.781 | 0.000 |
| DISTRIBUTION | 0.098 1.165 | 0.244 |
| EXCLUSION | 0.514 6.101 | 0.000 |
| MOTION | 0.653 7.750 | 0.000 |
| PERCEPTION | 0.693 8.227 | 0.000 |

According to this classification, the central meaning or proto-scene of *out, exteriority,* is extended into various meanings, which can be interpreted to have developed as metaphorisations. Among other meaning extensions, not included here given their low frequency, they mention the following major senses: a) entry into/presence in conceptual/cognitive field (Lee 2001), which would correspond to *perception* and *visibility* (Tyler & Evans 2003) (e.g., *find out what was going on*) (BofE); b) exit/absence from conceptual/cognitive field (Lee 2001), which would include Tyler & Evans' (2003) *exclusion* and *lack of visibility* (e.g., *I've crossed out his name*) (BofE); c) increase in size (Lee 2001) roughly corresponding to distribution and reflexivity (*He stretched out his right leg*) (BofE); and d) completion (*You have to cut down the tree and let the wood dry out*) (BofE) which is only included in Tyler & Evans (2003).

Once I had manually carried out the meaning categorisation of all the 1998 hits, I checked on its validity by asking two other judges to categorise a randomly chosen sample of 50 concordances. After applying a Fleiss' Kappa statistical analysis, since more than 2 raters were involved, the results were statically significant ($p < 0.000$) and the resulting kappa coefficient was 0.622, which can be interpreted as "substantial agreement" on the categorisation performed by the judges. In fact, after performing a category-wise kappa and the corresponding test statistics (see Table 2) for each category, it can be seen that the 'distribution' category, which is the least frequent, is the only one where no agreement among the raters was reached.

*Elaboration of path*
Another important aspect that I analyzed following the findings by Slobin and associates when dealing with motion events, concerns the elaboration of path, i.e., the prepositional phrases providing information about the ground. These prepositional phrases usually make reference to the source, the medium or the goal of the motion event (Slobin 1997: 22) and allow for a classification of verbs into two main groups: 'minus ground' and 'plus ground'.

According to Slobin (1996), 'minus ground verbs' would be those verbs "that appear alone or with a path satellite (English *fall* and *fall down*) (cited in Cadierno 2004: 31). For their part, 'plus ground verbs' would be those "that are accompanied by some path complement" (English *fall down into the fireplace below*)" (Cadierno 2004). Obviously, it is only in the latter group that a distinction can be made between simple paths, which contain one piece of path information, and more complex ones, which include two or more path elements.

I applied this categorisation to *out*-PVs. Thus, under the category 'minus ground' I classified those *out*-PVs followed by an intransitive preposition (Huddleston & Pullum 2002) or, to use a more traditional terminology, by a particle (cf. Cappelle 2005 for a discussion). This is the case for sentences such as *They sent him out* (BofE) where, using Lindner's (1981) expression, we say that the landmark is sublexicalized, i.e., not expressed. On the other hand, under 'plus ground', I included all the verbs which are either immediately followed by a transitive preposition or by a group of them. It is true that there are very few contexts where *out* is used transitively, since they are restricted to those cases where *out* is followed by NPs headed by *door, window,* etc. (*He went out the back to remove a few leaves*) (BofE). However, I also consider here the cases where *out* is followed by other prepositions, especially those where it is followed by *of,* to form to what traditional grammar has called complex prepositions (*So they went out of the locker room*) (BofE). In these cases, the landmark or ground is expressed.

### Tokens and types

Table 1 lists the number of tokens and types of *out*-PVs found in the different corpora analyzed. They are ordered according to the number of types and it can be seen that the number of *out*-PV tokens are higher in one of the corpora of native speakers of English used as a reference (i.e., the BNC) whereas the lowest is the corpus of Italian speakers (i.e., ITICLE). There are also differences both in the number of tokens and types of *out*-PVs use by the speakers of different languages.

**Table 3.** Number of tokens and types by sub-corpus

|  | Tokens | Types |
| --- | --- | --- |
| BNC-Essays | 368 | 123 |
| LOC | 352 | 94 |
| DUTCHICLE | 276 | 78 |
| SWICLE | 247 | 73 |
| RUSSICLE | 216 | 56 |
| BULGICLE | 213 | 59 |
| SPICLE | 175 | 38 |
| ITICLE | 151 | 40 |
| TOTAL | 1998 | 227 |

## Results and Discussion

### out-PVs: Types and tokens

In the first place, I wanted to test whether learners with an S-language background had an advantage over learners with a V-language background in the use of *out*-PVs (hypothesis 1), thus mirroring what has already been found for motion events (e.g. Cadierno 2004; Martínez 2008). In the context of my analysis, this would mean that learners whose L1 belongs to the group of S-languages will consistently use not only more *out*-PV tokens but also a greater number of out-PV types than those learners whose L1 belong to the group of verb-framed languages.

The analysis of the number of *out*-PV tokens used by the learners of the different language groups shows that overall the L1 background of the learners seems to play a significant role (see Figure 1), which is evidenced by the decreasing trend observed. More specifically, learners from both the Germanic and Non-Germanic S-language groups use, respectively, 60% and 30% more *out*-PV tokens than learners from the V-language group. That is, S-language learners use more out-PV tokens than V-language learners. It has to be borne in mind, however, that learners belonging to the Germanic S-languages use around 20% *out*-PVs more (123 tokens) than learners from a non-Germanic S-language background and that no homogeneity can be assumed between these two groups. Finally, the group of native speakers (NS) use more than twice as many out-PV tokens than

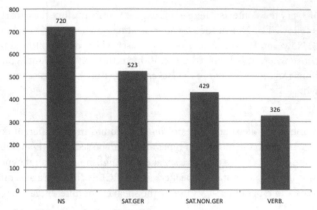

**Figure 1.** number of out-PV tokens by language group

those belonging to the V-language group, around 70% more (720 vs 429) than the Non-Germanic S-language group and around 40% more (720 vs 523) than the Germanic S-language group.

It has to be acknowledged that these results only refer to a group of PVs, those containing the particle *out*, and therefore could not be taken to hold true for the whole group of PVs. However, this particle is, together with *up* (cf. Gardner & Davies 2007; O'Dowd 1998) one of the most frequently used in English and it seems unlikely that things could change for other particles. In fact, they have been confirmed for the particle *up* by other unpublished analyses[3] (Gilquin 2009).

For its part, the analysis of the number of types (see Figure 2) gives a very similar picture to the one described by my analysis of tokens, accentuated in certain aspects. Thus, both Germanic and non-Germanic S-language learners show an increase in the number of *out*-PV types that they use with respect to V-language learners (100% and 66% respectively). Similarly, the group of native speakers shows a pattern of use more clearly differentiated from the rest of groups. They use over 50% more types (167 vs 110) than the group ranking second, the Germanic S-language learners and three times more than those ranking last, V-language learners. Only the difference between the two groups of S-language learners remains constant at approximately 20%.

The results for the markedly greater number of types used by S-language learners and native speakers can easily be interpreted by reference to the salience of manner verbs, typical of S-

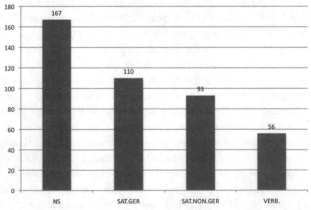

**Figure 2.** Number of out-PV types

languages (Slobin 2003). By contrast, the scarce number of types used by learners of V-languages may be explained in terms of the lack of attention that the L1 of these learners pays to manner verbs. *Out*-PVs would therefore be another area where the 'thinking for speaking hypothesis' is present.

*Extended meanings of out-PVs*
The findings in the above section seem to broadly confirm for *out*-PVs some of the predictions made by the 'thinking for speaking hypothesis' for motion events. However, the question remains whether the analysis carried out is only valid in so far as the majority of PVs analyzed have a motional meaning and therefore it does not add anything new to the hypothesis put forward by Slobin and associates. In this section, I will analyze whether the predictions I made hold not only for *out*-PVs with a motional meaning but also for those with an extended or metaphorical meaning (hypothesis 2).

In Figures 3 and 4, the number of tokens and meaning types for both groups of verbs are presented, together with the overall totals. It has to be taken into account that in the analysis of types the totals are slightly different from Figure 2 above. The unit of analysis used in this section is not the verb type but the meaning type, since the focus here is precisely on meaning. This means that for the same verb type (e.g., *carry out*) with different meanings ('to perform' or 'to take out') two different meaning types have been computed.

As can be seen, the number of tokens and types of non-motional *out*-PV meanings (labelled 'REST' in the figures) shows the same pattern found for all *out*-PVs. In other words, both NS and S-language learners also use a greater number of *out*-PV tokens and meaning types than V-language

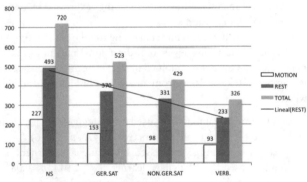

**Figure 3.** Out-PV meaning tokens

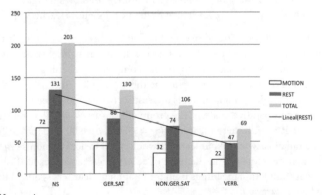

**Figure 4.** Out-PV meaning types

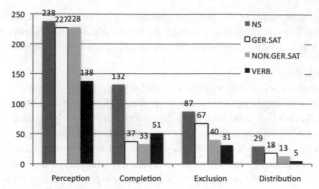

**Figure 5.** Non-directional *out*-PV meanings: tokens

learners not only with verbs whose meanings are clearly motional but also with verbs expressing other non-motional meanings, which can be conceived of as meaning extensions or metaphoric uses from the basic or prototypical directional meaning. These results are particularly relevant given that the latter group of verbs are used with greater frequency by all groups of learners and therefore have a greater weight in the overall results. The only result that does not fit the whole picture is the small number of tokens with a motional meaning (98) used by Non-Germanic S-languages learners, which is a mere 5% greater than the tokens used by V-language learners.

However, a more granular analysis of the main meanings expressed by non-motional *out*-PVs can provide us with some additional insights.

From this analysis we can see that the typical declining trend from left to right described above, in which S-language learners tend to use fewer non-directional meanings than NS and a greater number than V-language learners, is not maintained in all the meanings considered here, in particular if we look at the number of tokens. Thus, from an analysis of Figure 5 and Table 4, it is possible to notice the following:

1.  The number of completion *out*-PV meanings used by V-language learners is significantly greater than the number used by S-language learners ($\chi^2 = 19.476$, $p = 0.000$)
2.  The number of perception meanings expressed by S-language learners is also significantly greater than the number used by V-language learners ($\chi^2 = 2.914$, $p = 0.08$). It is mostly non-Germanic language learners who are responsible for this trend.
3.  The number of exclusion/invisibility *out*-PVs meanings used by V-language learners does not greatly differ from the number used by non-Germanic S-language learners ($\chi^2 = 0.755$, $p = 0.385$)

These findings suggest that there are idiosyncratic elements that interplay with the 'thinking for speaking hypothesis' and that may be said to moderate it. They may have to do with the saliency of certain meanings for learners. Thus, for example, the 'completion' meaning of *out* may be said to be highly salient for speakers of V-languages, whereas the 'perception' meaning may be more salient for speakers of non-Germanic S-languages. It is interesting to note, however, that both meanings are frequent and that in a comparative analysis, the group of non-native speakers taken as a whole uses significantly more *out*-PVs with these meanings ($\chi^2 = 33.762$, $p = 0.000$) than NS. This would mean that in learning the radial network of *out* learners would tend to access and use more readily those meanings which are more frequent and that ease of access may sometimes lead to overuse. In fact, the high frequency of completion meanings used by V-language learners is due to the overuse of the highly entrenched form *carry out*.

**Table 4.** Comparison of S-languages/V-languages meanings

| Meaning | S. Lang. | | V. Lang. | |
|---|---|---|---|---|
| | # | % | # | % |
| PERCEPTION | 455 | 47.8% | 138 | 42.3% |
| COMPLETION | 70 | 7.4% | 51 | 15.6% |
| EXCLUSION | 107 | 11.2% | 31 | 9.5% |
| DISTRIBUTION | 31 | 3.3% | 5 | 1.5% |
| OTHER | 38 | 4.0% | 8 | 2.5% |

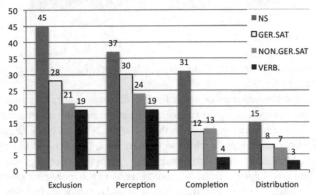

**Figure 6.** Non-directional out-PV meanings: types

However, these data should be considered in the light of meaning types (see Figure 6). When these are considered, the behaviour of individual non-directional meanings is not very different from that which has already been described for them as a whole. Some of the homogenizing effects found for some of the meanings disappear and V-language learners show a lower number of out-PV constructions in all the meanings analyzed than S-language learners.

What these results show is that, at more granular levels, the cross-linguistic effects of the L1 posited by the 'thinking for speaking hypothesis' may be seen to interact with frequency effects. Once learners have access to well entrenched forms expressing highly frequent meanings, they do not seem to have a problem acquiring them, in fact their overuse may serve as a way to compensate for their lack of vocabulary or appropriate constructions (Cobb 2003). These frequency effects, however, disappear when V-language learners are faced with the task of generalizing those meanings to new PVs.

*Elaboration of path*
Following the findings by Cadierno (2004) on the use of minus and plus ground verbs by L2 learners to express motion events, it may be hypothesized that V-language learners analyzed in this study will use fewer plus ground *out*-PVs than S-language learners and NS, given the tendency of the former to provide less information about the ground (hypothesis 3).

As can be seen from Figure 7, and as corroborated by performing a chi-square, the overall pattern is repeated and V-language learners do not use a significantly smaller number of plus ground out-PVs constructions than S-language learners ($\chi^2 = 0.166$, $p = 0.684$). If anything, one can observe a decrease in the number of plus ground constructions by the group of Non-Germanic S-language learners. But this difference is not statistically significant ($\chi^2 = 3.713$, $p = 0.294$) in the same way that

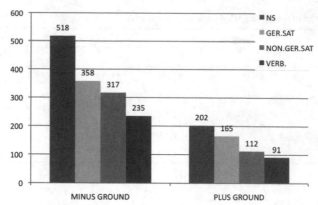

**Figure 7.** Minus/plus ground out-PVs

no statistically significant differences in the use of minus and plus ground was found between NS and NNS ($\chi^2 = 0.123$, $p = 0.725$).

As a consequence, the well-attested trend to provide more elaborated paths of motion events by S-languages seems therefore not to be transferred by learners to the meanings expressed by out-PVs. Neither does it seem to be a phenomenon that separates NS from NNS, i.e., a learning effect.

However, the elaboration of path, which as we have seen, is not found to be significant on its own, happens to be significant when combined with a particular meaning, namely, extended or metaphorical motion (see Table 5). Thus, S-language learners use more plus ground out-PVs than V-language learners when they are expressing non-motional meanings ($\chi^2 = 3.849$, $p = 0.05$).

On the other hand, it is worth mentioning that, while there is no interaction between elaboration of path and motion events, when we compare S-language learners and V-language learners, this interaction is found to be significant when NS and NSS are compared ($\chi^2 = 9.571$, $p = 0.002$). However, contrary to the predictions made by the 'thinking for speaking hypothesis', NNS, taken as a group, tend to use more out-PVs providing elaboration of path than NS. In particular, NNS have a preference for the elaboration of path by means of the complex preposition 'out of'.

From a CL point of view, this result could be explained in terms of cognitive effort. Thus, by including an explicit elaboration of path (metaphorical or directional), NNS's would be saving themselves the cognitive effort to decide whether the landmark can be sublexicalized as it is recoverable from the linguistic context.

**Table 5.** Extended motion vs. motion events

| Typology | Meaning | Plus Ground | | Minus Ground | |
|---|---|---|---|---|---|
| | | # | % | # | % |
| VERB.LANG | EXTENDED MOTION | 27 | 11,59 | 206 | 88,41 |
| SAT.LANG | | 119 | 16,98 | 582 | 83,02 |
| Total | | 146 | 15,63 | 788 | 84,37 |
| VERB.LANG | MOTION EVENT* | 64 | 68,82 | 29 | 31,18 |
| SAT.LANG | | 158 | 62,95 | 93 | 37,05 |
| Total | | 222 | 64,53 | 122 | 35,47 |

* Not sigfinificant

## Conclusion

To summarize this analysis, it can be argued that the 'thinking for speaking hypothesis', which has been found to be predictive in the acquisition of motion events by L2 learners (Cadierno 2004; Cadierno & Ruiz 2006), has also been found to be useful when applied to the acquisition of PVs. As expected, S-language learners do seem to use a greater number of *out*-PVs tokens and types than V-language learners, which may be indicative of the greater difficulty that the latter group of learners may have in learning a construction which is either non-existent or has very low frequency in their L1. Besides, this trend does not only show in PVs with a directional meaning, something which would amount to a replication of what had already been found for motion events, but also in those PVs which have other meanings. This finding would seem to extend the validity of the 'thinking for speaking hypothesis' beyond its original boundaries and, in addition, it would emphasize that the CL analysis of the meaning of particles and prepositions as metaphorical extensions from a basic or literal meaning is fundamentally correct.

However, not all the predictions made by the 'thinking for speaking hypothesis' have been sustained. The initial hypothesis regarding the elaboration of path has not been confirmed as no difference between V- and S-language learners has been found. Besides, other effects blurring the distinction between these two groups of language learners have been identified and, for example, all learners have been found to overuse, in comparison to NS, some of the most frequent meanings of the particle. This comes as no surprise as the tendency of NNS to overuse a limited number of meanings has already been attested in the literature (e.g., Cobb 2003). Finally, it has to be observed that S-language learners are not a homogeneous group as a distinction between Germanic and non-Germanic S-language learners can also be established.

Overall, the picture that emerges from this study is a complex one. The effects predicted by the 'thinking for speaking hypothesis' seem to be present at a very basic level, while at the same time they seem to interact with many other factors that the SLA literature has already emphasized. It is important to note, however, that these findings are also an indication that CL has something to offer to SLA research and that many results can be expected from the cross-fertilization of these two subjects. At the same time, there are limitations to the present study since only the particle *out* has been considered and different topics of the essays analyzed may also have had an impact on the results.

## Notes

1. SLA researchers have realized how some learner data can be described using Zipf's statistical law, which can be summarized as follows: "Zipf's law (Zipf, 1935) describes how the highest frequency words account for the most linguistic tokens" (Ellis & Cadierno 2009:119).

2. Talmy also includes a third group. He also states that this classification is best understood as the result of tendencies rather than in terms of clear cut distinctions. More recent research (see Cadierno 2008 for an overview) has put this into question and has even proposed additions to this typology.

3. According to Gilquin (2009), the use of *up*-PVs by Italian learners in the written corpus (ICLE) is highly frequent, at the same level as that of Bulgarian learners, whereas the same group of phrasal verbs features last, together with Spanish learners, in the spoken corpus (LINDSEI).

## References

Alejo, R. 2010. L2 Spanish acquisition of English phrasal verbs: A cognitive linguistic analysis of L1 influence. In *Corpus-Based Approaches to English Language Teaching*, M.C. Campoy, B. Bellés-Fortuno & M.Ll. Gea-Valor (eds), 149–166. London: Continuum.

Alejo, R., Piquer, A. & Reveriego, G. 2010. Phrasal verbs in EFL course books. In *Fostering Language Teaching Efficiency Through Cognitive Linguistics*, S. De Knop, F. Boers & A. De Rycker (eds), 59–78. Berlin: Mouton de Gruyter.

Boers, F. 2000. Metaphor awareness and vocabulary retention. *Applied Linguistics* 21: 323–363.

Boers, F. & Demecheleer, M. 1998. A cognitive semantic approach to teaching prepositions. *English Language Teaching Journal* 53: 197–204.

Boers, F. & Lindstromberg, S. 2008b. How cognitive linguistics can foster effective vocabulary teaching. In *Cognitive Linguistic Approaches to Teaching Vocabulary and Phraseology*, F. Boers & S. Lindstromberg (eds), 1–61. Berlin: Mouton de Gruyter.

Boroditsky, L. 2001. Does language shape thought? Mandarin and English speakers' conception of time. *Cognitive Psychology* 43:1–22.

Brugman, C. 1981. Story of Over. MA thesis, Department of Linguistics, University of California at Berkeley.

Cadierno, T. 2004. Expressing motion events in a second language: A cognitive typological perspective. In *Cognitive Linguistics, Second Language Acquisition, and Foreign Language Teaching*, M. Achard & S. Niemeier (eds), 13–49. Berlin: Mouton de Gruyter.

Cadierno, T. 2008. Learning to talk about motion in a foreign language. In *Handbook of Cognitive Linguistics and Second Language Acquisition*, P. Robinson & N.C. Ellis (eds), 239–275. New York/London: Routledge.

Cadierno, T. & Ruiz, L. 2006. Motion events in Spanish L2 acquisition. *Annual Review of Cognitive Linguistics* 4: 183–216.

Campoy, C. 1996. *Semantic Analysis of Adverbial, Prepositional and Adverbial Prepositional Verbs*. Castellón: Unversitat Jaume I.

Cappelle, B. 2004. The particularity of particles, or why they are not just 'intransitive prepositions'. In *Adpositions of Movement* [Belgin Journal of Linguistics 18], H. Cuyckens, W. De Mulder & T. Mortelmans (eds), 29–57. Amsterdam: John Benjamins.

Cappelle, B. 2005. *Particle Patterns in English. A Comprehensive Coverage*. PhD Dissertation at the Faculteit Letteren, Katholieke Universiteit Leuven.

Cappelle, B., Shtyrov, Y. & Pulvermüller, F. 2009. The magnetism between verbs and particles: an MEG perspective. Paper presented at a workshop on particles, prepositions and particle verbs, SESYLIA, Université Paris III – Sorbonne Nouvelle, 5 June 2009.

Cardini, F.E. 2010. Evidence against Whorfian effects in motion conceptualisation. *Journal of Pragmatics* 42:1442–1459.

Cobb, T. 2003. Analyzing late interlanguage with learner corpora: Quebec replication of three European studies. *Canadian Modern Language Review* 59: 393–423.

Condon, N. 2008. How cognitive linguistic motivations influence the phrasal verbs. In *Cognitive Linguistic Approaches to Teaching Vocabulary and Phraseology*, F. Boers & S. Lindstromberg (eds), 133–158. Berlin: Mouton de Gruyter.

Coventry, K.R. & Garrod, S.C. 2004. *Saying, Seeing, and Acting: The Psychological Semantics of Spatial Prepositions*. New York: Psychology Press.

Cuyckens, H., Sandra, D. & Rice, S. 1997. Towards an empirical lexical semantics. In *Human Contact Through Language and Linguistics*, B. Smieja & M. Tasch (eds), 35–54. Frankfurt: Peter Lang.

Dagut, M. & Laufer, B. 1985. Avoidance of phrasal verbs: A case for contrastive analysis. *Studies in Second Language Acquisition* 7: 73–79.

Davidoff, J., Davies, I. & Roberson, D. 1999. Colour categories in a stone-age tribe. *Nature* 398: 203–204.

Deane, P.D. 1993. At, by, to, and past: an essay in multimodal image theory. *Proceedings of the Annual Meeting of the Berkeley Linguistics Society* 19: 112–124.

Deane, P.D. 2005. Multimodal spatial representation: On the semantic unity of *over*. In *From Perception to Meaning. Image Schemas in Cognitive Linguistics*, B. Hampe & J.E. Grady (eds), 235–282. Berlin: Mouton de Gruyter.

Dehé, N., Jackendoff, R., McIntyre, A. & Urban, S. (eds) 2002. *Verb-Particle Explorations*. Berlin: Mouton de Gruyter.

Dirven, R. 2001. English phrasal verbs: Theory and didactic applicaton. In *Applied Cognitive Linguistics*, 2 Vols, M. Pütz, S. Niemeier & R. Dirven (eds), 3–27. Berlin: Mouton de Gruyter.

Ellis, N.C. & Cadierno, T. 2009. Constructing a second language: Introduction to the special section. *Annual Review of Cognitive Linguistics* 7: 111–39.

Ellis, N.C. & Ferreira-Junior, F. 2009. Constructions and their acquisition: Islands and the distinctiveness of their occupancy. *Annual Review of Cognitive Linguistics* 7: 187–220.

Espinal, M.T. & Mateu, J. 2010. On Classes of idioms and their interpretation. *Journal of Pragmatics* 42: 1397–1411.

Evans, V. & Green, M. 2006. *Cognitive Linguistics. An Introduction*. Edinburgh: Edinburgh University Press.

Evans, V. & Tyler, A. 2004. Applying cognitive linguistics to pedagogical grammar: The case of over. In *Cognitive Linguistics, Second Language Acquisition, and Foreign Language Teaching*, M. Achard & S. Niemeier (eds), 257–280. Berlin: Mouton de Gruyter.

Fraser, B. 1976. *The Verb-Particle Combination in English*. New York NY: Academic Press.

Gardner, D. & Davies, M. 2007. Pointing out frequent phrasal verbs: A corpus-based analysis. *TESOL Quarterly* 41: 339–359.

Gentner, D. & Goldin-Meadow, S. 2003. Wither Whorf. In *Language in Mind: Advances in the Study of Language and Thought*, D. Gentner & S. Goldin-Meadow (eds), 3–14. Cambridge MA: The MIT Press.

Gibbs, R.W. & Nayak, N.P. 1989. Psycholinguistic studies on the syntactic behavior of idioms. *Cognitive Psychology* 21:100–38.

Gilquin, G. 2009. The (non-)use of phrasal verbs in L2 varieties of English. Paper given at the ICAME 30 conference in Lancaster, UK.

Goldberg, A. 1995. *Constructions. A Construction Grammar Approach to Argument Structure*. Chicago IL: Chicago University Press.

Goldberg, A. 2006. *Constructions at Work: The Nature of Generalizations in Language*. Oxford: OUP.

Gonzalez-Álvarez, E. & Doval-Suárez, S.M. 2008. Testing the cognitive categorisations of at in native and non-native English speakers. Evidence from a corpus study. *The Linguistics Journal* 3: 100–135

Gries, S. 2003. *Multifactorial Analysis in Corpus Linguistics: A Study of Particle Placement*. London: Continuum.

Huddleston, R.G. & Pullum, G.K. 2002. *The Cambridge Grammar of the English Language*. Cambridge: CUP.

Hulstijn, J.H. & Marchena, E. 1989. Avoidance: Grammatical or semantic causes? *Studies in Second Language Acquisition* 11: 241–255.

Ishii, Y. & Sohmiya, K. 2006. On the semantic structure of English. Spatial particles involving metaphors. In *Readings in a Second Language Pedagogy and Second Language Acquisition: In Japanese Context*. A. Yoshitomi (ed.), 381–402. Amsterdam: John Benjamins.

Jackendoff, R. 1997. Twistin' the night away. *Language* 73: 534–59.

Jackendoff, R. 2002. English particle constructions, the lexicon, and the autonomy of syntax. In *Verb-Particle Explorations*, N. Dehé, R. Jackendoff, A. McIntyre & S. Urban (eds), 67–94. Berlin: Mouton de Gruyter.

Jackendoff, R. 2010. *Meaning and the Lexicon. The Parallel Architecture 1975–2010*. Oxford: OUP.

Jarvis, S. & Pavlenko, A. 2008. *Crosslinguistic Influence in Language and Cognition*. London: Routledge.

Kellerman, E. & Van Hoof, A. 2003. Manual accents. *International Review of Applied Linguistics* 41: 251–69.

Konopka, A. & Bock, K. 2009. Lexical or syntactic control of sentence formulation? Structural generalizations from idiom production. *Cognitive Psychology* 58: 68–101.

Kövecses, Z. & Szabó, P. 1996. Idioms: A view from cognitive semantics. *Applied Linguistics* 17: 326–355.

Kurtyka, A. 2001. Teaching English phrasal verbs: A cognitive approach. In *Applied Cognitive Linguistics*, II: *Language Pedagogy*, M. Pütz, S. Niemeier & R. Dirven (eds) 29–53. Berlin: Mouton de Gruyter.

Lakoff G. 1987. *Women, Fire, and Dangerous Things: What Categories Reveal About the Mind*. Chicago IL: University of Chicago Press.

Langlotz, A. 2006. *Idiomatic Creativity: A Cognitive Linguistic Model of Idiom Representation and Idiom Variation in English*. Amsterdam: John Benjamins.

Laufer, B. & Eliasson, S. 1993. What causes avoidance in L2 learning: L1-L2 difference, L1-L2 similarity, or L2 complexity? *Studies in Second Language Acquisition* 15: 35–48.

Lee, D. 2001. *Cognitive Linguistics: An Introduction*. Oxford: OUP.

Liao, Y. & Fukuya, Y.J. 2004. Avoidance of phrasal verbs: The case of Chinese learners of English. *Language Learning* 54: 193–226.

Lindner, S. 1981. A Lexico-Semantic Analysis of Verb-Particle Constructions with Up and Out. PhD dissertation, University of California at San Diego.

Lindstromberg, S. 1998. *English Prepositions Explained*. Amsterdam: John Benjamins. (Revised edition published 2010).

Martínez Vázquez, M. 2008. Constructions in learner language. *Círculo de Lingüística Aplicada a la Comunicación*. 36: 40–62

Mateu, J. & Rigau, G. 2007. Romance paths as cognate complements. A lexical-syntactic account. In *Romance Linguistics 2007. Selected Papers from the 37th Symposium on Romance Languages*, P.J. Masullo, E. O'Rourke & C.H. Huang (eds), 227–42. Amsterdam: John Benjamins.

Morgan, P.S. 1997. Figuring out *figure* out: Metaphor and the semantics of the English verb-particle construction. *Cognitive Linguistics* 8: 327–357.

Navarro, I. 2002. Towards a description of the meaning of *At*. In *Perspectives on Prepositions*, H. Cuyckens & G. Radden (eds), 211–230. Tübingen: Max Niemeyer.

Nunberg, G., Sag, I.A. & Wasow, T. 1994. Idioms. *Language* 70: 491–538.

Odlin, T. 1989. *Language Transfer:Cross-linguistic Influence in Language Learning*. Cambridge: CUP.

O'Dowd, E.M. 1998. *Preposition and Particles in English. A Discourse-Functional Account*. Oxford: OUP.

Papafragou, A., Li, P., Choi, Y. & Han, C. 2007. Evidentiality in language and cognition. *Cognition* 103: 253–299.

Phillips, W. & Boroditsky, L. 2003. Can quirks of grammar affect the way you think? Grammatical gender and object concepts. In *Proceedings of the 25th Annual Meeting of the Cognitive Science Society*. R. Alterman & D. Kirsh (eds), 928–933. Boston MA.

Pütz, M. 2007. Cognitive Linguistics and Applied Linguistics. In *The Oxford Handbook of Cognitive Linguistics*, D. Geeraerts & H. Cuyckens (eds), 1139–1159. Oxford: OUP.

Quirk, R., Greenbaum, S., Leech, G. & Svartvik, J. 1985. *A Comprehensive Grammar of the English Language*. London: Longman.

Radden, G. & Dirven, R. 2007. *Cognitive English Grammar*. Amsterdam: John Benjamins.

Rice, S. 1999. Patterns of acquisition in the emerging mental lexicon: the case of *to* and *for* in English. *Brain and Language* 68: 268–276.

Rice, S. 2003. Growth of a lexical network: Nine prepositions in acquisition. In *Cognitive Approaches to Lexical Semantics*, H. Cuyckens, R. Dirven & J.R. Taylor (eds), 243–280. Berlin: Mouton de Gruyter.

Rice, S., Sandra, D. & Vanrespaille, M. 1999. Prepositional semantics and the fragile link between space and time. In *Cultural, Typological and Psycholinguistic Issues in Cognitive Linguistics*, M. Hiraga, C. Sinha & S. Wilcox (eds), 107–27. Amsterdam: John Benjamins.

Robinson, P. & Ellis, N.C. (eds) 2008. *Handbook of Cognitive Linguistics and Second Language Acquisition*. London: Routledge.

Rudzka-Ostyn, B. 2003. *Word Power: Phrasal Verbs and Compounds. A Cognitive Approach*. Berlin: Mouton de Gruyter.

Sandra, D. & Rice, S. 1995. Network analyses of prepositional meaning: Mirroring whose mind — the linguist's or the language user's? *Cognitive Linguistics* 6: 89–130.

Silvestre, A.J. 2009. *Particle Semantics in English Phrasal and Prepositional Verbs*. Saarbrücken: VDM.

Siyanova, A. & Schmitt, N. 2007. Native and non-native use of multi-word vs. one-word verbs. *IRAL* 45: 119–139.

Sjöholm, K. 1995. *The Influence of Crosslinguistic, Semantic, and Input Factors on the Acquisition of Phrasal Verbs*. Åbo: Åbo Akademi University Press.

Skoufaki, S. 2008. Conceptual metaphoric meaning clues in two L2 idiom presentation methods. In *Cognitive Linguistic Approaches to Teaching Vocabulary and Phraseology*, F. Boers & S. Lindstromberg (eds), 101–132. Berlin: Mouton de Gruyter.

Slobin, D.I. 1996. Two ways to travel: Verbs of motion in English and Spanish. In *Grammatical Constructions: Their form and Meaning*, M. Shibatani & S.A. Thompson (eds), 195–220. Oxford: Clarendon Press.

Slobin, D.I. 1997. Mind, code, and text. In *Essays on Language Function and Language Type: Dedicated to T. Givón.* J. Bybee, J. Haiman & S.A. Thompson (eds), 437–467. Amsterdam: John Benjamins.

Slobin, D.I. 2000. Verbalized events: A dynamic approach to linguistic relativity and determinism. In *Evidence for Linguistic Relativity*, S. Niemeier & R. Dirven (eds), 107–138. Amsterdam: John Benjamins.

Slobin, D.I. 2003. Language and thought online: Cognitive consequences of linguistic relativity. In *Language in Mind: Advances in the Study of Language and Thought*, D. Gentner & S. Goldin-Meadow (eds), 157–192. Cambridge MA: The MIT Press.

Stam, G. 2006. Thinking for speaking about motion: L1 and L2 speech and gesture *International Review of Applied Linguistics* 44: 143–169.

Svorou, S. 1994. *The Grammar of Space*. Amsterdam: John Benjamins.

Talmy, L. 1985. Lexicalization patterns: semantic structure in lexical forms. In *Language Typology and Syntactic Description*. T. Shopen (ed.), 36–149. Cambridge: CUP.

Talmy, L. 1991. Path to realization: a typology of event conflation. *Berkeley Linguistic Society* 7: 480–519.

Talmy, L. 2000. *Toward a Cognitive Semantics*, Vol. 1: *Concepts Structuring Systems*. Cambridge MA: The MIT Press.

Tomasello, M. 2003. *Constructing a Language: A Usage-Based Approach to Child Language Acquisition*. Cambridge MA: Harvard University Press.

Tyler, A. & Evans, V. 2003. *The Semantics of English Prepositions*. Cambridge: CUP.

Vandeloise, C. 1991. *Spatial Prepositions: A Case Study from French*, Chicago IL: Chicago University Press.

Vandeloise, C. 1994. Methodology and analyses of the preposition *in. Cognitive Linguistics* 5: 157–184.

Verhagen, A. 2007. Construal and Perspectivization. In *The Oxford Handbook of Cognitive Linguistics*, D. Geeraerts & H. Cuyckens (eds), 48–81. Oxford: OUP

Waibel, B. 2007. *Phrasal Verbs in Learner English: A Corpus-Based Study of German and Italian Students.* Freiburg: Albert-Ludwigs-Universität Freiburg.

Waibel, B. 2008. *Phrasal Verbs. German and Italian Learners of English Compared*. Saarbrücken: VDM.

Wray, A. (2002). *Formulaic Language and the Lexicon*. Cambridge: CUP.

Wulff, S. 2008. *Rethinking Idiomaticity: A Usage-based Approach*. London: Continuum.

Zlatev, J. 2007. Spatial semantics. In *The Oxford Handbook of Cognitive Linguistics*, D. Geeraerts & H. Cuyckens (eds), 319–350. Oxford: OUP.

*Author's address*

Rafael Alejo González
Facultad de Educación
Universidad de Extremadura
Avda. de Elvas s/n
06006 Badajoz, Spain

ralejo@unex.es

# Why cognitive grammar works in the L2 classroom

## A case study of mood selection in Spanish

Reyes Llopis-García
Columbia University

This paper presents a series of experiments that tested the usefulness of teaching Spanish mood using an approach to Cognitive Grammar specifically developed for the foreign language classroom: *Operational Grammar.*

Mood selection is one of the most difficult aspects of learning Spanish as a FL, and it is one of the last features acquired. It is unquestionably complex, involving issues of subordination, alternation, and speaker's communicative intent. This complexity has been amplified by the traditional approach to mood, which has changed little over the last 50 years.

The alternative presented here sees language as a symbolic representation of the speaker's mental model of the world. Grammar is closely linked to this model as the tool used in class to help learners communicate meaning through form. This enables them to understand how native speakers choose to communicate. Language, then, portrays an outcome of the speaker's own selection, guided by communicative intent and not as part of a taxonomic set of rules.

The empirical study showed that the combination of a cognitive approach to mood with a Processing Instruction methodology had positive effects on how the students identified mood selection in both input and output learning situations.

### Introduction: An overview

The present paper discusses a series of experiments aimed at proving that a meaningful teaching of L2 Grammar with cognitive-based approaches will result in better L2 learning. Current teaching methods of L2 structures generally consist of separately considering forms and meanings, giving the students a list of forms to memorize and practice within a number of possible contexts.

It is the view sustained here, however, that learners who gain explicit knowledge from instruction based on cognitive grammar will be able to express meaningful and communicative intents because they will be able to make a form-meaning connection in the L2.

In the present study, the target form was mood selection in Spanish by German learners. Mood (indicative vs. subjunctive) is perceived as the most difficult structure to learn by German learners of Spanish as a foreign language (SFL) (Vázquez 1991).

The teaching methodology used was a combination of a cognitive-based approach to an explicit and meaningful teaching of grammar and the so-called *Processing Instruction* for the practicing part (VanPatten, see References). The former draws on pedagogical grammar approaches and is called

*AILA Review* 23 (2010), 72–94. DOI 10.1075/aila.23.05llo
ISSN 1461–0213 / E-ISSN 1570–5595 © John Benjamins Publishing Company

*Operational Grammar* (Ruiz Campillo 2006, 2007, 2008), whereas the latter uses both structured input and output tasks to ensure interpretation and production of mood selection in three types of clauses.

The analysis of the data elicited showed that the combination of these two approaches had indeed very positive effects on how the students identified mood selection to construe meanings in both input and output learning situations. The results of the study, then, suggest why Cognitive Grammar works in the L2 classroom and why it is promising to continue testing cognitive L2 *"teaching for learning"*.

## Second language teaching and SFL

In the world of Second Language Acquisition (SLA), there is a tendency to separate natural contexts (SLA occurring naturally through exposure, without instruction) from *instructed* SLA, which takes place when the learner relies on external aids to learn the language (typically, the foreign language classroom).

Within this second context, Doughty (2004) stresses the need to compare the efficacy of different methodologies and approaches to grammar instruction, in order to enhance the learner's interlanguage and competence. Arguments in favor of this view stipulate that instructed SLA does influence a variety of aspects of learning. For instance, a learner's L2 *processing strategies* can be positively modified. Instruction can motivate the strategies that lead to interlanguage development and also try to alter those that are negative, that hinder or hold back comprehension. Instruction also affects the *degree of fluency* that the learner may reach through teaching programs that focus on providing controlled practice to correct, modify, and consolidate acquired knowledge. For the cases where there is no immersion context, instruction may also provide the learner with sufficient *quality opportunities* to learn the foreign language.

Robinson & Ellis, in a recent review of instruction effects in SLA research (derived from the 2000 Norris & Ortega study), stated that *explicit* instruction that directs learners to making form-meaning connections has been "found to be more effective in promoting successful post-treatment assessments of construction learning compared to *implicit* conditions where such awareness is not promoted or demonstrated by learners" (2008, 498 f.).

Considering all the previous arguments, it can be argued that explicit instruction could be beneficial for learners dealing with complex grammatical features[1] (see Housen & Pierrard 2005, for a number of studies supporting this view). Since learners perceive mood selection in Spanish as a complex grammatical task, formal instruction and explicit grammar teaching could help them to understand and process its meaning in a more effective manner.

The next step to take into consideration, then, is *what kind* of grammar instruction is needed. Lee & VanPatten (2003:123) talk about traditional uses of grammar in American classrooms (although their arguments are highly applicable to other countries) as being "largely mechanical, with the focus exclusively on using a grammatical feature to *produce* some sort of utterance".

The 1980s and 90s in SFL saw a rise of the so-called "communicative approach" (also known as "Communicative Language Teaching" — CLT — in the SLA literature), where grammar was almost suppressed from the curriculum or taught "under the table", without specific reference to metalanguage. The focus was mainly on linguistic notions that used forms to be construed.[2]

Nowadays, there are many attempts to reconcile grammar with CLT. However, the question continues to be problematic, since many teachers tend to consider grammar as a disconnected set of linguistic forms used in many contexts (as linguistic categories, types of tenses, constructions, phrases…) regardless of meaning, or as meaningful events to be used with a number of forms (see Byrd 2005 for a further discussion on teacher beliefs). As CLT continues to prevail in classrooms everywhere, Byrd states that one of the most important issues related to grammar within this approach lies in the focus: on form or on forms? We will deal with *focus on form* (FonF) here.

FonF "consists of an occasional shift of attention to linguistic code features — by the teachers and/or one or more students — triggered by perceived problems with comprehension or production" (Long & Robinson 1998: 23). This way, FonF establishes a cognitive relationship between the learner and the linguistic form, allowing a processing based more on noticing and understanding and less on memorization. Cadierno (2008: 264), after reviewing approaches to grammar present in the L2 classroom for the last 30 years, concludes: "grammar instruction [...] is best implemented as a focus-on-form approach where linguistic expressions are presented in communicative contexts designed to promote learners' awareness of their form-meaning relationships".

There is one more matter to think about when confronted with L2 teaching, and that is the gap between the reality of the classroom and the scope of research conducted by linguists. Achard (2004: 167) points out that:

> Linguists often complain that the methods they see being used in language classrooms do not conform to what they know of language, and they regret that their expertise is overlooked in the design of methods and activities. On the other hand, language teachers complain that the linguists' expertise is simply of little help with practical classroom related matters, because they do not find in current linguistic theories the elements which would help them in their daily activities by providing strong theoretical guidelines on which to base a teaching methodology.

In recent years, many linguists and teachers have come to share this view, to name a few: Collentine (2003), Grove (2003), Ruiz Campillo (2007), Tyler (2008), Langacker (2008 ab), or Llopis-García (2007). Already in the 21st century, this significant lack of agreement between theoretically-informed research and generalized classroom practice continues to pose a serious challenge for the field. Research that focuses on empirical assessment of different SLA approaches to classroom instruction is highly needed. Furthermore, it should be valued as a useful resource for material development, teacher training, instructional planning and evaluation procedures. This is true for L2 teaching in general, but definitely so for SFL.[3]

The present contribution is an attempt to inform about the effects of grammar instruction in the SFL classroom by combining two separate SLA frameworks into one big methodological approach to mood selection: a FonF methodology named *Processing Instruction* (PI) and Cognitive Grammar. The goal is to provide learners of SFL with the necessary tools to *perceive* mood in Spanish and, through conscious understanding of the target structure, allow them to *control* their own production.

On the one hand, PI gives learners a chance to make form-meaning connections by cognitively processing target forms in especially designed input (and output) activities. This leads to an understanding of the target form and to the development of their L2 competence. Cadierno (2008: 264) stresses the advantages of working with the FonF approach to grammar, because "with its key in focus on form and meaning relations, and the use of language in communicative contexts, is thus more in consonance with the language view advocated by cognitive linguistics, and is expected to benefit from its insights."

On the other hand, the view of language advocated in cognitive linguistics focuses on the inseparable relationship between form and meaning. Language is seen as part of our general cognitive system. Hence, all speakers (native and non-native) express meaning on the basis of how they perceive reality and wish to express their perspective. Grammar, under this consideration, is not an arbitrary set of forms and rules used in contexts (meaningful or not), but rather the necessary tool that allows learners to construct reality in an L2.

Within cognitive linguistics, it is possible to find ways to operationalize form-meaning connections so that students need not work with form listings, but rather manage L2 prototypes that condense all possible usages of a structure to formal decisions based on communicative intents. And here is where *Operational Grammar* (Ruiz Campillo 2006, 2007, 2008) comes into play.

Operational Grammar is a cognitive approach to teaching grammatical forms in SFL. It attempts to reduce all possible uses of a linguistic form to a minimum of so-called *operational values*. The idea is that learners should then be able to produce an unlimited number of utterances without having to learn each usage individually. This is accomplished by working with metaphors, prototypes and radiality "by extension". Operational Grammar allows the learner to *own* her communication and master in each moment what she wants to say and why.

## Mood selection in SFL: A brief impression

Traditional language description methods have supported the claim that syntax reigns over meaning, and that the speakers of a language construct this meaning by means of correctly combining syntactic structures. These methods give priority to the linguistic form, detaching it from meaning. Hence, they teach the learner when to use forms in combination with other forms, in order to express meaning in a given context.

That is how, in the specific case of mood selection in SFL, learners are taught that the subjunctive has to do mostly with subordination and that at least the intermediate level is required for them to correctly understand and begin to use it. According to Collentine (1993: 2), until this level:

> The interlanguage is not sufficiently developed in resources to produce structures involving complex syntactic and morphological rules, especially in spontaneous speech, since successful spontaneous communication greatly depends on the efficient use of attention and memory.

It is assumed, then, that learners will need to master both morphological and syntactic principles before they can begin to face some mood selection cases. Achard (2004: 185) accurately describes what happens in the L2 classroom: "grammatical rules traditionally given in a language class are considered a property of the system, and not a result of the speaker's choice." Students are then faced with teaching materials like the following, where form and meaning are detached from each other:

> The subjunctive is used to express doubt with affirmative constructions such as *dudo que* + SUBJ [*I doubt that*] and negative constructions like *no creo que* + SUBJ [*I don't think that*].

Students then apply this rule to incorrect sentences like *\*supongo que + llueva*[4] [*I suppose that it rains*], which also expresses doubt but triggers indicative. However, their logical inferences are truncated with counter-explanations like: *Suponer* belongs to the so-called *thinking verbs* [*verbos de pensamiento*], which are used with indicative, along with others like *creer* [*believe*], *pensar* [*think*], *parecer* [*reckon*], etc. In these learning situations, students are given lists of forms on the one hand, and list of meanings on the other. How to combine them is left to morphological rules and syntactic principles, rendering the speaker passive in the communication process.

## Cognitive viewing of language: A change in perspective

One of the most basic tenets of Cognitive Grammar has always been the claim that language is meaningful, and that linguistic forms are symbolic in nature because they are made up of both semantic and phonological associations (see Langacker 2008a,b for an updated version of this argument).

In Cognitive Grammar terms, the speaker's conceptualization of the surrounding world determines the meaning he gives to linguistic forms, and his communicative intent will strongly determine how he will formulate what he wants to say. Form and meaning, from this perspective, are inseparable and respond to a normative language usage[5] within a given linguistic community. Language users select and combine linguistic forms in certain ways because that combination conveys the exact meaning they have in mind.

Language, then, is the vehicle through which we express our thoughts, impressions and perceptions of the world we live in: it allows us to put highly abstract concepts — and how we perceive them — into words. Viewing language from this standpoint gives speakers the leading role in communication. It makes them independent from taxonomies and linguistic rules based on apparently random criteria.

If this were to be the starting point when considering L2 language learning, a whole new world of teaching possibilities could open — a world where the student consciously selects a linguistic form because it carries the exact meaning she wants to express, and where fixed rules become prototypes that can be managed through their form-meaning relationship.

A Cognitive Grammar approach to L2 needs to look for the prototypical principle that governs the link between a linguistic form and its meaning. Then, it needs to see how to extend its properties to fit all incidences of usage by means of analyzing its radiality. This concept of *radiality*, if applied to L2 teaching, needs to be understood as the maximum scope of usages that can be inferred from the primary meaning of a prototype. Metaphors usually play an important role in these extensions.

Also, a cognitive, *pedagogical* grammar needs to focus on explicit teaching that helps students *understand* both the prototype and its radiality and how to use them *meaningfully* when constructing communication in the L2.

This paper provides evidence of such an approach to grammar, and empirically assesses the claim that it results in better L2 learning.

### What is Operational Grammar?

*Operational Grammar* (Ruiz Campillo 2006, 2007, 2008) is a pedagogical grammar[6] approach based on teaching form and meaning as one unit. It searches for the so-called "operational values", which are based on form-meaning connections. They are prototypical in nature and can be extended to fit usage through logical radiality and perspective, which will be determined by the speaker's communicative intent.

Through Operational Grammar, the number of occurrences of a form (such as the subjunctive) is dramatically reduced because it can be managed with a minimum of operational values based on form-meaning connections. In this way, learners themselves, and not the linguistic situation, will determine which form is selected every time.

This approach, then, gives the leading role in communication back to the speaker: based on what she wants to say, she will select certain linguistic forms because they will exactly transmit her message. Grammar, then, will be the ultimate means of communication, and not the tool with which to try and communicate. "Puzzle combinations" (*with "creo que", use indicative, but with "no creo que", use subjunctive*) are thus eliminated from the L2 formal instruction and the real challenge begins, i.e., to find evidence that this approach can feed comprehensible data to the learner's interlanguage.

### Operational Grammar and mood.

In order to understand how Operational Grammar is applied to mood selection, it is important to explain that there is one "Law for Meaning" and one "Law for Use". The first one defines what each mood prototypically conveys, and the second will extend the meaning of the prototype to fit different usage situations.

The "Law for Use" draws on the concept of *claim* [original: *declaración*] and *no-claim* [*no-declaración*]. It states the following argument:

> *Indicative represents a claim of the fact it states*
> *Subjunctive represents a no-claim of the fact it states* (Ruiz Campillo 2006: 15)

This means that indicative will convey a meaning that the speaker, *from his own perspective*, ratifies or claims as it is. The subjunctive, on the other hand, will convey *anything* else that the speaker may wish to communicate with his utterance, but never a claim. To clarify this with an example, let us consider the following conversation:

> – *Mira, Cristina, está diluviando, ¡ahora no podremos ir al jardín! [Look, Cristina, it's pouring down, we won't be able to go out and play in the garden!]*
> – *Pues da igual, nosotras vamos a salir a jugar aunque esté diluviando. [It doesn't matter, we are still going out to play although it's raining]*

In this example, Cristina does not deny that it is raining (that is, she does not *claim* that it is **not** *raining*). She is even probably looking out of the window and is in fact seeing that it is really pouring down. What Cristina does when she selects the subjunctive (for she could have equally constructed the very same sentence using indicative instead), is *avoiding* the claim that it, indeed, rains. Since she does not declaratively identify the problem (*llueve/it rains*), she can then go ahead and make the decision she wants: to go out and play.

The "Law for Use" then identifies when either mood is to be selected:

> *Does the meaning of the matrix imply that the subordinate clause is a claim?*
> *Yes: use indicative. No: use subjunctive.* (Ruiz Campillo 2006: 16)

To understand what the statement above means, the term "matrix" needs to be explained. In current L2 grammars, mood is selected from its relationship to other verbs, adjectives, fixed constructions, adverbs, etc., which are classified independently from each other. These relationships have a syntactic base combined with a pragmatic focus: '*noun clauses to talk about personal preferences*', '*relative clauses to describe things*', '*temporal clauses to talk about the relationship between events*', etc.

From a cognitive point of view, however, meaning is what will determine which mood to select. The matrix, then, will be any symbolic unit that, given its meaning, will need either indicative to construe a claim, or subjunctive if a no-claim is to be expressed (that is, everything else). The following examples will help clarify this:

*Está claro que/creo que/supongo que/sé que/es obvio que/por eso* [*it is clear that/I think that/I guess that/it is obvious that/for that reason*] will all, irrespective of syntactic properties, need an indicative, because the meaning they all have in common expresses something that can be claimed from the speaker's point of view. On the other hand, matrixes such as: *Es fantástico que /ojalá /me alegra que/quiero que/es necesario que* [*It is fantastic that/I wish that/I am glad that/I want that/It is necessary that*] will always convey meanings that are no-claims: wishes, criticisms, judgments, morals, etc., and they will always trigger the subjunctive.

The "Law for Use", thus, establishes a clear concept for selecting mood, and it moves away from syntactic taxonomies or pragmatic values: the speaker has a meaning to express and only the correct mood will get that meaning across.

The instruction groups in this study all received an explicit introduction to mood that adapted all the previous information to the SFL classroom setting.

*Operational values for the study*

There were three types of mood selection clauses in the experimental study. They were introduced according to the proficiency level established by the Common European Framework of Reference (CEFR): relative clauses (A2/B1), temporal clauses (B1/B2), and concessive clauses (B2/C1), which were also introduced in that order during the study. The "easiest" occurrence (relative clauses) was established as the prototypical value, and then its meaning was extended for the other two by means of strategic radiality:

**Relative clauses** (OR).[7] Stating a claim about an entity that is being described equals identifying its content, presenting it as known: *Un piso que tiene 4 habitaciones* [*An apartment that has 4 rooms*]. Indicative will be used to express this. However, the speaker may wish to describe other entities without having to identify them: *Un chico que me quiera* [literally: *a boy who loves me*]. These cases would trigger the subjunctive, which conveys the no-claim about the boy, namely, that the speaker does not or cannot identify this person but may still describe him. Given this explanation, then, the best translation for *un chico que me quiera* would be *A boy to love me* (Appendix A shows the explicit information that students received).

**Temporal clauses** (OC). When considering a moment in time, we may identify it and claim something about it. These claims about time may then naturally be identified as routine actions, moments the speaker is familiar with and can describe, as in *Bebo zumo de tomate cuando viajo en avión* [*I drink tomato juice when traveling by plane*]. Indicative will be used to claim something like: "(1) *Traveling by plane is something I do and know about*, (2) *Every time I take a plane, I drink tomato juice*".

On the other hand, making a no-claim about a moment in time means not being able to identify it, which in temporal terms is a clear reference to the future: *Hoy llamo a mi madre cuando llegue a casa* [*I (will) call my mother today when I get home*]. The moment "*I get home*" cannot be identified because it lies in the future. Therefore, although the speaker may use other constructions with it such as *later on this evening* or even *at seven pm*, subjunctive will still be needed because the actual moment cannot be controlled by the speaker: it has not happened yet, regardless of how limited and exact its specifics about when it will take place might be.

**Concessive clauses** (OA). When making a claim, it should be clear by now that the speaker identifies its content. OA always present an obstacle to the fulfillment of the proposition made (which however does not hinder the proposition from really happening). Using indicative in these clauses means directly *identifying* that problem, acknowledging the obstacle and giving it credit: *Voy a ir al concierto aunque cuesta mucho dinero* [*I am going to the concert although it costs a lot of money*]. In this example, the speaker identifies the problem of the price for the concert tickets, acknowledges and informs about its "presence", but will still ignore it in the end, since she is going to the concert anyway.

But the speaker also has the option of stating a no-claim about the price and not identifying it as a problem: instead, she can comment on it or judge it, but never declare it as a problem: *Voy a ir al concierto aunque cueste mucho dinero* [*I am going to the concert even though it costs a lot of money*]. Using the subjunctive here frees the speaker from openly identifying her problem and enables her to present it in light of a comment, a judgment, an opinion — it makes going to the concert (and paying, too) less arguable.

Treating mood selection as a single value to be logically understood and used to express a very concrete meaning gives the learners power over their grammatical decisions. Students can free themselves from learning a linguistic structure as the product of a foreign language system that functions independently from them.

Explicit grammar from a cognitive perspective helps learners take the leading role in their communication. It teaches them to treat the foreign grammar as the means for expressing their ideas, not as a list of countless rules and exceptions. In other words, cognitive grammar instruction through ONE operational value and its extended radiality allows students to handle different uses of the same linguistic form because they understand the "logical" decisions needed to convey meaning with each one of them.

## What is Processing Instruction?

Before defining what Processing Instruction (PI) is, the Input Processing Model must be briefly addressed. This model, developed by VanPatten (1996, 2002, 2004, 2007), deals with the strategies learners use to determine a form-meaning connection. This connection establishes the relationship between a linguistic form and the meaning or function it conveys. Although its origins are to be found within the field of psycholinguistics, its endeavor to make learners link linguistic form and meaning makes it very compatible with cognitive and pedagogical grammar approaches.

The Input Processing Model considers learners' processing resources when attending to made-available input as limited. In every input situation there is an overload of information ready to be processed and also many influential factors (word order, lexical preferences, communicative value of the forms, attention to the input, etc.) to take into account.

All these factors need to be controlled if the processing of the right form-meaning connection is to be ensured. And it is precisely here where PI appears, for it is the Model's application to the "real L2 classroom-world": it helps learners *process* these connections. PI searches for learning strategies that hinder acquisition of certain target forms and seeks to alter them.[8] This is done using so-called "structured input" activities,[9] which direct learners' attention to the target form and its meaning. Students then need to make the connection between both or they will not be able to complete the task (Appendix B includes examples of these types of activities).

## The present study: Research hypotheses and purpose

The research goal of this study was to examine the effects of formal instruction on the possible acquisition of mood selection in relative, temporal and concessive clauses. This formal instruction methodology consisted of a cognitive operational approach to grammar and practice based on the interpretation and production of target structures through structured activities. In short, the potential efficacy of the combination of Ruiz Campillo's Operational Grammar with an extended version of VanPatten's Processing Instruction (applied both to input and output) was to be researched.

The original study formulated five hypotheses that addressed methodological issues for the study in general, task type differences, and validity of the assessment materials. However, given the pedagogical focus of this paper, only two of these hypotheses will be tackled here:

H1. Instruction of mood selection in relative, temporal and concessive clauses will yield positive learning results:
– for both instruction groups on indicative and subjunctive from pre- to posttests
– for instruction groups in comparison with the control group

H2. There will not be significant differences between instruction groups for the processing of both indicative and subjunctive during assessment for relative, temporal, and concessive clauses.

## Methodology

**Participants.** 81 university students from the RWTH Aachen University in Germany participated in the study during the winter semester 2007/2008 (October to February).

All informants completed a survey about their level of Spanish, their understanding of the target structure, contact with native speakers, use of Spanish outside of class, and previous learning materials.

There were 26 male and 55 female students. The average age was 22. None of the informants reported having any impairment or disability that could affect their performance during the study. All of them had given their consent to participating and knew they would be involved in the study throughout the semester.

All participating students had a proficiency level of A2 (in CEFR standards, low intermediate). This means that they were all familiar with the indicative mood and had seen some uses of the subjunctive already, mostly when studying the imperative and in uses with the interjection *ojalá* [*I wish*]. The course in which they were at the time of the study was going to introduce the mood selection areas studied here for the first time. OR (relative clauses) and some uses of the OC (temporal clauses) belonged to the A2/B1 level, whereas the OA (concessive clauses) were meant for much more advanced levels.

The students who received instruction belonged to three intact classes. Two of them were randomly assigned to be the interpretation group (IG, with input tasks only) and the production group (PG, with output tasks only). The third class was also randomly divided into students belonging to the IG and PG and they were separated only during instruction practice, where the IG worked with interpretation and the PG with production tasks. There were, in total, N = 35 in the IG, and N = 31 in the PG.

The students from the control group (CG) (N = 15), who did not receive any instruction and only completed the assessment tests, had a CEFR level of B1+ (intermediate) and were already familiar with two of the mood selection areas (relative and temporal). These students had studied mood using traditional approaches to grammar, with a presentation of rules for each case and output practice in communicative tasks. Their level was higher than that of the instruction groups because one of the goals of the study was to see whether the methodology proposed would be better at teaching mood selection than what the other courses usually did in class.[10]

**Materials.** Aside from the initial survey mentioned before, there was an introductory session to the subjunctive that offered an explanation of mood from an Operational Grammar perspective: its *Law for Meaning* and its *Law for Use*. For the actual experimental part, there was a set of materials per mood selection area (OR, OC, OA). Each set contained an instructional packet with activities and three assessment tests. All activities were designed following PI's guidelines for the design of structured input (and its extension to output) tasks.

All vocabulary items were taken from the textbooks used in class. Additionally, for all activities in the study, students had a glossary of terms (following from procedures of other studies, like DeKeyser & Sokalsky 1996). This ensured that the students understood all content in the activities, avoided depletion of processing resources while trying to comprehend unknown words, and enabled them to work independently from the teacher and/or the other fellow students. This was particularly important for the target verbs: in each glossary, every single verb that the students had to work on was conjugated in the first person singular of the present indicative/subjunctive. The reason for this was that the study only targeted mood *selection*, that is, their ability to connect the form with its meaning, not to conjugate it. Also, the number and type of activities was balanced across clause types for all materials.

The last general issue was the language used: only the core content of each activity was in Spanish. The rest (directions, questions) was written in German to ensure full understanding of all procedures and help students focus their processing resources only on mood selection issues.

The <u>instructional packets</u> included a grammar explanation handout and a set of eight activities with structured input for the IG and structured output for the PG. The <u>grammar handout</u> was identical in structure for all three areas and the time devoted to it in each instruction session was initially 30 minutes. However, this time was only true for the first area (OR) and progressively decreased for the other two (less than 20 minutes for the OA). The reason was that only the explanation of the operational value was changed each time.

The handout was given out at the beginning of the instruction session and taken away for the activities. It addressed the following questions: (1) *What are OR/OC/OA?* (2) *How are they formed?* (3) *Where are IND/SUBJ placed within the clause?* (4) *When to use IND/SUBJ* (5) *How to correctly process mood in OR/OC/OA.* This last question explicitly addressed the learning strategies that were to be avoided in order to process mood successfully and made students conscious of their own ability to connect form with meaning.

The <u>set of activities</u> had two versions, one for each instruction group (structured input activities only or structured output only). All activities were exactly identical (see Appendix B) in number of items and content.[11]

Structured input activities consisted of making decisions on mood through interpretation of statements. Students from the IG had to read each statement and, solely based on the mood form, decide on the meaning conveyed. All statements were structured so that the main clause and the nexus appeared only once and all subordinate clauses immediately underneath, which positioned the mood form in sentence-initial position and made it easier to process (see Appendix B for examples).

On the other hand, structured output activities consisted of decision making about the meaning of each statement *after* having previously selected one mood form. In these activities, students had to write the form first, and then assign the correct meaning to it.

There were three <u>assessment tests</u> for each mood selection area: pretest, posttest1, and posttest2. They were versions of one same master test, randomly named A, B and C. They were used in different random orders (ABC, BAC, ACB, CBA) for each experimental group. All versions were identical and only the content varied. The total number of activities per test was four.

**Procedure.** The semester had a total duration of 13 weeks and the empirical study took up eight 90-minute sessions. As already mentioned, there were three mood selection areas: relative clauses (OR), temporal clauses (OC) and concessive clauses (OA). Three sessions were dedicated to each area as shown in Figure 1.

**Figure 1.** Procedure for each mood selection area

The protocol for each clause type was as follows:

-   Session 1: 20 minutes for the pretest, then classroom content related to the general program of the course.

–    Session 2 was entirely taken for the study: 30 minutes for the explicit grammar presentation with the handout, and practice for 45 minutes with eight activities (IG with interpretation and PG with production exercises). The students corrected every activity but did not receive feedback from the teacher at any point. After that, the teacher took all materials away and posttest1 was taken during the last 15–20 minutes.

–    Session 3: 20 minutes for posttest2, 50 minutes for content related to the general syllabus and the last 20 minutes for the next pretest.

Each experimental group (IG, PG, CG) had a different assessment test order. The control group only completed the assessment tests in the same week as the instruction groups. The rest of the time, they engaged in the usual contents and activities of their course, which was one for creative writing.

The instructor in all courses and for the whole duration of the study was the researcher herself, who was also the usual teacher of all students.

**Scoring.** Scoring procedures for the assessment tests were based upon three criteria: correct (CORR), incorrect (INC) and blank. Students were strongly encouraged not to guess if they were not sure and to leave the answer blank to refrain from randomly using the 50% choice.

A verb was scored as CORR and given 1 point if the students interpreted or produced the right mood-meaning connection, and as INC (with 0 points) if this connection was interpreted or produced wrongly. If a student had misspelled, failed to see concordance or written an irregular form as regular, but the mood was correctly selected, the answer still counted as CORR. Blank answers were not counted.

The statistical analyses used for H1 were:

–    Efficacy of the methodology for both moods in OR, OC and OA clauses: a multivariate variance analysis (MANOVA 3x3x2). The dependent variable was the number of correct answers.
–    Superiority of learning results in comparison with the control group: variance analysis (ANOVA) for each mood selection area.

The statistical analyses used for H2 were:

–    Equal performance of instruction groups on the processing of both moods during assessment for the three areas: a T-test for independent measures using raw and gain scores.

## Results

*A) Hypothesis 1 for methodology effects: confirmed for both instruction groups*
Table 1 shows the results for the within-group variables (assessment, mood and area) for IG and PG:

**Table 1.** MANOVA for instruction groups

| Source | Df | Mean square | F | Sign. |
| --- | --- | --- | --- | --- |
| Effects of instruction | 2 | 1925.984 | 213.945 | 0.000 |
| Mood | 1 | 39.862 | 17.415 | 0.000 |
| Work area | 2 | 1038.912 | 58.736 | 0.000 |
| Effect of instruction x mood | 2 | 41.147 | 21.881 | 0.000 |
| Effect of instruction x work area | 4 | 364.403 | 38.302 | 0.000 |
| Mood x work area | 2 | 10.011 | 4.743 | 0.011 |

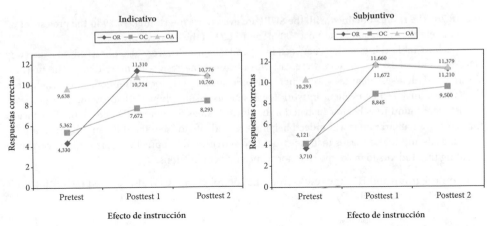

**Figure 2.**  Correct answers for each work area in both moods[12]

The first independent variable found statistically significant was 'assessment' (F[2] = 213.945; $p < .001$), so there was a difference between the pre- and posttests. 'Mood' was also significant (F[1] = 17.415; $p < .001$), so the methodology had a different impact on subjunctive (SUBJ) and indicative (IND). Lastly, 'work area' was also significant (F[2] = 58.73; $p < .001$), and this means that the number of correct answers varied for OR, OC and OA clauses. Figure 2 shows the positive impact of the instruction methodology in all three areas, since the values considerably increase from pretests to posttests for both moods:

The most striking instruction effect is found in the OR for IND, for the initial 4.33 values for the pretest go up to 11.31 in posttest1 and stabilize at 10.76 in posttest2. For the SUBJ, OR start at 3.71 correct answers and then go up to 11.66 in the posttest1 and 11.38 in posttest2. These data show a remarkable mood selection processing for the OR, and the interesting thing about it is that OR with IND are seen in the A2 level for the first time, whereas the SUBJ is first encountered in the B1 level. The participants in this study had all level A2, but found no apparent trouble in successfully processing the complex syntax of these subordinate clauses for either mood.

This result disagrees with Collentine's "syntactic-deficiency hypothesis" (2003 [1995]), which states that intermediate-level learners "are not yet at the syntactic stage where they can process in short-term memory both complex syntax and the semantic/pragmatic relationships (e.g., volition, doubt/denial) existing between two clauses" (p. 79).

If the OC are observed, a progress in learning can also be detected for both moods. For IND, correct answers in the pretest at 5.36 are already high with respect to the OR, which started out lower. This means that the students were already starting to extend the operational value for the IND by themselves. After instruction, correct answers raised to 7.87 and up to 8.29 in posttest2. This increase is even more striking for SUBJ, where pretest values are 4.12, then double up to 8.84 after instruction and increase to 9.5 a week later during posttest2. The differences to the OR pretest are not so relevant here, but make sense since the SUBJ is the marked, novel structure and presents a bigger challenge for the students, who at the time had not received any instruction yet. However, the elevated complexity of the OC seems to be overcome after instruction.

If Figure 2 is observed again, the most impressive results lie within the OA (which belong to the more advanced B2/C1 CEFR standards). The results show an almost ideal operationalization of the value for mood, since already in the pretest for both moods the results show near mastery of the structures. For the IND mood, the pretest values start at 9.64 and after the instruction move to 10.72

and 10.76. The results obtained with the SUBJ are even more interesting: 10.29 in the pretest, 11.67 immediately after instruction (almost 100%!) and 11.21 in the delayed posttest.

Back to Table 1, interactions between independent variables were also observed, so a one-way ANOVA and a Post-hoc Scheffé were carried out to see the results in more detail. The first test showed that all assessment tests were highly significant ($p < .001$) for both moods. The Scheffé test, on its part, analyzed assessment in work areas, and its results showed that the highly significant results were found mostly after instruction in all work areas for both IND and SUBJ. This means that Operational Grammar was indeed helping the students to "see" the difference in meaning for both moods and it also means that the structured activities of the practical part were successful in enabling the students to make the right form-meaning connections.

**The control group and H1.** The results from the control group (CG) also showed interesting findings (see Figure 3 and Table 2):

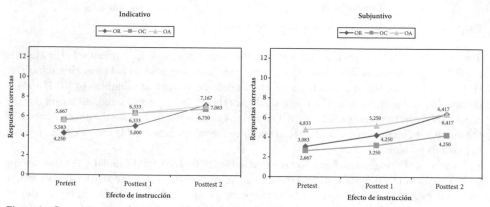

**Figure 3.** Correct answers for each work area in both moods[13]

Table 2. MANOVA for CG

| Source | Df | Mean square | F | Sign. |
|---|---|---|---|---|
| Instruction effect | 2 | 73.852 | 92.744 | 0.000 |
| Mood | 1 | 126.042 | 91.667 | 0.000 |
| Work area | 2 | 25.560 | 2.472 | 0.107 |
| Inst. Effect x mood | 4 | 6.428 | 7.631 | 0.000 |
| Mood x work area | 2 | 23.014 | 8.784 | 0.002 |

There was a significant effect for assessment ($F[2] = 92.744$; $p < .001$), which means that correct answers varied across testing phases. Mood was also found to be significant ($p < .001$), and from Figure 1 it is clear that the number of correct answers is higher for IND than for SUBJ. This is not surprising, since IND was the more familiar mood, and the students did not receive an instruction to explicitly clarify its differences with SUBJ. They used their already existing knowledge of both moods to answer all test items. The 'work area' variable was not found significant ($p = .107$), which means that this group essentially chose the correct answers constantly through the whole study.

Since there were interactions also between variables, another ANOVA and Post-hoc Scheffé test were implemented. For the IND, the only significant effect was for the pretest and there were no significant effects for work areas. The SUBJ, on the other hand, had significance in all the assessment moments. This significance, however, if Figure 3 is closely examined, happens over very small numeric values. The CG was able to slowly increase the number of correct answers along the study, which makes sense since the students were already familiar with OR and OC. The fact that the right answers also increase for the OA is a positive sign that the structured activities helped them focus on the target structure and gain knowledge of the new one. All in all, however, the results achieved by this group are still not comparable to those obtained by the instruction groups, which were much higher.

*H1 in relative clauses: methodology effects confirmed*

In order to confirm the hypothesis that the instruction groups would be superior to the control group, a repeated measures ANOVA test was performed in each work area. Figure 4[14] shows the results.

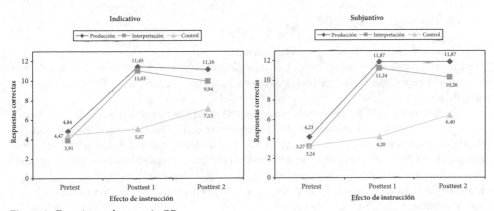

**Figure 4.** Experimental groups in OR

As seen in the graphs, all three groups start out similarly in the pretest. However, after instruction and for both moods, the IG and the PG sharply increase their correct answers. The CG is left behind with a much lower rate of success. Then, a significant value for all experimental groups was found ($F[2] = 1.724.821$; $p < .001$) and another Post-hoc Scheffé cleared the issue (Table 3):

**Table 3.** Post-hoc Scheffé for group interactions in OR

| (I) Group | (J) Group | Sign. |
|---|---|---|
| Production | Interpretation | 0.043 |
| | Control | 0.000 |
| Interpretation | Production | 0.043 |
| | Control | 0.000 |
| Control | Production | 0.000 |
| | Interpretation | 0.000 |

All three experimental groups were different from each other, but a close look at Figure 4 and the values in Table 3 reveals that the instruction groups (IG and PG) were very close to each other, whereas the CG was distanced from both. The instructional method has very clear and marked effects on PG and IG and therefore, it can be safely concluded that the increase in correct answers for OR is much more defined and clear for both instruction groups.

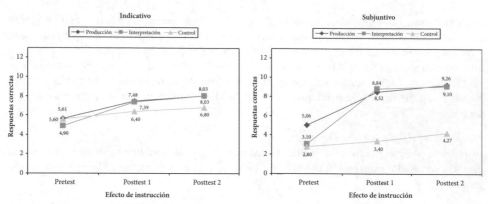

**Figure 5.** Experimental groups in OC

*H1 in temporal clauses: methodology effects confirmed*

The case of the OC differs from the one just seen, although the first results found for the OR were also present here (differences between all three groups: F[2] = 8.985; p < .001). Figure 5 shows OCs in both moods:

The effects for IND are interesting, since the CG started out with better results than the IG, which by the end of the assessment had duplicated their correct answer count. Both IG and PG clearly progress after instruction, whereas the CG evolves lightly, but still below both instruction groups. The SUBJ results are to be expected from the predictions raised: instruction groups upgrade their correct answers to high levels, and the CG stays in a slightly ascending line. The Post-hoc Scheffé confirmed these results: instruction groups (IG, PG) are no different from each other, but both are different from the CG (Table 4).

**Table 4.** Post-hoc Scheffé for group interactions in OC

| (I) Group | (J) Group | Sign. |
| --- | --- | --- |
| Production | Interpretation | 0.660 |
| | Control | 0.000 |
| Interpretation | Production | 0.660 |
| | Control | 0.004 |
| Control | Production | 0.000 |
| | Interpretation | 0.004 |

*H1 in concessive clauses: methodology effects confirmed*

The OA offer the most outstanding difference between instruction and control groups. When the ANOVA was first executed, group differences were found both for IND and SUBJ (F[2] = 23.731; p < .001). Then, the Post-hoc Scheffé clarified once more that these differences were significant only between the control group on the one hand and the instruction ones on the other hand. PG and IG were no different from each other (see Table 5). Figure 6 confirms these findings and shows the remarkable distance between the instruction groups and the control one:

For the OA, already in the pretest the differences show (for both moods) that the progress of all three experimental groups evolves in a very steady way: PG and IG in levels close to complete success, and the CG in its improved but lower level.

B) Hypothesis 2: Equal performance of instruction groups: confirmed[15]

*H2 in relative clauses*
The T-test implemented for the H2 data analysis with gain scores showed no statistically significant differences, so it cannot be concluded that the instruction groups were different from each other during assessment. Both were equally successful. Figure 7[16] shows these results graphically:

**Table 5.** Post-hoc Scheffé for group interactions in OA

| (I) Group | (J) Group | Sign. |
|---|---|---|
| Production | Interpretation | 0.700 |
| | Control | 0.000 |
| Interpretation | Production | 0.700 |
| | Control | 0.000 |
| Control | Production | 0.000 |
| | Interpretation | 0.000 |

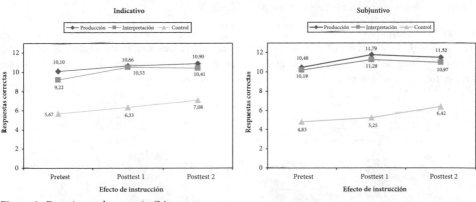

**Figure 6.** Experimental groups in OA

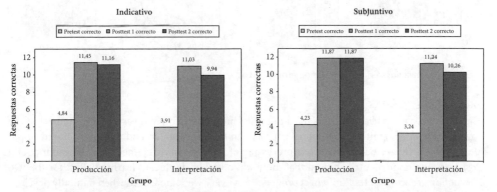

**Figure 7.** Correct answers for instruction groups in OR

## H2 in temporal clauses

The T-test for the OC with gain scores also failed to detect statistically significant results and therefore it may not be concluded that one instruction group had any advantages over the other in either mood. Both performed equally well, especially after instruction. Figure 8 illustrates this argument:

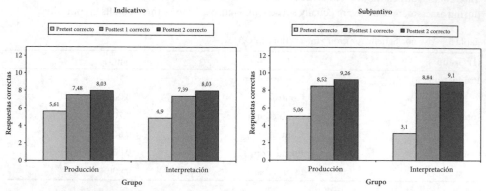

**Figure 8.**  Correct answers for instruction groups in OC

## H2 in concessive clauses

The results from the analysis of gain scores rendered no differences at all in any variables for OA, and it may be concluded that there was no difference at all between the interpretation and production groups for mood selection in these clauses. Figure 9 supports this argument:

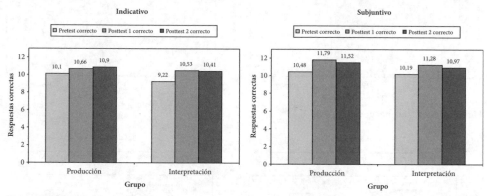

**Figure 9.**  Correct answers for instruction groups in OC

## Discussion

The data analyzed for H1 confirms the *a priori* assumptions, namely, a very positive impact of the combination of a cognitive, operational approach to mood grammar, and of the structured (input and output) activities based on correct processing of form-meaning connections. All variance and Post-hoc tests implemented showed that there was a highly significant learning effect for the two instruction groups, and that this effect progressed in every work area, even when naturally developing syntax and/or pragmatic complexities were factored out. This means that the students were able to operationalize the prototypical value for mood given in the OR and correctly apply its radiality to the OC and OA.

The OR show the steepest progress after instruction and this is consistent with the fact that these clauses belonged to the A2 level of the students: they had no trouble in correctly interpreting and producing both moods in this work area.

Although the OC were more complex and difficult (levels B1/B1+ of the CEFR) and the learning progress was not as striking as for the OR, the students were still able to progress, especially after having received the instruction. They consistently increased their correct answers in IND and duplicated them for the SUBJ.

The OA, contrary to what might be expected given their difficulty and inclusion in advanced CEFR levels, were the most successful work area of the three. Students understood the more than subtle differences that come from selecting either mood and could, even before instruction, choose the correct answers with a high success percentage. After working with OR and OC, they could consciously connect mood morphology with meaning. It is also relevant to stress that, when the instruction for the OA was due, the time devoted to the explicit information handout did not reach 20 minutes: students were familiar with the operational value, had already learned the importance of focusing on the subordinate verb, and knew that linking it with the meaning was the key to success.

The control group, not having received any type of instruction during the study, still progressed in all work areas. This success might partly be due to the efficacy of the structured activities, which directed learners' attention to the target form (VanPatten & Oikkenon 1996 proved the validity of these structured materials).

At any rate, in no case after instruction was the control group comparable to the other groups, which supports the strong learning effects of the methods under discussion.

Considering now the second hypothesis presented in this paper, both the interpretation and production groups performed equally well in all three work areas of mood selection. This also confirms the methodological advantages proposed here. The students who produced mood selection performed as well as those who interpreted it during instruction (and vice versa). Both benefitted equally from instruction and progressed in their control of the target structures with every assessment test. These results support those obtained by Llopis-García (2007) and Morgan-Short & Wood Bowden (2006), and indicate that a proper managing of output also renders positive learning results, because it enables the students to make correct form-meaning connections not only in interpretation, but also in production tasks. Both types of tasks are a reality and a necessity in every foreign language classroom.

## Conclusions: Cognitive teaching = better learning

This study proves that, in the L2 classroom, a cognitive approach to teaching grammar results in better learning for the students.

Traditional methodologies focus on teaching form and syntax on the one hand, and meaning and pragmatics on the other. This results in a taxonomy of rules, exceptions and usage situations that do not help the students to truly understand the L2. Instead, it contributes to the general idea that languages are arbitrary and syntax-dominated, and that nobody (apart from native speakers) can understand why a certain linguistic form is used in some cases and not in others.

Langacker (2008a: 66) challenged linguists to prove the benefits of teaching with a cognitive approach in the FL/L2 classroom: "it remains to be seen whether language teaching will fare any better when guided by notions from cognitive linguistics". The present study suggests that applying cognitive principles to formal mood instruction in SFL is highly beneficial and will hopefully encourage further research with other complex grammatical structures and/or other languages.

Operational Grammar helps close the gap between form and meaning and as such can help students to understand that language is not a system that exists for its own sake, but that it comprises a set of choices available to the speaker. This approach can help learners to understand that the ability to communicate lies within themselves and that their communicative intent can always find an appropriate linguistic form.

"Making the communicative classroom also a cognitive one does not raise any contradictions. On the contrary, cognitive linguistics provides an enhancement, or better still, a product" (Ruiz Campillo 2007: 17). From this point of view, grammar is seen as communication itself, containing tangible and helpful resources for the construction of output and the understanding of input in the L2. Learning a foreign language then becomes *understanding* the world of its native speakers and realizing that their communicative perspectives might be, after all, not so different from one's own.

## Notes

1. By 'complex grammatical feature' we are referring to forms that have either a heavy grammatical load, a low lexical and semantic value, a limited perceived salience, or all of these factors combined. Mapping of these forms in the input does not usually happen unless some kind of instruction directs the learners' attention to them.

2. See Santos Gargallo 1999 for a history of methodology in SFL.

3. See the author's doctoral dissertation for a full account and justification of this claim.

4. All examples given in this paper are taken either from the author's dissertation or from the study conducted within.

5. It is important to observe that this *normative use* does not refer to the morphosyntactic norms and rules outlined in grammar books, but to the tacit cognitive rules that govern native language usage: how we construct and convey meaning by selecting linguistic forms that communicate our thoughts, and that are very much the same within our linguistic community.

6. Operational Grammar may be termed as *pedagogical* because it fits the definition that De Knop & De Rycker present: "both an inventory of all the form-meaning units of the target language, and a didactic approach to their acquisition" (2008: 1).

7. Please note that, for coherence's sake, the notation of the original study has been kept here. *Relative clauses* relate to *oraciones de relativo* (thus OR), *temporal clauses with 'when'* relate to *oraciones con 'cuando'* (OC), and *concessive clauses with 'although'* relate to *oraciones con 'aunque'* (OA).

8. One example of a negative processing strategy for mood in Spanish is word order. The mood form is usually located in the middle of the sentence, and learners tend to process structures in sentence-initial position first, then those in final position and those in sentence-medial positions last. Dealing with mood, sentences are usually syntactically complex, and learner's processing resources will be depleted or nearly so before mood can be made available for processing. See VanPatten (1996 and elsewhere) or Llopis-García (2009) for more details.

9. It is important to mention that, for this study, PI was adapted to work with output learning situations as well, since production of target forms is a necessity and a reality in the FL classroom. Neither the Input Processing Model nor PI share this view. See Llopis-García (2007, 2009) and Morgan-Short & Wood Bowden (2006) for a full argumentation in support of including output within PI.

10. The original study documents in detail the methodologies used normally in SFL classrooms.

11. There were no distractor activities in any of the materials. Although their use is quite common in empirical research, they were considered superfluous in this eight-week study, where the students completed a total of nine assessment tests and more than 100 activities.

**12.** Translation of Figure 2: *indicativo* = indicative, *subjuntivo* = subjunctive, *respuestas correctas* = correct answers, *efecto de instrucción* = effect of instruction.

**13.** Translation of Figure 3: *indicativo* = indicative, *subjuntivo* = subjunctive, *respuestas correctas* = correct answers, *efecto de instrucción* = effect of instruction.

**14.** Translation Figure 4: *indicativo* = indicative, *subjuntivo* = subjunctive, *producción* = production group, *interpretación* = interpretation group, *control* = control group, *respuestas correctas* = correct answers, *efectos de instrucción* = effect of instruction.

**15.** It has already been mentioned that the T-Tests for this hypothesis were performed on both raw and gain scores. Any differences found relevant from the analysis of the raw scores was settled with the gain score testing afterwards. This paper will therefore only present the analyses of the gain scores.

**16.** Translation of Figure 7: *indicativo* = indicative, *subjuntivo* = subjunctive, *correcto* = correct, *respuestas correctas* = correct answers, *grupo* = group, *producción* = production, *interpretación* = interpretation.

## References

Achard. M. 2004. Grammatical instruction in the Natural Approach. In *Cognitive Linguistics, Second Language Acquisition and Foreign Language Teaching,* M. Achard & S. Niemeier (eds), 165–194. Berlin: Mouton de Gruyter.

Byrd, P. 2005. Instructed Grammar. In *Handbook of Research in Second Language Teaching and Learning,* E. Hinkel (ed.), 545–561. Mahwah NJ: Lawrence Erlbaum Associates.

Cadierno, T. 2008. Motion events in Danish and Spanish: A focus on form pedagogical approach. In *Cognitive Approaches to Pedagogical Grammar,* S. De Knop & T. De Rycker (eds), 259–294. Berlin: Mouton de Gruyter.

Collentine, J. 1993. The Development of Complex Syntax and the Selection of Mood by Foreign Language Learners of Spanish. PhD dissertation, University of Texas at Austin. http://jan.ucc.nau.edu/~jgc/cv_research.php.

Collentine, J. 2003. The development of subjunctive and complex-syntactic abilities among FL Spanish learners. In *Spanish Second Language Acquisition: State of the Science,* B. Lafford & R. Salaberry (eds), 74–97. Washington DC: Georgetown University Press.

Common European Reference Framework. http://www.coe.int/t/dg4/linguistic/CADRE_EN.asp.

DeKeyser, R. & Sokalsky, K. 1996. The differential role of comprehension and production practice. *Language Learning* 46(4): 613–642.

De Knop, S. & De Rycker, T. (eds). 2008. *Cognitive Approaches to Pedagogical Grammar.* Berlin: Mouton de Gruyter.

Doughty, C. 2004. Effects of instruction on learning a second language: A critique of instructed SLA research. In *Form-Meaning Connections in Second Language Acquisition,* B. VanPatten, J. Williams, S. Rott & M. Overstreet (eds), 181–202. Mahwah NJ: Lawrence Erlbaum Associates.

Grove, C. 2003. The role of instruction in Spanish second language acquisition. In *Spanish Second Language Acquisition: State of the Science,* B. Lafford & R. Salaberry (eds), 287–319. Washington DC: Georgetown University Press.

Housen, A. & Pierrard, M. 2005. *Investigations in Instructed Second Language Acquisition.* Berlin: Mouton de Gruyter.

Langacker, R.W. 2008a. Cognitive grammar as a basis for language instruction. In *Handbook of Cognitive Linguistics and Second Language Acquisition,* P. Robinson & N.C. Ellis (eds), 66–88. London: Routledge.

Langacker, R.W. 2008b. The relevance of Cognitive Grammar for language pedagogy. In *Cognitive Approaches to Pedagogical Grammar,* S. De Knop & T. De Rycker (eds), 7–36. Berlin: Mouton de Gruyter.

Lee, J.F. & VanPatten, B. 2003. *Making Communicative Language Teaching Happen.* New York NY: McGraw-Hill.

Llopis García, R. 2007. Procesamiento del *input* y mejora en el *output* para el aprendizaje de segundas lenguas: un estudio basado en la Instrucción de Procesamiento para el subjuntivo español. *Revista Nebrija de Lingüística Aplicada a la Enseñanza de Lenguas* 1(1): 100–123.

Llopis García, R. 2009. Gramática Cognitiva e Instrucción de Procesamiento para la enseñanza de la selección modal: Un estudio con aprendientes alemanes de español como lengua extranjera. PhD dissertation, Universidad Nebrija, Madrid. [https://biblioteca.nebrija.es/cgibin/opac/.]

Long, M. & Robinson, P. 1998. Focus on form. Theory, research, and practice. In *Focus on Form in Classroom Second Language Acquisition*, C. Doughty & J. Williams (eds), 15–41. Cambridge: CUP.

Morgan Short, K. & Wood Bowden, H. 2006. Processing instruction and meaningful output-based instruction: Effects in second language development. *Studies in Second Language Acquisition*. 28: 31–65.

Norris, J.M. & Ortega, L. 2000. Effectiveness of L2 instruction: A research synthesis and quantitative meta-analysis. *Language Learning* 50(3): 417–528.

Robinson, P. & Ellis, N.C. (eds). 2008. *Handbook of Cognitive Linguistics and Second Language Acquisition*. London: Routledge.

Ruiz Campillo, J.P. 2006. El concepto de *no-declaración* como valor del subjuntivo. Protocolo de instrucción operativa de la selección modal en español. En *Actas del programa de formación para profesorado de ELE 2005-2006*, Pastor C. Villalba (ed.). Munich: Instituto Cervantes de Múnich. [http://www.cervantes-muenchen.de/es/05_lehrerfortb/02.html].

Ruiz Campillo, J.P. 2007. (Revista *MarcoELE*). Entrevista a José Plácido Ruiz Campillo: gramática cognitiva y ELE. *MarcoELE*, n°5. [http://www.marcoele.com/num/5/index.html].

Ruiz Campillo, J.P. 2008. El valor central del subjuntivo: ¿informatividad o declaratividad? *Revista MarcoELE* n°7. [http://marcoele.com/el-valor-central-del-subjuntivo-%C2%BFinformatividad-o-declaratividad/].

Santos Gargallo, I. 1999. *Lingüística aplicada a la enseñanza-aprendizaje del español como lengua extranjera*. Madrid: Ed. Arco/Libros.

VanPatten, B. & Oikkenon, S. 1996. Explanation versus structured input in processing instruction. *Studies in Second Language Acquisition* 18(4): 495–510.

VanPatten, B. 1996. *Input Processing and Grammar Instruction: Theory and Research*. Norwood NJ: Ablex.

VanPatten, B. 2002. Processing instruction: An update. *Language Learning* 52(4): 755–803.

VanPatten, B. (ed.) 2004. *Processing Instruction: Theory, Research, and Commentary*. Mahwah NJ: Lawrence Erlbaum Associates.

VanPatten, B. 2007. Input processing in adult second language acquisition. In *Theories in Second Language Acquisition: An Introduction*, B. VanPatten & J. Williams (eds), 115–136. Mahwah NJ: Lawrence Erlbaum Associates.

Vázquez, G. 1991. *Análisis de errores y aprendizaje de español/lengua extranjera*. Frankfurt: Peter Lang.

## Appendix A: Explicit Information about Learning Strategies in OR. An Example

**4. ¿CUÁNDO SE USA IND O SUBJ EN LAS OR?**

En las OR utilizamos el *indicativo* cuando hablamos de un sustantivo que **CONOCEMOS**, que sabemos que **EXISTE**, que hemos visto...

*Javier es el chico que conoce a tu hermana*

*Chicago es una ciudad donde puedo ver arquitectura moderna*

Pero a veces necesitamos describir algo que **NO CONOCEMOS** y que buscamos, que queremos tener, que **NO SABEMOS si existe**. Entonces utilizamos el subjuntivo:

*Necesito un piso que tenga cuatro habitaciones*

*Busco un restaurante donde se coma paella valenciana*

## Appendix B: Examples of Structured Input and Output Activities

### EINE GENIALE WOHNUNG, OBWOHL...

SILVIA HAT SICH IN EINE WOHNUNG VERLIEBT UND MÖCHTE SIE KAUFEN. SIE HAT SICH DIE WOHNUNG NICHT GENAU ANGESCHAUT ABER ES IST IHR EGAL, SIE WILL SIE HABEN.

(1) SCHAU DIE VERBEN IN DEN FOLGENDEN SÄTZEN AN UND ENTSCHEIDE MIT EINEM ✓, OB SILVIA VON EINER REALEN TATSACHE (HECHO REAL) DER WOHNUNG ODER VON EINEM HYPOTHETISCHEN PROBLEM (PROBLEMA HIPOTÉTICO) SPRICHT.

(2) ÄUSSERE DEINE MEINUNG ZU DEN SÄTZEN! SIND DIESE DETAILS FÜR DICH WICHTIG, WENN DU EINE WOHNUNG SUCHST? SCHREIBE ☺ WENN JA ODER ☹, WENN ES DIR EGAL IST:

#### 🖳 VOY A COMPRAR ESTE SUPERPISO, AUNQUE...

|   |   | HECHO REAL | PROBLEMA HIPOTÉTICO | MI OPINIÓN |
|---|---|---|---|---|
| 1. | deba pagar una hipoteca | ___ | ___ | ___ |
| 2. | gaste todos mis ahorros | ___ | ___ | ___ |
| 3. | está lejos del parque | ___ | ___ | ___ |
| 4. | haya vecinos ruidosos | ___ | ___ | ___ |
| 5. | tiene un salón pequeño | ___ | ___ | ___ |
| 6. | oigo el tráfico de la calle | ___ | ___ | ___ |
| 7. | es un 4° piso sin ascensor | ___ | ___ | ___ |
| 8. | necesite hacer reformas | ___ | ___ | ___ |
| 9. | viven cerca los padres de mi novio | ___ | ___ | ___ |
| 10. | camine 20 minutos al supermercado | ___ | ___ | ___ |

### EINE GENIALE WOHNUNG, OBWOHL...

CRISTINA HAT SICH IN EINE WOHNUNG VERLIEBT UND MÖCHTE SIE KAUFEN. SIE HAT SICH DIE WOHNUNG NICHT GENAU ANGESCHAUT ABER ES IST IHR EGAL, SIE WILL SIE HABEN.

(1) SETZE 5 VERBEN IN IND UND 5 IN SUBJ UND MARKIERE DEINE ANTWORT MIT EINEM ✓ UM ZU ENTSCHEIDEN, OB CRISTINA VON EINER REALEN TATSACHE (HECHO REAL) DER WOHNUNG ODER VON EINEM HYPOTHETISCHEN PROBLEM (PROBLEMA HIPOTÉTICO) SPRICHT.

(2) ÄUSSERE DEINE MEINUNG ZU DEN SÄTZEN! SIND DIESE DETAILS FÜR DICH WICHTIG, WENN DU EINE WOHNUNG SUCHST? SCHREIBE ☺ WENN JA ODER ☹, WENN ES DIR EGAL IST:

#### 🖳 VOY A COMPRAR ESTE SUPERPISO, AUNQUE...

|   |   | HECHO REAL | PROBLEMA HIPOTÉTICO | MI OPINIÓN |
|---|---|---|---|---|
| 1. | _____ (deber) pagar una hipoteca | ___ | ___ | ___ |
| 2. | _____ (gastar) todos mis ahorros | ___ | ___ | ___ |
| 3. | _____ (estar) lejos del parque | ___ | ___ | ___ |
| 4. | _____ (haber) vecinos ruidosos | ___ | ___ | ___ |
| 5. | _____ (tener) un salón pequeño | ___ | ___ | ___ |
| 6. | _____ (oír) el tráfico de la calle | ___ | ___ | ___ |
| 7. | _____ (ser) un 4° piso sin ascensor | ___ | ___ | ___ |
| 8. | _____ (necesitar) hacer reformas | ___ | ___ | ___ |
| 9. | _____ (vivir) cerca los padres de mi novio | ___ | ___ | ___ |
| 10. | _____ (caminar) 20 minutos al supermercado | ___ | ___ | ___ |

*Author's address*

Reyes Llopis-García
Columbia University
Department of Latin American and Iberian Cultures
Casa Hispánica
612 West 116th Street
New York, NY 10027

rl2506@columbia.edu

# Helping learners engage with L2 words

## The form–meaning fit

Julie Deconinck, Frank Boers and June Eyckmans
Free University of Brussels / Erasmus University College

The pace at which new words are acquired is influenced by the degree of engagement with them on the part of the learner. Insights from cognitive linguistics into the non-arbitrary aspects of vocabulary can be turned into stimuli for such engagement. The majority of Cognitive Linguists' proposals for vocabulary teaching aim at helping learners appreciate the way a single word form can develop different meanings. This, however, presupposes knowledge of the 'basic' meaning of that word. We report an experiment in which learners under an experimental treatment were stimulated to consider the possibility that the form–meaning link in target words might not be fully arbitrary. The mnemonic effect of this task-induced engagement was assessed in relation to comparison treatments in immediate and delayed post-tests measuring both receptive and productive knowledge. Results show that simply prompting learners to evaluate the form–meaning match of words can foster vocabulary acquisition, although not all target words lends themselves equally well to this type of engagement.

## Introduction

The chances of an L2 word becoming entrenched in long-term memory are influenced by the degree of cognitive (and affective) involvement on the part of the learner (e.g., Laufer & Hulstijn 2001). Schmitt (2008: 339–340) uses "engagement" as an umbrella term to refer to any activity on the part of the learner that involves more attention to or manipulation of lexical items. Others (e.g., Barcroft 2002) have adopted the term "elaboration" to describe the various mental operations learners can perform with regard to a lexical item. Learners can engage in such elaborative processing spontaneously, but they may also benefit from teacher-initiated interventions that stimulate it. Such an intervention may simply cater to the kind of elaboration which the learner would otherwise engage in spontaneously. Additionally, the intervention may extend the scope of the given elaboration strategy to embrace more L2 words, or it might even reveal a pathway for elaborative processing which the learner has not yet considered herself. We will illustrate this complementary relationship between learner-initiated and teacher-prompted engagement with reference to the well-known keyword technique.

In this technique, learners associate an L2 word with a familiar word (usually an L1 word), and they use the latter as a key to retrieve the L2 word from memory (see Nation 2001: 311 ff. for a review). A suitable keyword shows some phonological (and/or graphemic) resemblance to the target word (otherwise it would not assist in retrieving the L2 word form). The learner then creates a semantic association between the keyword and the target word. In its simplest form, the L2 word could simply be a cognate (in which case the semantic association is very straightforward).

*AILA Review* 23 (2010), 95–114.  DOI 10.1075/aila.23.06dec
ISSN 1461–0213 / E-ISSN 1570–5595 © John Benjamins Publishing Company

Learners are known to resort to cognates spontaneously (e.g., Hall 2002), but a teacher can guide this type of engagement by pointing up suitable cognates for the learners. Crucially, the keyword technique extends beyond straightforward cognates that learners are likely to recognise themselves. Most often — especially when it is teacher-initiated — the technique rests on creative imagery to establish connections between a target word and a keyword whose semantic relatedness is less than direct. For example, a Dutch-speaking learner of English may be advised to associate the target noun *puncture* with the Dutch noun 'puntje' (meaning sharp end) because a punctured tyre and a sharp pointed object can easily be pictured together in a single scene. She may be advised to associate the target verb *frolic* with the Dutch adjective 'vrolijk' (meaning merry) through an image of merrily frolicking chimpanzees. She may be advised to associate the target adjective *brave* with the exclamation 'bravo!', since brave acts merit an applause. These are the kinds of potentially useful mnemonic associations which the learner might not have turned to when left to her own devices, and so it is the intervention by the teacher (or materials writer) which helps her substantially stretch the use of cognates in the narrow sense.[1]

In the study we report below we shall explore the merits of an intervention which, unlike the keyword technique, is not meant to teach learners a new mnemonic strategy in its own right, but rather to stimulate a type of engagement which learners may sometimes resort to spontaneously but whose full potential is not yet realized. The intervention, in which learners are prompted to consider the degree to which the form of a word might fit the word's meaning, is placed in the framework of applied cognitive linguistics insofar as it relies on the thesis that language is far less arbitrary than has often been assumed.

### The contribution of applied cognitive linguistics so far

The principal contribution of pedagogy-oriented cognitive linguistics (CL) to L2 vocabulary instruction has been to propose and validate interventions that exploit non-arbitrary dimensions of lexis. More particularly, several authors with a CL background have in recent years suggested methods of showing learners how seemingly distinct meanings and uses of a single word are actually related in ways that are 'motivated' (i.e., explainable in retrospect) (see Boers &Lindstromberg 2008a for a review). In the CL view, polysemy is not at all the result of a word taking on new meanings in a random fashion, but rather the outcome of semi-systematic meaning extensions from a word's 'core' sense. For example, familiarity with the physical-motion use of *stumble* may help learners appreciate the 'accidental' nature of a discovery described figuratively as "she stumbled on a piece of evidence" (e.g., Lindstromberg & Boers 2005; Verspoor & Lowie 2003). CL case studies of motivated polysemy and their potential pedagogical applications have not only featured 'content' words, but also such high-frequency 'function' words as prepositions. For example, a chain of meaning extensions can readily be recognised from the literal use of *over* as in "the ball went over the hedge" via a semi-figurative use as in "let's discuss this over a beer" to the fully figurative use as in "they had a dispute over the use of Boolean networks" (cf. Boers & Demecheleer 1998; Cho 2010; Tyler & Evans 2004; Lindstromberg 2010).

In addition to single words, multi-word items such as phrasal verbs and idioms have also been found highly suitable targets for CL approaches to motivated polysemy. For example, the conventionalised, figurative uses of expressions such as *find out (the truth)* and *behind the scenes* can be explained with reference to conceptual metaphors such as KNOWING IS SEEING (e.g., Beréndi, Csábi and Kôvecses 2008; Boers 2000; Boers, Demecheleer & Eyckmans 2004; Condon 2008a; Hu & Fong 2010; Kövecses & Szabó 1996; Skoufaki 2008). The results of several small-scale experiments collectively lend support to CL-inspired vocabulary instruction (see Boers & Lindstromberg 2009, Ch. 5, for a review), although some questions remain as to the generalisability of the findings.[2]

CL proponents will need to concede, however, that these proposed approaches focus on *meanings*, and more particularly *extensions* of meanings; they do not help learners much in the way of mapping the initial *form–meaning connection* of the words at the root of those meaning extensions.

At the other extreme, some recent CL-connected endeavours have focused on certain non-arbitrary *formal* properties of lexis. One example of a minimally intrusive intervention in that regard is to briefly alert students to sound patterns such as alliteration in the multiword units they come across in reading or listening texts (e.g., *bunk bed, to wage war, time will tell*) (Lindstromberg & Boers 2008a). Despite the brevity of the intervention, it appears sufficient to facilitate students' recollection of the lexical makeup of multiword units that happen to display such phonemic repetition (on similar evidence regarding assonance, see Lindstromberg & Boers 2008b; on the high incidence of phonemic repetition in multiword lexis, see, e.g., Boers & Lindstromberg 2009, Ch. 6).

After having found ways of exploiting motivated meaning–meaning connections (as in polysemy) and motivated form–form connections (as in alliterative multiword units), CL now faces the challenge of finding *form–meaning* motivations that could be used to foster the initial stage of learning new L2 words. Form–meaning matches are commonly referred to as cases of *iconicity*. As one starts to consider the possibility that words might be iconic, one inevitably enters the field of sound symbolism.

## Sound symbolism

Sound symbolism refers to non-arbitrary correspondences between phonology and semantics. Some theorists have in fact speculated that early human languages were very much sound-symbolic, and that arbitrary correspondences between semantics and phonology only developed with the need to expand the linguistic means to express more complex messages (e.g., Lecron Foster 1978). Although sound symbolism now appears to be the exception rather than the rule in Indo-European languages (but see below), in many other languages of the world word classes (e.g., so-called ideophones; Doke 1935: 118) remain that display strong systematic sound-meaning mappings (see Nuckols 1999 for a review). Interestingly for language pedagogues, experimental research provides ample evidence that many of the phonological patterns which descriptive linguists have intuited to be iconic are indeed experienced as such by language users generally (see below).

Sound symbolism that is motivated extra-linguistically stands the best chance of being shared by many languages, and may therefore provide useful scaffolding in second language vocabulary learning. Examples of sound symbolism that spring to mind most readily, of course, are onomatopoeia. These indeed show a fair degree of resemblance across languages, although there is obviously also some variation in the way they have been conventionalised (e.g. English *cock-a-doodle-do* vs. Dutch *kukeleku*; English *hiss* vs. Dutch *sissen*). However, several other cases of potentially universal sound symbolism have been examined. One is that of 'shape sound symbolism' (e.g., Ramachandran & Hubbard 2001), for instance, where people are more likely to associate words containing rounded vowels (e.g., "bouba") with rounded shapes and words containing unrounded vowels (e.g., "kiki") with angular shapes. The fact that this strong association has been attested not only in adults but also in toddlers (Maurer, Pathman & Mondloch 2006) lends support to the thesis that it is more than a mere by-product of language learning, i.e., of becoming accustomed to hearing and using words which happen to reflect this particular association.

An example of sound-symbolic use of consonants which is language-specific is the phenomenon of so-called phonesthemes (Bloomfield 1933). These are consonant clusters that recur in several words that convey a similar idea. For example, the occurrence of /sw-/ in as many verbs as *swab, sway, sweep, swing, swipe, swirl, swish, swivel*, and *swoop*, is unlikely to be a coincidence. Bloomfield (1933: 245) lists several such sets of words that share a consonant-cluster onset that is potentially sound-symbolic (e.g., *slime, slip, slide* and *crash, crack, crunch*). In a series of experiments, Parault & Schwanenflugel (2006) presented adult speakers of English with sets of unfamiliar words which — on the basis of lists such as Bloomfield's — were deemed to be either sound-symbolic or non-sound-symbolic. The participants were encouraged to make guesses at the meaning of the words and to match the words with the appropriate definition in a multiple-choice task. The participants obtained significantly better scores on the sound-symbolic words than on the matched controls.

In many languages semantic and/or grammatical classes are signalled pretty systematically through sound. In Japanese, for example, different kinds of motion events are described by means of words that share the same combination of consonants. Imai et al. (2008) report a series of experiments in which participants were asked to match novel instances of Japanese motion words with actions displayed on video. This task posed no problems whatsoever for adult speakers of Japanese, arguably because they were familiar with the language-specific conventions for marking different kinds of motion events. Young Japanese children obtained lower scores, but these were still significantly above chance level. Interestingly, however, a group of adult speakers of English *without* any prior knowledge of Japanese also obtained significantly above-chance scores on the matching tasks. This can only be explained with reference to a sound-symbolic effect that carries over across the two languages. Findings like these give reason to believe that learners' appreciation of non-arbitrary sound-meaning connections might not only provide scaffolding for vocabulary acquisition in L1 but possibly also for vocabulary learning in L2.

The main research objective of this study is to explore the possibility of turning students' subjective appreciation of the form–meaning motivation of words into a pathway for their engagement with those words. To be clear, although we have resorted to research in sound symbolism as part of establishing the rationale for study, the study itself is not intended to provide objective evidence in support of iconicity *per se*. The nature of said appreciation may not be due to sound symbolism in any strict sense, but also by 'coincidental' resemblances with known words in the L1, the L2 or an additional familiar language (i.e., interlinguistic and/or intralinguistic associations). Hall (2002) reports evidence of learners' spontaneous inclination to relate new L2 words to prior knowledge of word forms — in whichever language they have at their disposal — and their associated meanings. Hulstijn (2001; 262) writes: "If a new word appears to the learner as having a form unrelated to its meaning, it will need more attention and mental elaboration than if it has a transparent appearance." If it is true that language learners implicitly gauge whether a particular word meaning more or less 'fits' the phonological (or graphemic) form they have somehow come to associate with (aspects of) that meaning, then we ask whether this implicit evaluation could be turned into a conscious elaboration strategy, benefiting the initial mapping of meaning onto the form of a new L2 word. This type of elaboration would be explicit, yet minimal in terms of time and cognitive investment.

### Research questions
Our general objective led to the following research questions:

1.  Does a prompted elaboration of the form–meaning connection of a new L2 word lead to higher learning and retention gains as measured on a *form recall* test in relation to comparison treatments?
2.  Does a prompted elaboration of the form–meaning connection of a new L2 word lead to higher learning and retention gains as measured on a *meaning recall* test in relation to comparison treatments?
3.  Is the effect of this prompted form–meaning elaboration of a new L2 word influenced by the degree of fit between the form and the meaning as perceived by the learners?

Most studies investigating either L1 word memory (e.g., Eagle & Leiter 1964; Hyde & Jenkins 1969) or L2 word learning (e.g., Barcroft 2002) have instructed subjects to engage with either the meaning of the target words (i.e., semantic elaboration), or the form (i.e., structural elaboration), but rarely to engage explicitly with the form–meaning connection.[3] Expectations concerning the effect of drawing learners' attention simultaneously to meaning *and* form depend on the processing model one adheres to. Simply put, Levels of Processing theory (LOP) (Craik & Lockhart 1972) holds that semantic elaboration induces superior processing to structural elaboration, in turn leading to better recall on a test. Transfer-Appropriate-Processing theory (TAP) (Morris, Bransford & Franks 1977), on the other hand, proposes that tasks which stimulate structural elaboration will result in better recollection of form, whereas tasks that encourage semantic elaboration will result in better recollection of meaning. Lastly, Barcroft's (2002, 2003, 2004) Type of Processing Resource Allocation (TOPRA) model holds that learners' processing capacity is limited, so attention to word form would be at the expense of the acquisition of meaning, and vice versa. In this light, as it seems to require dispersion of students' attentional resources, the task of evaluating the form–meaning match of a novel L2 word may arguably be overambitious. However, when participants are encouraged to process items for 'mapping', this could stand them in good stead on a *cued* recall test, where the mapping of meaning onto form or vice versa is exactly what is required. It is this initial, but crucial, step in the word learning process that is under investigation in our study.

## Design

### General design
The experiment was designed as a between-subjects study which examined the effectiveness of three different learning treatments on the cued recall of 24 new L2 words. The three treatments corresponded to the following three tasks:

1. 'Familiarity assessment'. The participants were told that they were helping the researchers with a norming study to find out which of a series of words were likely to be unknown to learners of a similar level of proficiency. This task was intended not to stimulate any particular elaborative processing of the words.
2. 'Form–meaning-fit assessment'. The participants were asked to evaluate the degree to which they felt the form of L2 words they were presented with matched their meaning. This is the experimental treatment we are putting to the test in this study.
3. 'Utility assessment'. The participants were told they were helping the researchers select words they felt to be sufficiently useful to be included in a new advanced learners' dictionary. This task was intended to stimulate engagement with the meaning of the words, i.e., semantic elaboration.

Like several previous L2 word learning studies (e.g., De Groot & Keijzer 2000; Lotto & de Groot 1998; Schneider, Healy & Bourne 2002), we presented the new L2 words paired with their L1 translations.

The 24 target words were presented to the participants in two sets, separated by a break. After having tackled the first set according to one of the three tasks, the students were given an unannounced post-test. First the L1 word was given and participants were requested to produce the corresponding L2 word (*form* recall, traditionally known as "productive" testing), and subsequently the L2 word was given and participants were asked to provide the corresponding L1 word (*meaning* recall, traditionally known as "receptive" testing).

The second set of words was tackled by the participants along the same task instruction they were given for the first, but this time the participants knew there was going to be a test afterwards. On the one hand, we wanted to include a sufficient number of L2 words to enhance the validity of any conclusions drawn from the results, and to enable us to estimate the scope of applicability of the experimental treatment if it were shown to be effective. On the other hand, springing an un-announced test on the participants after they had been presented with a considerable number of unknown words in a row risked yielding poor scores and thus a floor effect. The result of the set-up is thus a sequential combination of incidental and intentional learning conditions.[4] Let it be clear from the start, however, that the experiment was not designed to compare gains under incidental and intentional learning conditions *per se*. For one thing, the target words in each set were different and not deliberately matched. For another, both sets of words were tackled in one session, and so fa-tigue was more likely to affect performance on the second set (i.e., the intentionally studied words). It is the effect of the form–meaning-fit-assessment task in comparison with other treatments that we are interested in here. While it may be interesting to find out if this effect — if any — becomes more noticeable if students perform the task purposefully as part of a mnemonic strategy, the results obtained from our study can only be suggestive in that regard.

Two weeks later, a delayed post-test was administered. This consisted of the same test items as the immediate post-test. For a general outline of the experimental design, see Table 1.

### Participants

Our participants were 56 university students (20 male, 36 female) in Brussels, Belgium, enrolled in the 1st or 2nd year of an English Language degree. Their average age was 20.2 (SD: 4.7), and their English proficiency was judged by their teachers to approximate level B2 according to the descrip-tors in the Common European Framework of Reference. Participants' native language was Dutch or a combination of Dutch with another language, mostly French. All participants were highly expe-rienced language learners; in combination with English their university degree involved one other foreign language, and many of them reported working knowledge of at least one more additional language. The experiment was carried out in four intact classes, and students were randomly as-signed to one of three treatments: 'familiarity assessment' (n = 17); 'form–meaning-fit assessment' (n = 20), designed to induce an elaboration of the form–meaning connection; and 'utility assess-ment' (n = 19), devised to encourage semantic elaboration. Two weeks later, 39 participants took part in the delayed post-test.

Given our choice of target words (see below), prior knowledge of these was extremely unlikely. As far as their general proficiency in English was concerned, the three treatment groups were found well matched on the basis of the students' end of semester grades (p = .68).

### Target words

As it was essential to control for prior word knowledge, 24 very rare, mostly obsolete words were culled from an obscure word list on the internet (http://www.obscurewords.com). These words were of various lengths, and they belonged to three word classes: nouns, verbs, and adjectives. The 8 nouns used in the study were: *foppotee* 'idiot', *seraglio* 'palace', *welkin* 'sky', *yawd* 'mare', *meed* 're-ward', *bandobast* 'settlement', *cant* 'hypocrisy', *mattoid* 'madman'. The 8 verbs were: *blandish* 'flatter', *hie* 'leave', *sough* 'sigh', *tope* 'drink', *madefy* 'moisten', *vitiate* 'damage', *fub* 'postpone', *gledge* 'squint'. Finally, the 8 adjectives included in the study were: *cinnabar* 'dark red', *voluble* 'talkative', *harageous* 'brutal', *gibbous* 'round', *sere* 'dry', *mim* 'modest', *mellifluous* 'harmonious', *luculent* 'clear'.

These stimuli were not manipulated in any way or controlled for the effects of frequency, con-cept familiarity, imageability, cognate status, phonotactic regularity, or any other psycholinguistic

Table 1. General experimental design

| | Subexperiment 1 (incidental) | | | Subexperiment 2 (intentional) | | | 2 weeks later: |
|---|---|---|---|---|---|---|---|
| | Study phase | Testing phase | | Study phase | Testing phase | | Delayed testing phase |
| Group 1 (familiarity assessment) | First series of 12 words (L2 – L1) +rating exercise | | | Second series of 12 words (L2 – L1) + rating exercise | | | |
| Group 2 (form-meaning-fit assessment) | First series of 12 words (L2-L1) +rating exercise | Form Recall L1 – L2 | Meaning Recall L2-L1 | Second series of 12 words (L2 – L1) + rating exercise | Form Recall L1 – L2 | Meaning Recall L2 – L1 | Form Recall + Meaning Recall |
| Group 3 (utility assessment) | First series of 12 words (L2-L1) +rating exercise | | | Second series of 12 words (L2 – L1) + rating exercise | | | |

aspect that could inform word memorability. We only ensured the 24 words were grouped into two groups of equal length, i.e., two series of 12 words each — constituting our separate sets which would fuel either the incidental or the intentional learning condition —, comprising a total of 24 syllables each.

The words targeted in our experiment were not selected on the basis of previously identified sound-symbolic patterns either. Neither did any of the authors — who shared the participants' L1 — anticipate that any of the words was likely to call up an L1 cognate. Using a mixed bag of items adds to the ecological validity of the study, and it can help to estimate what fraction (if any) of (English) words are amenable to the type of processing we are putting to the test here. Such an estimate would not be possible if we were to use a pre-selection of likely sound-symbolic items (as was done by, e.g., Parault & Schwanenflugel 2006).

## Procedure
The experiment was carried out in the participants' regular computer classroom, during scheduled class hours. At the start of the lesson students were informed, in Dutch, that they were taking part in a survey, and that their answers would have no negative influence on their marks for English. They were invited to sit down at a computer, to fill in a language background questionnaire, and to log onto the software programme (Question Mark Perception, version 3) using the individual log-in and password provided on their questionnaires. Unbeknownst to the students, this automatically —

and randomly — assigned each of them to one of the three treatments/tasks: familiarity assessment, form–meaning-fit assessment or utility assessment.

Each target word was then shown in the middle of the screen, accompanied by its translation. The students also heard the target word pronounced once. They were then given 12 seconds to perform the task, which involved making an indication on a five-point Likert scale. Students assigned to the familiarity assessment treatment were asked to indicate the extent to which they were familiar with the words. Students assigned to the form–meaning-fit assessment treatment indicated the degree to which they felt the form/sound of each word went together with its meaning. Students assigned to the utility assessment treatment rated the words according to how useful they felt them to be.

After giving students the opportunity to ask questions about the procedure, a first set of 20 words, including 12 of our target words, was presented to them, and the students individually tackled their respective rating tasks. The first 3 words given were 'dummy' items, so that participants could familiarize themselves with the procedure, as well as to control for primacy effects. To counteract recency effects, the last 2 stimuli given were also excluded from the analyses. For affective reasons, we included in the set three filler words ('pity', 'dwell', 'brave') which we expected the students to be familiar with.

The presentation and rating of the first 20 words was followed by an unannounced, immediate post-test. This testing phase consisted of 2 blocks: a form recall test followed by a meaning recall test. In the form recall test, learners were given 15 questions, each presenting the Dutch translation of an English word they had just evaluated, as well as the first letter of said English word, and they were asked to produce it. After this test block, learners were presented with 15 questions again, each providing the English word, and learners were then asked to provide the Dutch translation, for which they were not given the first letter. This was the meaning recall test. Both testing blocks were self-paced.

After completing this part of the assignment, participants were asked to note down on their questionnaires whether they had expected to be tested on the vocabulary presented. None of the students reported in the affirmative.

A short break was given, after which participants were invited to proceed with the second series of words. They were again instructed on the screen to carry out the rating exercise as in the previous series but also — since they knew it was to be followed by a post-test — to do their best to learn the words as well as they could. This time, the filler words that we expected the participants to be familiar with were 'herd', 'toss', 'slender'. After the retention test on the second set of words (which followed the same pattern as the test administered after the first set), the students were thanked for their participation and told that they would be informed about their test results in due course.

Two weeks later, 39 original participants were given an unannounced delayed post-test, identical to the immediate one. The entire procedure lasted approximately 70 minutes (learning phase + immediate post-test: 50 minutes; delayed post-test: 20 minutes).

## Scoring and analysis

For the meaning recall test, dichotomous scoring was applied: one point was awarded to each word **correctly** and **completely** translated into Dutch, zero points to incorrect translations. In the case of the form recall test, however, we applied a less stringent scoring protocol. As participants were only exposed to each lexical item once, and new words are learnt incrementally, we needed a recall measure that was sensitive to both complete and partial word learning. This measure was supplied by the well-established *Lexical Production Scoring Protocol* (Barcroft 2000), which awards **.25, .50, .75, or 1 point** to each word **partially** or **completely** produced (see Appendix). By giving the first letter of the target words and by asking the participants to try and reproduce the words they had been presented with in the previous stage of the experiment, we prevented the participants from filling in known synonyms of the targets.

We submitted the scores for each testing block to an analysis of variance (ANOVA). To provide an answer to all three research questions we needed to include both an analysis by participants and one by items. As our selection of target words had not been controlled for item effects, we could not simply compare students' test scores obtained under the incidental with those under the intentional learning condition (given the possibility that item effect might interact with learning condition). Therefore, the analysis by participants was run on the test scores for the two sets of 12 words separately, with treatment ('familiarity assessment', 'form–meaning-fit assessment, 'utility assessment') as between-subject factor and retention interval (immediate, delayed) as within-subject factor. The ANOVA by items added learning condition (incidental, intentional) as a between-subject factor to this model, but since the items were not crossed across learning condition, items were *nested* within that factor to control for potential item effects.[5]

## Results

### Analysis by participants

#### Form Recall Scores
In the incidental learning condition (first series of words), the analysis reveals a significant effect of treatment, with a moderate effect size: $F(2,89) = 3.254$, $p < .05$, $\eta2 = .068$. Table 2 shows recall rates across conditions. It reveals that the form–meaning-fit-assessment group outperforms the two other groups in both post-tests. The delayed post-test amplifies the divergence between our experimental group and the utility-assessment group.

**Table 2.** Mean form recall rates across treatment groups and retention intervals (max score: 10) in the incidental learning condition.

| Treatment: | 'familiarity' | 'form–meaning-fit' | 'utility' |
|---|---|---|---|
| | n = 17 | n = 20 | n = 19 |
| Retention interval: | | | |
| immediate | 5.59 (1.67) | 5.88 (1.47) | 4.98 (2.47) |
| delayed | 3.87 (2.02) | 3.82 (1.21) | 2.56 (2.05) |

The average recall rates for words in the intentional learning condition (i.e., our second series of words) across treatments and post-tests are shown in Table 3. The form–meaning-fit-assessment group outperforms the other two groups in both the immediate and the delayed post-test under this condition as well. The divergence falls short of statistical significance, however, which could be due to the high standard deviations recorded.

**Table 3.** Mean form recall rates across treatment groups and retention intervals (max score:10) in the intentional learning condition.

| Treatment: | 'familiarity' | 'form–meaning-fit' | 'utility' |
|---|---|---|---|
| | n = 17 | n = 20 | n = 19 |
| Retention interval: | | | |
| immediate | 4.11 (1.83) | 5.13 (2.36) | 4.52 (1.86) |
| delayed | 1.01 (1.15) | 1.72 (1.83) | 1.09 (1.37) |

## Meaning Recall Scores

There are no significant main effects in the incidental learning condition. Meaning recall scores are higher than form recall scores generally, yet remarkably similar across all treatment groups: participants in the familiarity assessment group score an average of 7.34 (1.98) across both post-tests, those in the form–meaning-fit-assessment group achieve a mean of 7.24 (1.58), and those in the utility assessment group an average of 7.06 (1.93). Moreover, the word meanings are retained remarkably well between the immediate and the delayed post test; there is **no** effect of retention interval ($p = .503$).

As regards our second series of 12 words (intentional learning condition), the analysis does reveal a significant effect of retention interval, $F(1,87) = 11.367$, $p = .001$, $\eta2 = .116$. On the immediate post-test, the form–meaning-fit-assessment group returns a higher mean score (5.61) than the other two groups: 4.59 (familiarity assessment) and 5.21 (utility assessment). However, in the delayed post-test, the utility-assessment group shows less attrition than the others, with averages of 3.7 vs. 3.23 (form–meaning-fit assessment) vs. 3.23 (familiarity assessment) respectively. None of these differences are statistically significant, however, nor do they yield a significant interaction between treatment and retention interval.

## Analysis by items

### Form recall scores

The item analysis confirms the significant effect of treatment: $F(2, 44) = 6.654$, $p = .003$, $\eta2 = .232$. Post-hoc paired comparisons (Tukey) indicate that the difference between the form–meaning-fit-assessment group and the familiarity-assessment group is significant at $p = .022$, and even highly significant at $p < .0001$ between the former and the utility-assessment group. Table 4 presents the mean form recall scores by items across all conditions.

**Table 4.** Mean form recall scores (max score = 10) across all conditions by items

| treatment | retention interval | learning condition | |
|---|---|---|---|
| | | incidental | intentional |
| 'familiarity' | immediate | 5.59 (1.63) | 4.11 (1.19) |
| | delayed | 3.87 (1.68) | 1.08 (1.3) |
| 'form–meaning-fit' | immediate | 5.88 (1.41) | 5.13 (1.46) |
| | delayed | 3.82 (1.35) | 1.72 (1.06) |
| 'utility' | immediate | 4.99 (1.37) | 4.52 (1.23) |
| | delayed | 2.55 (1.39) | 1.08 (0.95) |

The effect is not equally strong for all items, however. Although item effect falls (just) short of statistical significance ($p = .066$), it seems likely that the effect of the task(s) is likely to be qualified by the properties of individual items.

Our treatment variable is borderline significant in interaction with learning condition (i.e., incidental versus intentional) ($p = .059$). This is probably due to the divergence in recall rates obtained under the familiarity-assessment treatment: they are relatively high for the incidentally learned words but comparatively low for the intentionally learned words. Table 4 reveals a similar interaction between treatment and condition in the *delayed* form recall scores: it is with regard to the 'intentionally' learned words that the form–meaning-fit-assessment task appears mnemonically more effective in the long term than both of the other tasks. What is surprising is that words were retained less well through the utility-assessment task than the familiarity-assessment task, while we expected the former to stimulate more engagement with the words.

*Meaning recall scores*
The analysis by items uncovered no main effect of treatment here. As expected, word meanings were more likely to be recalled immediately after the presentation of the words than two weeks later, but the attrition rate (which is similar in the three groups) is much less pronounced than in the case of form recall. It may look surprising that the word meanings of the 12 words presented in the incidental learning condition were much better remembered than the 12 words shown in the intentional learning condition, with means of 7.19 and 4.25, respectively (F(1,22) = 20.662, $p < .0001$, $\eta2 = .484$). However, the lack of uptake despite the anticipation of a post-test may in this experiment simply be due to fatigue on the part of the students towards the end of the session, and we cannot be sure that the learning burden of the two sets of target words was equivalent in the first place. Table 5 shows that the retention interval had a much larger effect on the meaning recall of items that were learnt intentionally than on the items in the incidental condition; performance on the incidentally learned items nudged downwards ever so slightly, whereas performance on the intentionally learned items plummeted.

**Table 5.** Average meaning recall scores (max score = 10) for all treatments produced by the interaction between retention interval and learning condition.

| Retention interval | Learning condition | |
|---|---|---|
| | Incidental | Intentional |
| Immediate post-test | 7.34 (1.80) | 5.09(1.64) |
| Delayed post-test | 7.05 (2.21) | 3.40 (2.01) |

*Recall rates for 'motivated' items*
The 20 participants in the form–meaning-fit-assessment group rated each word according to how well they felt its meaning to fit its form. The average Likert score (on a scale from 1–5) given to our 24 stimuli was 2.71 (1.35). We used this mean as a cut-off point to organize our items into a 'more motivated' and a 'less motivated' group.

The 12 words in our 'more motivated' group were (in descending order according to motivation ratings, standard deviations between brackets): *harageous* 'brutal': 4.2 (.83), *voluble* 'talkative': 3.7 (1.17), *luculent* 'clear': 3.58 (1.31), *sere* 'dry': 3.47 (1.22), *mattoid* 'madman': 3.37 (1.21), *sough* 'sigh': 3.35 (1.23), *foppotee* 'idiot': 3.25 (1.25), *welkin* 'sky': 3.2 (.894), *seraglio* 'palace': 3.2 (1.32), *mellifluous* 'harmonious': 3.11 (1.37), *mim* 'modest': 2.79 (1.48), *blandish* 'flatter': 2.74 (1.37).

The remaining 12 words in our 'less motivated' group were: *tope* 'drink': 2.5 (1.43), *gledge* 'squint': 2.42 (.961), *madefy* 'moisten': 2.42 (.961), *gibbous* 'round': 2.3 (1.13), *hie* 'leave': 2.2 (1.47), *fub* 'postpone': 1.95 (1.05), *meed* 'reward': 1.95 (1.18), *cinnabar* 'dark red': 1.85 (.745), *vitiate* 'damage': 1.84 (1.07), *bandobast* 'settlement': 1.84 (1.12), *cant* 'hypocrisy': 1.84 (1.35), *yawd* 'mare': 1.8 (1.06).

Coincidentally, the 12 words from each of our 2 learning conditions (incidental and intentional) are equally distributed across these two groups, suggesting the items in each condition would have appeared comparably motivated to our raters.

We analysed the item recall scores using analysis of variance (ANOVA), this time including motivation strength (2) as between-subjects factor, and treatment (3) and retention interval (2) as within-subjects factors. Table 6 shows the recall scores for the 'less motivated' and 'more motivated'

**Table 6.** Average form and meaning recall rates for 'more motivated' and 'less motivated' items across treatment groups (max score = 10)

|  | 'more motivated' | | | 'less motivated' | | |
|---|---|---|---|---|---|---|
|  | 'fam.' | 'f-m-f' | 'util.' | 'fam.' | 'f-m-f' | 'util.' |
| Form recall | 3.69 (1.88) | 4.54 (1.94) | 3.09 (1.98) | 3.64 | 3.73 | 3.47 |
| Meaning recall | 5.92 | 6.03 | 5.74 | 5.33 | 5.56 | 5.76 |

items per treatment, collapsed across retention intervals. It reveals that most recall scores are remarkably similar across the board. This is confirmed by our analyses, which show neither a main effect of strength of motivation, nor a significant interaction effect between treatment and motivation strength. However, a divergence between *form* recall scores is found among the 'more motivated' items: form recall scores for those items in the form–meaning-fit-assessment group are higher (4.54) than in the familiarity-assessment group (3.69), and considerably higher than in the utility-assessment group (3.09).

When we split our data file and take an exclusive look at the form recall scores for the 'motivated' items, we do obtain a highly significant effect of treatment with a large effect size, $F(2,66) = 8.254$, $p = .001$, $\eta2 = .200$. Graph 1 shows the effect of treatment on the form recall rates of 'more motivated' items compared to the 'less motivated' items. Post-hoc analyses (Tukey) reveal that it is the divergence between the form–meaning-fit-assessment and utility-assessment groups that is most significant ($p < .0001$). This is not just a congruence effect; if we run a similar analysis on the items rated

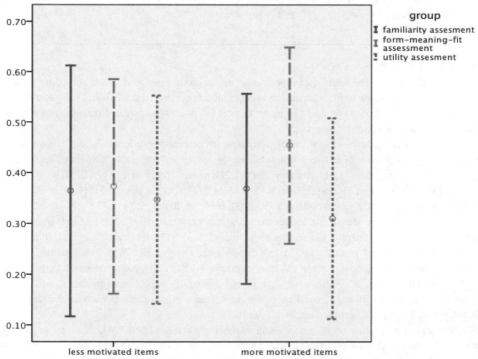

**Graph 1.** Effect of treatment on form recall scores of 'less motivated' and 'more motivated' items.

comparatively 'useful' by our participants in the utility-assesment group, no such treatment effect is revealed for either form or meaning recall rates.

## Discussion

This study aimed to compare the short-term and medium-term effectiveness of three different treatments for the receptive and productive recall of unknown L2 words. Each of the treatments involved a rating exercise pertaining to the words, which for the participants in the familiarity-assessment group was intended to induce little elaboration of any particular kind, in the form–meaning-fit-assessment group an engagement with the form–meaning connection, and in the utility-assessment group a semantic elaboration. The mnemonic effect of each treatment task was measured using immediate and delayed form and meaning recall tests over a two-week interval. The main findings will be discussed with reference to the 3 research questions.

1. Does the prompted elaboration of the form–meaning connection of a new L2 word lead to higher learning and retention gains as measured on a *form recall* test in relation to comparison treatments?

Our form recall scores reveal a significant effect of treatment. The form–meaning-fit-assessment task yields the highest form recall scores, in the immediate as well as the delayed post-test. This can probably be attributed to the engagement with word form that this task is likely to induce in participants, in line with the principles of Transfer Appropriate Processing (TAP) (Morris, Bransford & Franks 1977). Cued form recall on a test is the first step on the way to fluent, productive word knowledge, and as such it charts the most challenging and elusive aspect of word learning (Laufer 2005, 2006; Schmitt 2008). If the pedagogical aim is to enable learners to eventually use words productively, engagement with words must include a structural component. Moreover, an exclusive focus on semantic elaboration is likely to inhibit word form learning (Barcroft 2002, 2003, 2004), and this is corroborated by the comparatively poor scores on the form-recall tests generated by the utility-assessment task. In fact, even the familiarity-assessment task, which was meant not to stimulate any particular elaboration, seems to yield better form recall than the utility-assessment task (although the difference in scores is not statistically significant). This substantiates the thesis that semantic elaboration does not foster word *form* learning.

The superiority of our experimental treatment held out over time, although there was no interaction effect between treatment and retention interval, indicating attrition rates were similar across groups.

2. Does the elaboration of the form–meaning connection of a new L2 word lead to higher learning and retention gains as measured on a *meaning recall* test in relation to comparison treatments?

By rating words in terms of their usefulness to learners of English, participants in one of the two comparison conditions, namely the utility-assessment group, were encouraged to think about the meanings of these items, and possibly of available synonyms, thus inducing semantic elaboration. According to LOP-theory (Craik & Lockhart 1972), this engagement with meaning is expected to lead to superior results on a recall test in comparison to engagement with form. TAP-theory (Morris, Bransford & Franks 1977) posits that test scores are enhanced when testing measure is congruent with learning condition. Hence, both theories predict comparatively good scores on the meaning recall test after the utility-assessment task. On the other hand, learners who performed the form–meaning-fit-assessment task were coaxed into mapping meaning onto form, and so a cued meaning recall test must be congruent with that learning mode also. The meaning recall scores turned out uncannily similar across the groups. This suggests that our experimental treatment does not impede retention of semantics as compared to other treatments.

The performance of the familiarity-assessment group is perhaps the most surprising of all, especially in terms of the test scores on the items tackled in the incidental learning condition. This does not necessarily challenge the view that word meaning learning is always enhanced by engagement, as we cannot be sure that the participants in the familiarity-assessment task did not engage in any elaborative processing, despite the nature of the task.

Attrition rates were similar across the board, as there was no interaction between treatment and retention interval.

Before concluding our discussion with regard to form and meaning recall scores, we need to address how our findings relate to the TOPRA model (Barcroft 2002, 2003, 2004) of lexical processing. After all, the model predicts that attending to both form and meaning of lexical items leads to the dispersion of students' attentional resources. This would imply that meaning recall scores are impaired by treatments that include attention to form as compared to treatments that target meaning exclusively. Yet this is not corroborated by our meaning recall results. Likewise, it may suggest that treatments that include attention to meaning would inhibit form recall scores as compared to treatments that solely fixate on form. As our study does not include an exclusively 'form-focused' elaboration treatment, this cannot be substantiated at present. But our results do not actually contradict the TOPRA-model. Firstly, our experimental treatment does not induce participants to attend to form and meaning separately, but instead it encourages them to map them together — 'processing for mapping' in the model. Secondly, our dependent measures were *cued* recall tests. These necessitate the mapping of meaning onto form, in contrast to *free* recall tests, which, it could be argued, do not chart L2 word learning at all.[6] Of all the treatments induced, it is this 'processing for mapping' that is actually most congruent with a cued form and meaning recall tests, and its success is therefore not so unexpected after all. Our results show that the high form recall scores obtained by the form–meaning-fit-assessment group are not at the expense of meaning recall scores; unlike the utility-assessment task, our experimental task does not seem to trade off form recall gains for meaning recall gains. This suggests that our proposed type of elaboration is effective in enhancing both form and meaning recall, at least for our group of learners.

3.    Is the effect of this prompted form–meaning elaboration of a new L2 word influenced by the degree of fit between the form and the meaning as perceived by the learners?

In terms of form recall scores, the form–meaning-fit-assessment treatment was more effective for items rated linguistically motivated by the participants than items that were less so (4.54 vs. 3.73). This does not seem to be due to giving positive ratings to these words *per se*. If this were the case, the words rated as useful by participants in the utility-assessment group should then have yielded better scores than those rated less useful, and no such differences were observed in the test scores of these participants.

Rather, the question arises as to whether the success of these motivated items in the experimental treatment points to a possible congruence between internal and external salience. As proposed by Sharwood-Smith (1991, 1993), linguistic features that are noticed autonomously by the learner have internally-created salience, necessitating no further instructional intervention. Externally-created salience, on the other hand, is generated through pedagogical intervention, and is required when surface features are not noticed autonomously by the learner, whose attention then needs to be drawn to said features. More empirical research is needed to ascertain whether spontaneously occurring salience has a different learning effect than when salience is deliberately engineered through instruction (Sharwood-Smith 1991: 121). However, it would certainly make sense to consider instruction optimal when it can capitalize on learners' internal salience, forging a kind of harmony between the two types of salience (cf. Park & Han 2007: 110) (see also our brief discussion of the keyword technique in the introduction to this article). If the form–meaning connection of some words appears more 'naturally' motivated to learners than others, explicitly attending to this apparent motivation by way of a minimal, pedagogical intervention would certainly seem to capitalize on its internal salience. Moreover, even though word motivation might be an idiosyncratic affair at times, the standard deviations recorded for our Likert motivation ratings are moderate, pointing to an acceptable inter-rater agreement for many of these items. This suggests that teachers' subjective appreciations of form–meaning motivations could by and large be relied upon and provide the basis for short pedagogical interventions. More research needs to be done to ascertain this.

Incidentally, and interestingly in this respect, our filler items, i.e., *toss, dwell, herd, pity, brave,* and *slender,* scored very highly on this Likert scale for linguistic motivation; median 5. It suggests that language users collapse 'form' and 'meaning' entirely when a word is known, i.e., when its form–meaning connection is deeply entrenched and fluent.

## Limitations

A number of possible restrictions constrain the generality of our study's findings. First of all, the groups of participants were relatively small, and each participant received only one of the three types of treatments. We were compelled to use this between-subject design rather than compare the effect of different treatments on the same individuals, because a pilot study had revealed that each of the tasks encroached too much on the following if assigned in combination. Given the small size of the groups, individual differences in learning styles may accidentally have impacted the relative effectiveness of this or that treatment.

Secondly, whether the rating tasks given to the learners are good operationalizations of the constructs of 'zero elaboration', 'form–meaning elaboration' and 'meaning elaboration' is subject to debate. We deemed it essential for each treatment to involve a similar mental and motor task; i.e., assess the word on a scale, but we wanted the quality and quantity of the induced elaboration to be different. The most important concern in this respect is raised by the familiarity-assessment task, which we thought came close to a 'zero elaboration' treatment. Yet assessing to what extent one 'knows' a word might imply a type of elaboration after all, which, if induced, would involve attending to both meaning and form, as it encourages a reflection on the learner's side whether meaning and form are already associated with one other, presumably on the basis of possible previous encounters with the word — or similar words — in question.

Lastly, operational constraints also meant that our 12 words in the incidental learning condition were different from our 12 words in the intentional learning condition, yet identical for each treatment group, and presented in the same order. It may come as a surprise that recall scores were higher in the incidental learning condition than in the intentional learning condition (see the tables in the results section), but the effect of intentional learning is likely to have been eclipsed by other variables, such as primacy effects, fatigue and memory crowding. Given the different variables at play, we cannot say at this stage whether the effectiveness of our proposed pedagogical intervention is influenced by type of motivation for learning.

## Conclusion and implications for vocabulary learning and teaching

Our study suggests that an evaluation of the linguistic motivation of a word's form–meaning link can be an effective form of elaboration. As such, it could be turned into a conscious, simple, and time-efficient word learning strategy, providing an extra pathway to strengthen the form–meaning mapping of a new word. Lexical items whose form–meaning link is perceived to be motivated are particularly amenable to it. The 'processing for mapping' induced by our form–meaning-fit assessment appears equally beneficial for the learning and retention of word meaning as word form, with neither aspect of word knowledge being established at the expense of the other. What's more, findings suggest it has a competitive edge over comparison treatments when it comes to learning word *form*.

In terms of vocabulary teaching, the appreciation of the form–meaning motivation of words does not need to be scientific or universally shared; as long as it is there for a particular learner, it can have mnemonic potential (cf. Croft 1978). Still, the degree of agreement among our participants on which of the items were relatively motivated suggest that — for lack of a thesaurus of 'transparent' words — teachers could rely on their subjective appreciations of form–meaning motivations to justify short pedagogical interventions.[7] We propose that an elaboration of the form–meaning connection can help to enhance the mapping of meaning onto form and vice versa. As there may not be a 1:1 correspondence between meanings in the L1 and the L2, further semantic fine-tuning could still be required. Nor may this initial mapping be sufficient to achieve fluent word knowledge, but it does constitute the first essential step — or leap — towards it.

Teachers' interventions to tap this resource can be very simple and brief. For example, on encountering an unfamiliar L2 word during a classroom activity, the teacher might pronounce this word in a tone of voice that is compatible with the word's 'connotations', and with exaggerated articulation or lengthening of certain phonological features to hint at a certain degree of iconicity. One can do this with words as varied as *slime, whisper* and *smooth*. This kind of minimal intervention on an as-the-opportunity-arises basis is reminiscent of what Lindstromberg & Boers (2008a) have found to be measurably effective when applied to alliterative phrases. The auditory stimulus for elaboration can of course go hand in hand with others, such as awareness-raising of morphological clues (as *pro* and *long* in *prolonged*) and semi-cognates (as 'vol' in *voluptuous* — Dutch 'vol' means full). Student involvement can easily be invited when a phonestheme is encountered: on encountering the word *swirl* the teacher can easily ask students to pool other sw- verbs they happen to know and contemplate what semantic feature they have in common with the new word.

But also in exercises designed to teach vocabulary more directly, potential form–meaning fits can perhaps be put to good use, and more particularly to help avoid the risk of erroneous initial form–meaning correspondences. For example, matching exercises (e.g., connecting L2 words to corresponding L1 words or corresponding L2 synonyms) can be pedagogically sound only if the risk of erroneous matches is minimized. One way of doing this is by making sure that only some of the items in the exercise are new to the learners. A supplementary way suggested indirectly by the results of our study may be to reduce blind guessing by selecting words for the exercise that display a certain degree of form–meaning-fit. Whether a given word is suitable in this respect may have to be tested through piloting, however. This piloting would ideally have to be done with same-population students. As we mentioned in the introduction, whether or not the form–meaning connection of a given L2 word is perceived as 'motivated' is likely to be partially determined by cognate effects.

What we have attempted to do in this contribution is to complement the existing CL approaches to teaching L2 vocabulary, most of which exploit meaning–meaning motivation (as in polysemy) and some form–form motivation (as in alliterative word partnerships), by exploring the pedagogical potential of form–meaning motivation. Our intention has not been to provide evidence of iconicity *per se*, but rather to investigate whether making learners consider the possibility of such iconicity is a fruitful way of stimulating engagement with L2 words. We believe the preliminary results are encouraging.

### Suggestions for further research

A qualitative follow-up study is warranted to answer a number of questions. We wish to know whether the advantage of the experimental treatment for form recall is possibly informed by an *affective* dimension that the other two treatments might not afford. Reactions by the students indicated that they enjoyed the rating exercise, but further study could investigate to what extent they also appreciate the relevance of it, and how straightforward or natural it seems to them. Furthermore, the validity of our conclusions could be explored for students at lower levels of proficiency and with different learner characteristics. Finally, qualitative data could reveal whether individual learners can 'motivate' their ratings, be it on the basis of sound symbolism, loanwords and cognates, or idiosyncratic associations.

## Acknowledgements
The authors would like to thank Hélène Stengers for her invaluable assistance with QuestionMark Perception (3). We also thank two anonymous reviewers for their suggestions, which have helped us make this a more reader-friendly article — we hope — than the original version was. Last but not least we are grateful to the students who took part in the experiment.

## Notes
1. Some investigations of the keyword technique suggest that its efficiency decreases as the semantic link between keyword and target word becomes far-fetched (e.g., Wang & Thomas 1995).

2. Laufer (2005) likens the difference between the systematic teaching of pre-selected vocabulary (e.g., through word translation exercises) and the more occasional targeting of vocabulary during communicative activities to the distinction that in contexts of grammar instruction has become known as 'focus on forms' and 'focus on form', respectively (Long 1991). It is not always clear where CL proposals for language pedagogy are to be situated in this framework, although the input materials used in most CL experiments to date seem to suggest leanings toward forms-focused instruction.

3. To operationalize the construct of semantic elaboration, a significant number of studies have instructed participants to rate the experimental words in terms of the pleasantness of their *referents* (e.g., Barcroft 2002, in line with previous L1 experiments). Whether participants are able to divorce meaning entirely from the formal properties of these words in this kind of exercise, however, has never been ascertained.

4. In accordance with Hulstijn (2001: 266 f.), we have operationalized the difference between incidental and intentional learning as the absence or presence of a warning to participants that they will be tested afterwards.

5. A nested design is an experimental design in which the variables are not crossed, but have an implicit hierarchy. In our case, words 1–12 are nested (i.e., embedded) within the 'incidental' learning condition, and words 13–24 are nested within the 'intentional' learning condition.

6. Recalling the forms of target L2 words freely after a treatment is no evidence of word learning if you do not know what they mean, and recalling the meanings of target L2 words freely (i.e., by producing known L1 words) suggests you have a good episodic memory.

7. Given the likelihood that a fair number of subjective form–meaning associations might be due to cognate effects in a broad sense, the chances that a teacher's appreciation of such appreciations will correspond to the learners' may be reduced if the teacher is unfamiliar with the learners' L1.

## References
Barcroft, J. 2002. Semantic and structural elaboration in L2 lexical acquisition. *Language Learning* 52: 323–363.

Barcroft, J. 2003. Effects of questions about word meaning during L2 Spanish lexical learning. *The Modern Language Journal* 87: 546–561.

Barcroft, J. 2004. Effects of sentence writing in second language lexical acquisition. *Second Language Research* 20: 303–334.

Beréndi, M., Csábi, S. & Kövecses, Z. 2008. Using conceptual metaphors and metonymies in vocabulary teaching. In *Cognitive Linguistic Approaches to Teaching Vocabulary and Phraseology*, F. Boers & S. Lindstromberg (eds), 65–99. Berlin: Mouton de Gruyter.

Bloomfield, L. 1933. *Language*. New York NY: Holt, Rinehart and Winston.

Boers, F. 2000. Metaphor awareness and vocabulary retention. *Applied Linguistics* 21: 553–571.

Boers, F. & Demecheleer, M. 1998. A cognitive semantic approach to teaching prepositions. *English Language Teaching Journal* 53: 197–204.

Boers, F., Demecheleer, M. & Eyckmans, J. 2004. Etymological elaboration as a strategy for learning figurative idioms. In *Vocabulary in a Second Language: Selection, Acquisition and Testing* [Language Learning and Language Teaching 10], P. Bogaards & B. Laufer (eds), 53–78. Amsterdam: John Benjamins.

Boers, F., Eyckmans, J. & Stengers, H. 2006. Means of motivating multiword units: Rationale, mnemonic benefits and cognitive-style variables. In *EUROSLA Yearbook* 6, S. Foster-Cohen, M.M. Krajnovic & J.M. Djigunovic (eds), 169–190. Amsterdam: John Benjamins.

Boers, F. & Lindstromberg, S. 2009. *Optimizing a Lexical Approach to Instructed Second Language Acquisition*. Basingstoke: Palgrave Macmillan.

Cho, K. 2010. Fostering the acquisition of English prepositions by Japanese learners with networks and prototypes. In *Fostering Language Teaching Efficiency through Cognitive Linguistics*, S. De Knop, F. Boers & T. De Rycker (eds), 259–275. Berlin: Mouton de Gruyter.

Condon, N. 2008a. How cognitive linguistic motivations influence the phrasal verbs. In *Cognitive Linguistic Approaches to Teaching Vocabulary and Phraseology*, F. Boers & S. Lindstromberg (eds), 133–158. Berlin: Mouton de Gruyter.

Condon, N. 2008b. Investigating a Cognitive Linguistic Approach to the Learning of English Phrasal Verbs. PhD dissertation, Université Catholique de Louvain-la-Neuve.

Craik, F.I.M. & Lockhart, R.S. 1972. Levels of processing: A framework for memory research. *Journal of Verbal Learning and Verbal Behaviour* 11: 671–684.

Croft, L.B. 1978. The mnemonic use of linguistic iconicity in teaching language and literature. *Slavic and East European Journal* 22: 509–518.

De Groot, A.M.B & Keijzer, R. 2000. What is hard to learn is easy to forget: The roles of word concreteness, cognate status, and word frequency in foreign-language vocabulary learning and forgetting. *Language Learning* 50(1): 1–56.

Doke, C.M. 1935. *Bantu Linguistic Terminoloy*. London: Longman, Green.

Eagle, M. & Leiter, E. 1964. Recall and recognition in intentional and incidental learning. *Journal of Experimental Psychology* 68(1): 58–63.

Hall, C.J. 2002. The automatic cognate form assumption. Evidence for the parasitic model of vocabulary development. *IRAL* 40: 69–87.

Hu, Y.H. & Fong, Y.Y. 2010. Obstacles to CM-guided L2 idiom interpretation. In *Fostering Language Teaching Efficiency through Cognitive Linguistics*, S. De Knop, F. Boers & T. De Rycker (eds), 293–317. Berlin: Mouton de Gruyter.

Hulstijn, J.H. 2001. Intentional and incidental second language vocabulary learning: A reappraisal of elaboration, rehearsal and automaticity. In *Cognition and Second Language Instruction*, P. Robinson (ed.), 258–286. Cambridge: CUP.

Hyde, T.S. & Jenkins, J.J. 1969. Differential effects of incidental tasks on the organization of recall of a list of highly associative words. *Journal of Experimental Psychology* 82(3): 472–481.

Imai, M., Kita, S., Nagumo, M. & Okada, H. 2008. Sound symbolism facilitates early verb learning. *Cognition* 109: 54–65.

Kövecses, Z. & Szabó, P. 1996. Idioms: A view from cognitive semantics. *Applied Linguistics* 17: 326–355.

Laufer, B. 2005. Focus on Form in second language vocabulary acquisition. In *EUROSLA Yearbook* 5, S. Foster-Cohen (ed.), 223–250. Amsterdam: John Benjamins.

Laufer, B. 2006. Comparing focus on form and focus on formS in second language vocabulary teaching. *The Canadian Modern Language Review* 63(1): 149–166.

Laufer, B. & Hulstijn, J. 2001. Incidental vocabulary acquisition in a second language: The construct of task-induced involvement. *Applied Linguistics* 22: 1–26.

Lecron Foster, M. 1978. The symbolic structure of primordial language. In *Human Evolution Biosocial Perspectives*, S.L. Washburn & E.R. McCown (eds), 77–122. Merlo Park CA: Benjamin/Cummings Publishing.

Lindstromberg, S. 2010. *English Prepositions Explained*, 2nd edn. Amsterdam: John Benjamins.

Lindstromberg, S. & Boers, F. 2005. From movement to metaphor with manner-of-movement verbs. *Applied Linguistics* 26: 241–261.

Lindstromberg, S. & Boers, F. 2008a. The mnemonic effect of noticing alliteration in lexical chunks. *Applied Linguistics* 29: 200–222.

Lindstromberg, S. & Boers, F. 2008b. Phonemic repetition and the learning of lexical chunks: The mnemonic power of assonance. *System* 36: 423–436.

Long, M.H. 1991. Focus on form: A design feature in language teaching methodology. In *Foreign Language Research in Cross-Cultural Perspective*, K. de Bot, R.B. Ginsberg& C. Kramsch (eds), 39–52. Amsterdam: John Benjamins.

Lotto, L. & de Groot, A.M.B. 1998. Effects of learning method and word type on acquiring vocabulary in an unfamiliar language. *Language Learning* 48(1): 31–69.

Maurer, D., Pathman, T. & Mondloch, C.J. 2006. The shape of boubas: Sound-shape correspondences in toddlers and adults. *Developmental Science* 9: 316–322.

Morris, C.D., Bransford, J.D. & Franks, J.J. 1977. Levels of processing versus ransfer appropriate processing. *Journal of Verbal Learning and Verbal Behavior* 16: 519–533.

Nation, I.S.P. 2001. *Learning Vocabulary in Another Language*. Cambridge: CUP.

Nuckols, J.B. 1999. The case for sound symbolism. *Annual Review of Anthropology* 28: 225–252.

Parault, S.J. & Schwanenflugel, P.J. 2006. Sound symbolism: a piece in the puzzle of word learning. *Journal of Psycholinguistics Research* 35: 329–351.

Ramachandran, V.S. & Hubbard, E.M. 2001. Synaesthesia: A window in to perception, thought and language. *Journal of Consciousness Studies* 8: 3–34.

Park, E.S. & Han, Z. 2007. Learner spontaneous attention in second language input processing: An exploratory study. In *Understanding Second Language Process*, Z. Han & E.S. Park (eds), 106–132. Clevedon: Multilingual Matters.

Schmitt, N. 2008. Review article: Instructed second language vocabulary learning, *Language Teaching Research* 12(3): 329–363.

Schneider, V.I., Healy, A.F. & Bourne, L.E. 2002. What is learned under difficult conditions is hard to forget: Contextual interference effects in foreign vocabulary acquisition, retention, and transfer. *Journal of Memory and Language* 46: 419–440.

Sharwood-Smith, M. 1991. Speaking to many minds: on the relevance of different types of language information for the L2 learner. *Second Language Research* 7(2): 118–132.

Sharwood-Smith, M. 1993. Input enhancement in instructed SLA. *Studies in Second Language Acquisition* 15: 165–179.

Skoufaki, S. 2008. Conceptual metaphoric meaning clues in two idiom presentation methods. In *Cognitive Linguistic Approach to Teaching Vocabulary and Phraseology*, F. Boers & S. Lindstromberg (eds), 101–132. Berlin: Mouton de Gruyter.

Tyler, A. & Evans, V. 2004. Applying cognitive linguistics to pedagogical grammar: The case of *over*. In *Cognitive Linguistics, Second Language Acquisition, and Foreign Language Teaching*, M. Achard & S. Niemeier (eds), 257–280. Berlin: Mouton de Gruyter.

Verspoor, M. & Lowie, W. 2003. Making sense of polysemous words. *Language Learning* 53: 547–586.

Wang, A.Y. & Thomas, M.H. 2005. Effect of keywords on long-term retention: Help or hindrance? *Journal of Educational Psychology* 87(3): 468–475.

## Appendix
Lexical Production Scoring Protocol-Written (LPSPS written)

| 0.00 points | 0.25 points | 0.50 points | 0.75 points | 1 point |
|---|---|---|---|---|
| None of word is written; this includes:<br>– nothing is written<br>– the letters present do not meet any "for 0.25" criteria<br>– English word only is written | ¼ of word is written; this includes:<br>– any 1 letter is correct<br>– 25–49.9% of the letters are present<br>– correct # of syllables | ½ of word is written; this includes:<br>– 25–49.9% of letters correct<br>– 50–74.9% of letters present | ¾ of word is written; this includes:<br>– 50–99.9% of letters correct<br>– 75–100% letters present | Entire word is written;<br>– 100% letters correct |

"Correct" refers to any letter written and placed in its correct position within a word; "present" refers to any letter written but not placed in its correct position.
Adopted from Barcroft 2002:263.

*Authors' addresses*

Free University of Brussels (VUB),
Department of Languages and Literature,
Pleinlaan 2,
1050 Brussels, Belgium

Julie.deconinck@gmail.com
Frank.boers@ehb.be
June.Eyckmans@ehb.be

# Construction grammars

## Towards a pedagogical model

Randal Holme
Hong Kong Institute of Education

*Constructions* are the central unit of grammatical analysis in cognitive linguistics. In formal linguistics 'construction' referred to forms that were projected from lexical items rather than from an autonomous syntax. Thus, an expression, 'I danced the night away' requires an intransitive verb in a transitive construction provided 'away' is present. In cognitive linguistics, constructions comprise any grouping of words or morphemes that in combination possess meanings that cannot be predicted from the parts in isolation. This meaning belongs to the construction itself and is not necessarily dependent upon the presence of a given item of lexis. If this definition is accepted by second language teachers the fundamental interest is that language learning is about learning lexis, constructions, and the text types by which constructions are combined. This article first distills a concept of a construction useful to a pedagogical grammar and considers the relationship of this concept of form to better known language content 'packets' such as the structure and the lexical phrase. Last, it discusses how a CL concept of construction does and does not propose different pedagogical methods.

## Introduction

Central to the cognitive linguistic (CL) approach to language is an insistence upon the symbolic nature of grammatical form. Although this principle was a departure from the generative perspective, it was to some extent accommodated by earlier formalist approaches. Thus structuralism had treated meaning as inchoate and incoherent until organised by the symbolism of lexis and grammar. The symbolic principle also underwrote the functional premise that form was the systemized expression of the need to make meaning. CL formulates this symbolic assumption somewhat differently. In SFL (Systemic Functional Linguistics) linguistic form is a straightforward response to functional need. In the structuralist tradition, form is an architecture of differentiation imposed upon meaning (e.g., Bloomfield 1914; Saussure 1974). CL, on the other hand, sees the functional imperative of meaning-making as structured by the nature of our perceptual processes (e.g., Lakoff 1987; Langacker 1987). Far from being a blank slate, cognition structures experience. Cognition therefore performs such operations as categorizing experience, comparing and selecting phenomena or blending concepts to create new ones. Since these operations shape experience and experience is a function of how our bodies interact with the world, the meanings that cognition develops are also embodied.

In CL, language provides a series of access points to the network of categories derived from experience (e.g., Langacker 1990). As categories group meanings that sometimes seem to have stretched semantic relationships we need to anchor them with salient exemplars. The exemplars'

*AILA Review* 23 (2010), 115–133. DOI 10.1075/aila.23.07hol
ISSN 1461–0213 / E-ISSN 1570–5595 © John Benjamins Publishing Company

saliency may derive from some central perception of sense experience such as that of gravity. It might also come from some insistence of culture or affect. We call these exemplars prototypes (e.g., Lakoff 1987; Rosch 1978). The categories are networked together by different types of sense relations such as similarity or part-whole relationships and further presuppose extensive knowledge *frames* that may govern how their linguistic representations are used. For example, a verb, 'break', profiles a relationship between an agent and a patient that must have the property of being breakable. This makes example 2 difficult to conceptualise and example 1 straightforward.

(1)   I broke the milk jug (British National Corpus — BNC)

(2)   I broke a book*

When we move beyond the word, CL is also changing our approach to what the units of symbolism are. Words or morphemes combine to create another level of symbolism that we call constructions. Let us take the three elements that compose example 1: "I', 'broke' and 'the milk jug.' The first element, 'the milk jug', is already a complex of two elements, 'the' and 'milk jug' and this last is also composed of two more. The verb has been constructed from a verb stem to construe the event as past. Example 1 is therefore a construction that combines others. Each comes to possess a meaning that its components did not individually possess. Thus, 'I' is the agent of a breakage. 'Broke' specifies the relationship between the agent, 'I', and a patient, 'the milk jug'. 'The' grounds the milk jug as a particular instance of the sub-category 'milk jug' and 'milk' modifies 'jug' to create the subcategory.

We can explain this idea of a construction with the metaphor of a picture. A representational picture consists of different signs. These might represent walls, a door, a roof and windows. These signs have only the individual significances just mentioned but together compose something more than the sum of their parts and represent a house. This 'gestalt' is also evident in language. Just as the parts of the house can be recognized as combining into a single form so can those of a construction. Constructions are thus 'cognitive' in two senses. First, they are a 'gestalt' in the sense just outlined. Second, their meaning reflects how cognition structures perception.

Constructions therefore reflect the broader constructional process through which human cognition organizes many aspects of our existence, creating larger units from small. Language builds composite items from smaller elements, or syllables from phonemes and words from syllables, something illustrated by the grammatical conundrum shown in example 3 (Langacker 2008: 180–181).

(3)   the King of Denmark's castle

Here, the entity marked with -'s appears incorrect because it is 'the king' not 'Denmark' which possesses 'the castle'. The conundrum can be explained by seeing the construction as *bipolar* rather than *unipolar*. A unipolar structure is so called because it is a phonological construction with a meaning. Thus 'pic' and 'nic' mean nothing alone but together construct the meaning. The organization of 'picnic' is therefore unipolar. But example 3 has two poles. At one it is an assembly of symbolic elements that we could represent as: 'theking+of+Denmark'. At the other pole we have a picnic-like compilation that we could represent as 'thekingofDenmark'. Like 'picnic' or other composed items the last phoneme of the form, or 'k', must carry the possessive inflection -'s.

In a picture, the elements of the composition can be substituted within a category type without overly affecting the meaning of the composition. Thus, to return to our 'house' analogy, if we change the nature of the door or even exclude it altogether we will probably still recognize the drawing as showing a house. Equally, in a construction, when we change the meanings of some terms, the composition holds together but makes a different interpretation of what it represents. However, some word meanings cannot be construed by the construction. Accordingly, in example 2, we can note that it is difficult to construe 'books' as breakable. As all grammars recognize, however, there is still a relationship between 'I tore a book' and 'I broke a milk jug', even though the different verbs profile complements with different types of meanings. The relationship is generally described as one of transitivity, or can be seen as that of an agent affecting a change in a patient.

We can now see how the construction can be described at different levels of productivity. CL, then, does not see syntax as an autonomous organisational principle that is entirely distinct from the lexis it manipulates. Lexis and grammar are at opposite ends of the same continuum. To grasp this we should consider how we can analyse the construction, 'I broke the milk jug' in one of three ways, or as:

I.   simply the form of words shown with their quite specific meaning
II.  a form built around a specific verb, 'break', that allows such complements as 'glass' or 'eggs' but precludes others such as 'book' or 'cloth'
III. an agent, a process and a patient, or as an expression of any transitive meaning in other words

In the first case we can treat the construction as lexically filled. Such an instance is at the lexical end of the lexico-grammatical continuum. In the second case the form is more productive only in the way specified by its verb. The form therefore falls more towards a midway point on the continuum. The third case is a highly productive pattern than can be made precise with a large range of lexical forms. We are now at the grammatical end of the continuum. We can call this type of meaning schematic because of the fact that it is like an outline that can be filled by other more precise meanings

In this paper, we argue, therefore, that our notion of the construction should shape both the 'what' and the 'how' of teaching. The 'what' consists of the language content that our notion of a construction identifies. It also means deciding whether to treat it as a productive grammatical pattern or a closely specified lexical form. The 'how' originates in the principle of the embodied cognition from which the form and meaning of the symbolic complex have been fashioned and through which they will be learnt. It is about explaining meanings through CL's insights into how they have been conceptualised. To put forward this argument more concretely we will first elaborate upon the notion of a construction then discuss how it does and does not change a pedagogical approach to language content. Next we will consider how the identified differences should impact upon pedagogy, more directly.

### Construction controversies: Deriving a pedagogical perspective

Any attempt to identify constructions as a central unit of language pedagogy encounters disagreements among cognitive linguists about how these forms should be described. One of the most fundamental disagreements relates to the status of the grammatical classes used to classify a construction's elements. In Langacker's (1982; 1987; 1990; 2008) theory of Cognitive Grammar the word classes noun and verb represent meanings that arise from a universal perceptual distinction between a world of stable 'things' and the processes that construct relationships between them. In other words, nouns and verbs possess schematic meanings that are prototypically 'things' and 'processes', respectively. In Croft's (2001) Radical Construction Grammar, however, word classes are not based upon perceptions that can be generalized across languages in the way Langacker proposes. Word classes are metageneralisations that emerge from the construction itself. Thus, in example 1, 'break' is a verb and not a noun because of how it shows a relation between the agent, 'I', and the patient, 'the milk jug'.

Although the above disagreement is fundamental from the perspective of theoretical linguistics, it may have less consequences within language pedagogy. Much of the disagreement between Langacker and Croft concerns whether the same schematic characterization of nouns and verb is possible for all languages. If it is, then the learner will transfer this knowledge from their L1 without it being taught. But such knowledge is *implicit*, or is not something of which the learner can be aware. In other words, teachers who find formal grammatical categories useful in the classroom still have to teach them even if such teaching is asking learners to recognize what they already know. The larger question of whether formal grammar teaching is useful is not affected by the status of categories used. By Croft's argument teachers who take a formal approach are using metageneralisations to help learners understand a form. According to Langacker they are helping them to make use of their own intuitive knowledge. But in each case, the issue remains how far such explicit instruction is useful when the goal is implicit knowledge of the form.

### Compositional and non-compositional constructions: The lexico grammatical continuum

A teacher can approach constructions as *compositional or non-compositional*. Compositional means treating a form of words as an example of a productive grammatical pattern. One can therefore substitute some or all of the words in pattern with others that fit its or their meaning/s. To treat a construction non-compositionally means to regard it as a fixed expression. In theoretical linguistics, there is doubt about whether a construction can ever fit perfectly into one or another of these categories (Taylor 2002: 550–1). Yet, here, we explore compositionality as a pedagogical choice that is determined by the nature of the form in question and what the teacher wants learners to do with it.

To understand a compositional construction better, consider an indefinite article construction, 'a basket'. Formally, this is a noun phrase with a head, 'basket' that begins with the indefinite determiner, 'a'. If we treat the indefinite article 'a/an' as a fixed form and the noun as substitutable, the construction is compositional but within a fixed band of meaning. The meaning first expresses a 'thing' or an abstract idea that is conceptualized in the same way as 'a thing'. Furthermore, the phenomenon is construed as *bounded*, or as one example of an entity whose form makes it separate from others. It is therefore countable. We can create similar constructions by substituting different nouns, provided they too have *bounded* and countable meanings. We could use 'book', 'chair', or 'mountain', for example, saying 'a book/chair/mountain'. When we insert these types of meaning into the construction we can see that they *inherit* its reference to things that are countable or bounded.

The notions of schematicity and inheritance are clearly important to how compositional constructions work. Most people would not find it cognitively effortful to conceptualise 'horse'. Such animals or their images are common, making it easy to find a concrete exemplar of the meaning. 'Organism' would be more difficult to conceptualise, however. Many languages do not in fact make such general categorizations (e.g., Berlin, Breedlove & Raven 1966). It is notable, also, that if asked to think what an organism is, we must conjure a physical exemplar of it. Further, one person's exemplar may differ from another's. This is because 'organism' has a more schematic meaning than 'horse'. An organism's meaning can accommodate a more varied set of meanings as subordinate categories. Even if our language does not give a name to the organism concept, we cannot fully grasp the meaning of 'a horse' without understanding that it is a living thing. Whether the organism schema is named or not, our notion of a horse inherits that larger meaning of something living. If we reconsider the indefinite article construction, we can see that this principle of schematicity can also be used to describe the construction's meaning. The indefinite article has one meaning that is able to accommodate another's just as our sense of an organism accommodates that of an animal and horse. Our understanding of '*a* mountain', '*a* horse' or '*a* wine stain' *inherits* the understanding that these are singular, *groundable* instances of whatever category we want to discuss (Langacker 1987). It is also notable that this indefinite meaning is difficult to put across, perhaps because it is schematic. Teaching the grammar that encodes schematic meanings can therefore be challenging when the meanings do not match those in the learner's own L1.

A term such as 'a/an' can be described as opening a conceptual space into which some types of more specific meaning can be inserted and others cannot. For example, 'a furniture', is not found in the British National Corpus. This is because 'furniture' refers to an entire category of objects. Many meanings can be *construed* in different ways, however. 'Wine' is generally construed as unbounded and hence uncountable, or as (liquid) substance rather than form. In such a case we cannot use it in an indefinite article construction. However, we can also construe 'wine' as bounded, or as one type that is singled out from others as in example 4:

(4)   Pay about £45 a case for *a wine* from the Classico hillsides and it can be a revelation (BNC).

We can now see how the degree to which we regard an expression as grammatical depends on the match between the construction's schematic meaning and the meaning of the lexis that instantiates it.

Compositional constructions vary greatly, ranging from the combination of morphemes used to make past tense verbs, for example, 'call+ed', to clauses and co-ordinations. They are acquired through usage as multiple *tokens* of a *type*. The notion of 'type' refers here to the stored image of the construction and 'token' to the form produced. Let us suppose that a speaker stores the phrase 'a girl' as an example of the indefinite article construction. This then constitutes a type. Let us suppose they use this in a text as in example 5: The form that appears in this text is the token.

(5)   What is it, a boy or a girl? (BNC)

We can further note that apart from differences in how the form is stored and actually reproduced, the type is the same as the token. But let us now imagine that the speaker needs the same construction to talk about 'a baby' and that they have stored 'baby' but not 'a baby'. We can then say that they have generalised from their type, 'a girl', to a token, 'a baby', and type and token do not match. In the case of a construction such as the irregular verb, 'went', type will match token. In contrast, an utterance that is original for its speaker will by definition be a token that differs from a type.

### Non-compositional constructions

If we return to the noun, 'basket', we can add another term to obtain 'basket case'. The term 'basket' is now acquiring a new meaning from its combination with 'case'. The expression was first used in World War 2 to refer to soldiers who were so badly wounded they were spoken of as needing to be carried, as if in baskets. This shows how construal operations develop meanings. 'Basket' is now a container-for-contained metonymy (Lakoff 1987). The container is the conveyance, or basket, and the contained is the conveyed or injured person. The term was developed by metaphor to represent any hopeless case or situation. In example 6 it refers to an aircraft needing restoration.

(6)   Restored in 1960 for the Temora Aero Club she eventually fell into disuse and was sold to Ray Windred of Dungong, New South Wales, as a basket case (BNC).

'Basket case' is a non-compositional construction because its meaning depends on two fixed terms. This type of non-compositional construction is also called an idiom. In formal approaches to grammar idioms and other non-compositional constructions are treated in the same way as lexis. Sinclair's more descriptive view argued that they evidenced one of two basic choices made by their user. The choice was between the idiomatic, lexical principle shown by 'basket case' and more 'open' grammatical forms (Sinclair 1991). Many corpus-based studies have emphasised how this lexical principle is more central to language use than previously thought. Discourse, and speech in particular, consists of large numbers of memorized, formulaic sequences retrieved whole from memory (Altenberg 1998; Eeg-Olofson & Altenberg 1994; Kormos 2006; Moon 1998). In fact, apart from the subject-predicate construction, where 'almost anything can be a subject', it has been argued that English has 'few, if any, patterns' where the meaning is purely word-order dependent (Fried & Ostman 2004: 15).This has been used to argue for a stronger non-compositional emphasis in language teaching based upon lexical phrases (Nattinger & DeCarrico 1992) or a more general lexical approach (Lewis 1993, 1997).

CL's assumptions differ somewhat from Sinclair's, however. Both compositional and non-compositional constructions express the symbolic principle and are, therefore, not alternative in the way that Sinclair implies. When combined, 'basket' and 'case' assume meanings they did not have. As discussed, something similar happens in the sentence, 'I broke a milk jug'. The phrase, 'a milk jug', for example, has both its conventional meaning and that of a patient of 'break'. The compositional construction, therefore, changes the meaning of its elements, albeit in a way that is less strong than in an idiom such as 'basket case'.

CL positions constructions on a lexico-grammatical continuum. We can place constructions with little or no schematicity and not much prospect of formal variation towards the continuum's lexical end. Constructions such as the transitive, agent+process+patient ('I broke a milk jug'), are very schematic and more productive. They are therefore at the continuum's grammatical pole. From a construction-based perspective, therefore, teaching language content does not mean emphasising grammar over lexis or lexis over grammar. Rather it is a case of taking up different positions along the lexico-grammatical continuum.

Even when teaching an idiomatic or fixed form, the lexical objective can allow some grammatical exploration. Consider example 7:

(7)    Your goose is cooked Darina; Chef's show faces axe after Hubby's child porn shame. (The Mirror, London, June 21, 2004)

The construction 'your goose is cooked' puns the idiom, 'cook your own goose', which perhaps derives from another expression, 'killing the goose that lays the golden egg', and so comes to mean a mistake that ends future hope. Example 7 is interesting for how it makes compositional use of an idiom and so reminds us how fixed forms are only fixed to a degree. Students need, therefore, to understand how they can use such forms productively but within certain constraints. To grasp the form's productive nature teachers might use CL's notion of an *image schema*. Image schemas refer to how we build patterns of imagery from experience then use these to conceptualise meanings. For example, the 'goose laying an egg' uses schemas of procreation and reproduction to conceptualise wealth creation (e.g., Lakoff & Johnson 1999). Image schemas thus furnish language users with a creative resource whilst imposing constraints upon the same. One way to exploit this resource involves asking learners to think of expressions that use a schema in their L1. They can next consider how well any identified expressions translate into the TL and ask what adjustments have to be made. Such procedures draw upon work in Applied CL that researches teaching idiomatic forms by taking them back to their literal origins (Beréndi et al. 2008; Boers, 2000, 2001; Boers et al. 2004; Skoufaki, 2008). Littlemore (2009) and MacArthur & Littlemore (2008) have also explored how a judicious use of corpora can help learners explore the different ways in which non-compositional meanings are extended across contexts. A larger need is for students to grasp how they can use compositional constructions to rework the elements of fixed patterns in ways that both respect and exploit their underlying image schemas.

### Teaching along the lexico-grammatical continuum

Lexical approaches to language teaching also treat collocations as teachable entities that underpin language use (Lewis 1997). Teaching the collocations shown in example 8 might stop learners from saying 'heavy road', for example.

(8)    'heavy traffic'
      'busy road'

Unsurprisingly, 'heavy road' cannot be found in the British National Corpus while 'busy traffic' has only 11 occurrences against the 91 for 'heavy traffic'. But teachers should be aware of how a collocational or fixed term approach would miss the productivity of each expression. 'Heavy' exploits the complex and productive image schema of weight that develops from our experience of gravity. Understanding the nature of the schema has the potential to help students group and perhaps produce a larger network of useful expressions. In Figure 1, I group 'heavy-'constructions into different subcategories whilst giving some indications of the imagery used by each.

First our embodied experience of gravity means that we feel certain phenomena as having excessive weight. This straightforward, prototypical meaning is shown in the graphic in the centre circle (1). In the overlapping circles (2) I show various metonymic and metaphoric construals of weight. Learners can then explore how we use the idea of weight to capture abstract experience. The image schema is used to develop our grasp of abstract concepts. Thus, 'heavy demands' are more abstract than 'heavy rain' though the construal of rain as weight is as an accrual of volume and not conceptually straightforward. Some categories are treated as transitional. 'Make-up' may not be conventionally heavy but could arguably be felt as weight. It therefore leads us away from the concrete, physical experience of a burden towards the more abstract construal of emotions and cognitive states as burdensome. 'Heavy taxation' is also transitional in the sense that money was once felt as a weight in gold but also projects the less concrete sense of a fiscal burden. Through money we develop a more abstract understanding of demands and expectations as sometimes heavy. Circle 3 (heavy user) shows how metonymy extends meaning. Somebody who uses a lot of something expends a

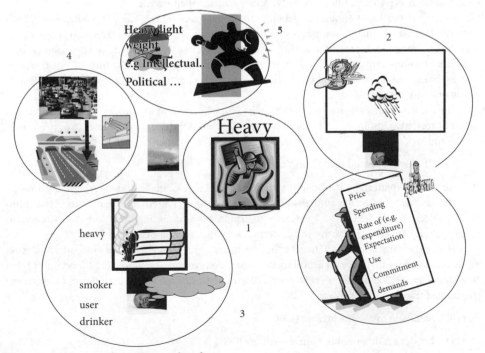

**Figure 1.**  Heavy: a productive approach to form

large weight of it. Use then is heavy and another metonymy construes the user as heavy also. 'Heavy cloud' takes us in the different direction of *objectification*. We treat other entities, whether earth or sky, as experiencing the weight that we ourselves feel. 'Heavy cloud' thus leads to 'heavy traffic' in circle 4 where the road takes the weight. Here, we also find a metonymy, this time, 'heavy fire' with gunfire being graded according to the weight of ammunition expended. The construction 'heavy-weight/light weight in circle 5 shows how the schema also creates a non-compositional form. In the cultural frame of sports and boxing we should note how weight becomes positive because it is associated with greater force. This gives us the laudatory 'political heavy-weight', and the pejorative 'intellectual light weight'. Taking this further, one can note how books and films can be over-sub-stantive or too 'heavy' but others may lack weight and so approach the trivial. Teachers may want to use such explorations of the positive and negative attributes of weight to stimulate the kind of cross-linguistic discussion just mentioned. My own speculation is that our notions of weight pivot around the ideal medium of a body that has strength without its mobility being encumbered. Though as shown, this will vary according to context and purpose. Last, other non-compositional forms could also be explored, for example, 'heavy industry' and 'heavy metal' (rock music).

My starting with quite concrete and physically-felt exemplars of the schema exploits the em-bodied learning principle outlined in my introduction. Using the embodied learning principle, we can re-associate the 'heavy' schema with the physical experience of gravity. Teachers can therefore ask students to enact the carriage of a burdensome object around the class. They can then repeat whilst talking about 'the weight of expectation'. In this vein, Lindstromberg & Boers (2005) have shown that enacting verbs of movement can help students with the use and retention of the forms whose meanings were mimed.

### Constructions as partially filled or empty: A compositional approach

Our analysis of the 'heavy+noun' construction shows how we can help students come to grips with constructions as productive meanings that are built around one or more fixed terms. As in the analysis of 'your goose is cooked', I also argued that teachers can treat the same construction as com-positional or non-compositional according to pedagogical objective. I now turn to constructions that are both clausal and which also lend themselves to this treatment as patterns where the lexis is partly or entirely unspecified.

The construction shown in sentence 9 can be treated in both of the two ways just mentioned. It might be treated as instantiating a pattern that is built around the mandatory presence of two words, 'make' and 'sick'.

(9)    The sight of blood made him sick (BNC)

It could also be a pattern built around the main verb 'make', (e.g., made him crazy). Finally it might be taken as what traditional grammars call a complex transitive pattern, or one with an object (him) and an object complement (sick). I now want to explore how far one might explore constructions as empty patterns that are productive within certain semantic constraints.

First, I should stress that CL treats a form as meaningful even if it is seen as a pattern of sche-matic relationships that have no lexical specification. For example, Goldberg (1995) points out that the ditransitive or double object construction illustrated in examples 10 and 11 always carries some meaning of transferred possession.

(10)    Someone gave her a present (BNC)

(11)    Bowler's mother knitted him a sweater (BNC)

CL argues that such meanings are obtained from the construction itself and not from the presence of a particular verb in the way assumed both by more traditional approaches and by lexical ones such as Sinclair's. For Goldberg, therefore, the verb 'knit' in example 11 has no meaning of 'giving' and must obtain that meaning from the schematic sense of the construction itself.

Yet it can sometimes be difficult to explain the meanings of such 'empty' patterns to learners. An additional difficulty lies in how Lakoff (1987) sees construction and lexical meanings as categories and therefore as extensible in quite complex ways. Thus the construction in example 11 adds to the sense of 'making' one of 'giving'. Goldberg (1995), however, talks of how certain verbs can be regarded as 'pathmakers' that help first language learners find the meanings of certain constructions. The pathmaker verb could help both first and second language learners associate constructions with image schemas derived from core human experiences. For example, we all experience changes of possession as letting go or taking hold. We may next *associate* the ditransitive and a pathmaker verb such as 'give' with that imagery. From that point we can use the imagery to build a more schematic and productive meaning from the other ditransitive constructions that we encounter. Teachers exploring clausal constructions should therefore look for appropriate pathfinder verbs when giving learners a prototypical form.

Yet finding pathmakers is not always straightforward. Goldberg (1995, 2009) calls a complex transitive such as example 9 a resultative construction because the verb 'made' maps a result, 'sick', onto an object, 'him'. But example 12 shows how the complex transitive pattern has a somewhat different meaning. Arguably, there is still some common sense of a meaning being mapped onto an object by the verb but it is far fetched to see 'consider' as having the resultative meaning expressed by 'make' and 'sick'.

(12)   He considered them necessary. (British National Corpus)

One straightforward response to this type of problem is to move second language teaching back towards the lexical end of the continuum and give up on any attempt to explore schematic meanings. Teachers dealing with the complex transitive would then give learners a list of the verbs that can take this type of pattern. Unfortunately, the list of verbs that can construct with complex transitives is quite long. Further this precludes a creative or genuinely compositional use of the construction. A more economical solution is to see how far one can bundle the verbs into subcategories of meaning. Previous lexical work can help here. For example, the Collins Cobuild Grammar (1991) associates the complex transitive with the following seven categories of verb, the last of which does not seem to have a resultative meaning at all. I describe these meanings as follows:

(13)   causing:
       They're driving me crazy
       She painted her eyelids blue

(14)   maintaining
       I kept her awake
       Leave the door open

(15)   appointing
       They made/elected Obama president

(16)   giving opinions
       I thought them crazy

(17)   describing and naming
       They declared her innocent
       I name this ship Titanic

(18)   proof
       They proved him wrong

(19)   depictives
       Serve it chilled (Cobuild Grammar, 1990)

Another problem with treating the complex transitive as an empty form is that a given verb allows a restricted range of object complements. For example, 'drive' seems to restrict its complement to meanings that suggest frenzied rather than straightforward emotion yet, according to the British National Corpus, is unlikely to construct with a term such as 'furious' in example 21, suggesting other rare internet uses are eccentric.

(20)   the roar of flames over their heads drove them wild (BNC)

(21)   their constant carping drove them furious*

One way forward is for teachers to adopt the principle illustrated with 'heavy' in Figure 1. They can then use the insights of CL to show learners the relatedness of apparently unrelated meanings whilst also pointing out resultatives which like 'the drive-crazy construction' are less compositional in kind. Like Figure 1, Figure 2 uses a process that Lakoff (1987) called conceptual projection to suggest how the construction's different meanings fold out of each other.

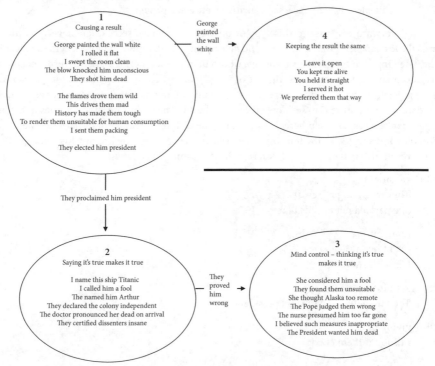

**Figure 2.**  Conceptual projection: extending the resultative construction

In Figure 2, circle 1 shows a group of meanings that give a clear sense of a fabricated 'result'. There is a further subdivision between abstract and concrete results. Concrete meanings may be easier to grasp so learners may find a better prototype among them. Among this group, we also find verbs such as 'wipe' or 'elect' that predicate a very limited range of object complements (e.g., for 'wipe', 'clean' or 'dry' but not 'clear'). I again treat some constructions as transitory because they show how one type of meaning develops from another. Thus, 'elected him President/proclaimed him President' at the bottom of the first circle provide a thematic linkage to the more abstract processes in circle 2 and 3. Naming, electing and proclaiming are linguistic processes of high illocutionary force. In other words, they speak their own result. If speech can make something true then thought can also. The diagram therefore gives students the idea of proof to carry us to the idea of creating a result out of intellectual activity or from thought. The constructions in circle 3 are therefore about considering or thinking. Circle 4 shows how the construction also extends in a different semantic direction. Here the verb 'painted' carries a shift from result creation to result maintenance. Once painted white, a house remains white, at least for a while.

Our suggestion is not that teachers engage in laborious and empirically suspect explanations about how one meaning extends into another. Rather teachers can present the construction as a productive group of connected category meanings. In other words, the presentation organises the compositional construction into groups of fixed forms whose meanings have a sometimes tenuous relationship. Priming experiments show how we can recall items more easily when they have a thematic or image schematic link (e.g., Feldman 2006). Giving learners a securer hold on how the meanings of a construction relate to each other might encourage them to treat it as a fully productive or 'empty' pattern rather than as one built around a handful of specific verbs.

### Construction generalisation

The above discussion shows how teaching language content, particularly to more advanced students, can be framed as a series of judgment calls about where to place one's teaching on the lexico-grammatical continuum, or about how compositional to be. The discussion also shows ways in which constructions can be bundled to help students learn and recognize them as forms whose related meanings show them to be tokens of a type. I now want to consider how one can actually help students to generalize a construction.

First, both L1 and L2 learners show a remarkable capacity to generalize constructions without being taught to do so (Goldberg & Casenhiser 2008). Tomasello (2003) counts what he calls 'pattern-finding' as one of the two cognitive processes that make language acquisition possible. Pattern-finding is part of our natural cognitive endowment and is probably common to most animals (Feldman 2006). This could also argue for simply concentrating on giving learners the lexically 'filled' forms on which their natural propensity for linguistic pattern finding and hence for generalization can work.

A problem with the above 'laissez-faire' approach to generalisation is that there is also a lot of research that questions how much it actually happens in the second language case. Both FLA and SLA researchers have realized that learners treat even compositional forms non-compositionally during the early stages of learning (Wong-Fillmore 1976: 640; Lindblom, 1992). When verb-based constructions are learnt, for example, the form is still treated semi-non-compositionally with one verb being used in one construction. This has given rise to the term 'verb island' and the understanding that it is only later that infants seem to make use of more productive adult type constructions. For example, one of my children used the verb 'fall down' almost exclusively in his first intransitive constructions. The 'rubbish', 'Christopher', 'The Prince' (in a computer game), all 'fall down' with no tense being marked. Thus, L1 learners may use different forms of the same verb in constructions with quite different and specific semantic representations. Achieving this productivity may be more problematic for L2 learners, however. Ullman (2005) justifies a generative model of SLA with the proposal that there are maturational constraints which make second language learners more dependent on the part of the mind associated with lexical processing. Accordingly, learners have a declining access to neurological functions associated with syntax. On-line studies by Silva & Clahsen (2008) have supported this view with evidence that when compared to native speakers, L2 users tend to reproduce regular past tense forms as if from a single stored unit instead of decomposing them into their morphemes. This storage of composed forms as single units is often called 'chunking'. For our purposes, the generative basis of this argument is less relevant than the issue of how such research indicates that generalisation can be a problem for L2 learners.

Yet if language teaching is not framed by some notion of universal grammar then we must treat its larger objectives as accelerating an extended process and compensating for an often poor level of exposure to the target language. Such a treatment suggests that teachers should try to help construction generalisation along whilst trying to put over the constraints placed upon it.

Second, the insistence upon chunking among L2 learners by certain scholars may be overdone, or may even be a product of how grammar is over-associated with the concept of an autonomous syntax. In this regard, a corpus study by Gries & Wulff (2005) noted how advanced German learners of English had acquired a knowledge of the interface between lexis and syntax that was similar to that of native speakers. Gries & Wulff further repeated an experiment with non-native German speakers that was originally conducted on native speakers by Bencini & Goldberg (2000). In this study subjects were asked to categorise English constructions written on cards. Their choice was between a verb based categorisation or one derived from a construction's argument structure. Thus they might sort the constructions 'I gave them a book', 'I gave them away' and 'I brought them their lunch' either as two ditransitives (I gave them a book/I bought them their lunch) or as two forms pivoting on 'give' (I gave them a book/I gave them away). The proportion of constructions categorized on the basis of argument structure did not differ greatly from that of native speakers. In other words, the learners perceived constructions not as chunks built round specific verbs but as patterns with matching argument structure to the same degree as native speakers.

If learners gravitate to chunks then teaching strategies should push them to generalize. The risk of not doing this is to leave learners with a discourse that moves between phrasal islands whose very correctness is made incongruous by a failure to control the compositional forms that can be manipulated to integrate them into text (Holme 2009). Consider, for example, sentence 22 from an assignment question about Wilfred Owen's poem 'Dulce et Decorum Est' that was written by a learner with Cantonese L1.

(22)  He was a patriot to fight for his country and believed it was his role to fight. (author's data).

(23)  He was a patriot who believed it was his role to fight for his country

A possible correction has been given in example 23. Example 22 shows appropriate and inappropriate phrases lying side by side with the inappropriate trying to compensate for a larger failure to find an appropriate clause structure. The first sentence runs into problems because the writer appears to avoid the relative clause construction that would modify 'patriot' and help them avoid the subsequent redundancy (patriot to fight/role to fight). It may be that the correct 'was his role to' has been acquired and overgeneralised to the 'patriot'. The passage typifies a larger failure to use compositional forms and the techniques of subordination that are required.

Finally, it is self-evident that one cannot recognize a pattern when a construction is repeated without lexical variation. To grasp a construction as compositional learners must encounter different tokens of it in text. In the sense that instruction involves some measure of 'forcing', teachers can arrange texts in ways that recycle new tokens of previously taught constructions. Thus they can consider adapting or doctoring texts in ways that insert or use taught forms. Though irritating to the author if discovered, this can be simpler in literary texts. Thus descriptive passages or dialogues need be only marginally diverted from a topic in order to contextualize some version or other of construction meaning. Teachers can also insist that these are 'noticed'. Research in the learning of lexis has shown how learning a word through explanation alone is not very effective. Simply leaving the learner to encounter lexis in context achieves greater uptake. Yet most effective is to combine such encounters with explanations (Qun et al. 2009). If we assume that the same holds true for constructions, teachers need to make sure that these are re-encountered consistently and that their different instantiations and related shifts in meaning are noticed. Encountering tokens that cannot be satisfactorily linked to types may itself promote learning. Hudson (2008) notes how a failure to integrate a token into an appropriate inheritance hierarchy or to find its type keeps that form cognitively hyperactive. In other words, it forces the mind to give it undue attention, even to the exclusion of other forms (Hudson 2008). The teacher can advance that construction's learning by ensuring that the guesswork is correct, or by helping the student to scaffold a hierarchy.

### Helping students generalize constructions

The use of explicit procedures to help learners use constructions compositionally can be a result of any three types of encounter with form. In the first the construction appears as a grammatical item on the curriculum. In the second the item is 'noticed' in a text that the learner needs to process. The teacher or learner then focuses class attention on a particular form. In the third, the teacher supplies a correct construction in response to an error.

There is some overlap between constructions and forms that language teachers know as structures, particularly where the construction can be reduced to a pattern without lexical specification. L2 curricula may be implicitly construction based. For example, the Primary Course English for Hong Kong (Smith & Ling 2005) gives its language content with some functional and some grammatical specification under such headings as 'Questions to find out someone's age', or 'articles 'a' and 'an' to refer to objects'. Like most such books it then gives its learners specific examples that could be learnt and generalised as constructions. Thus 'a/an' to refer to objects gives examples of the indefinite article construction that refer to classroom objects in the construction 'it's a computer' and the questions to find someone's age are exemplified with very specific instances of a more productive interrogative 'How old are you, Rosita?'. Such presentation forms may work simply because they give learners the necessary prototypes. These approaches may be supported in class with 'rules of thumb'. From a construction-based perspective such rules could do one or both of two things. First they may stipulate how to compose a form whose meaning is already clear. For example they tell learners to use 'V+ing' after 'look forward to'. Second the rules may link the use of a form to the expression of a meaning. Thus, the learner might be told that 'would' expresses a strong or impossible condition. CL cautions against an over-generalised and over-abstract approach to grammar teaching, however. If students leave one class with an established match between one type and token, they may be doing well. A larger capacity to treat the form schematically and as the constrained basis of pattern generalisation may require further encounters with other tokens in other contexts. Second, CL provides teachers with a stronger sense of the construal operations from which construction meanings emerge. For example, Tyler (2008, this volume) demonstrates a successful use of graphics with second language learners to illustrate the force dynamics implicit in different types of English modality. Thus, for the modal 'will', a stick figure is drawn with an arrow projecting from them to show how the 'force emanates from the doer' of the action. For 'would', the same graphic is given but is drawn in dotted lines to show a weakened commitment. For 'must', the lines are solid and another figure is added to show an external force projecting onto the agent of the action. Third, because CL understands how such schemas evolve from embodied experience, it also argues for the use of enactment and movement routines to help students build form–meaning relationships from the types of physical experience in which they originate. In a CL view, FLA advances when infants match what Feldman (2006) calls "the richness of their (cognitive) substrata" to the imagery implicit in a language's use of form. In other words, the infant's own development of imagery from embodied experience helps them grasp how language makes use of this. It is plausible that second language learners also need to redevelop their grasp of meaning from the physical imagery with which that meaning is associated. Fourth, grammar is often practised with cloze procedures or gapped sentences. This type of practice generally focuses on finding grammatical or closed class words such as prepositions in the way shown in example 24. A focus on grammatical terms seems to stress grammaticality. It also reduces the number of possible answers and so simplifies marking. Yet teachers could think more about asking students to provide appropriate lexical items. Example 25 asks learners to experiment with finding appropriate predicative adjectives to construct with 'of'. This builds awareness of the types of adjectival meaning that fit the construction and makes a more creative and compositional use of the cloze procedure.

(24)    He was conscious _____ something moving in the room.

(25)    He was _____ of something moving in the room

Last, the functional emphasis of many ELT materials may over-connect a construction to a particular context. The learner is then discouraged from treating a construction as a category. Even a category of tenuously related meanings may steer a creative use in multiple contexts. Our discussion of Figures 1 and 2 has also shown how CL can help teachers explore constructions as extendable semantic categories. Such figures can be used with only some of the examples provided, students can then be asked to sort other forms into the circle that best fits their meaning.

Visual devices such as category diagrams can steer the development and selection of form–meaning correspondences that are appropriate for a given construction. Designed for young learners, Figure 3 shows how hyponym charts or category diagrams can be used to help learners find appropriate category meanings for these slots. Thus, students working on the caused motion construction shown here can use the chart to explore categories for the goal of motion. At the same time another group could work on the object and another on the verb or process. When implementing this procedure, I have noticed a multiplier effect where classes create quite a large number of different exemplars from changes to a few category forms. The chart emphasises how the larger compositional construction requires that its parts retain certain meanings. Thus the object must be an entity put into literal or figurative motion and the prepositional phrase must profile that motion's destination.

As Tyler (2008, this volume) showed in her work on modality that was discussed above, thinking about how a meaning has been conceptualized may also give learners a securer understanding of the constraints it imposes on a form. Thus teachers faced with explaining different forms of English modality can use diagrams showing force applied to patients or agents to different degrees. In the same vein, much work in CL has been motivated by the way in which relational or grammatical meanings are often conceptualised through the experience of spatial relations. Thus causal relations are expressed through metaphors of spatial attachment (one thing leads to another) and containment (one thing comes from/out of another) (Lakoff & Johnson 1980). This interest has been expressed by a growing body of work in Applied CL that looks both at how prepositions are used to

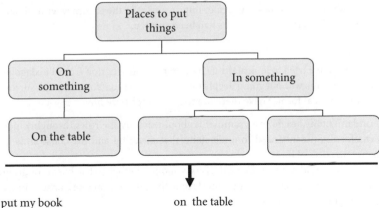

Grandpa   put my book                          on  the table

**Figure 3.** Using category diagrams to explore construction meanings

construe reality (e.g., Boers 1996; Lindner 1981; Tyler & Evans 2003) and at how such insights can be used in teaching (e.g., Dirven 2001; Coventry & Guijarro Fuentes 2008; de Knop & Dirven 2008; Kurtyka 2001; Littlemore & Low 2006; Littlemore 2009).

In Tyler (2010) I report on how I used a combination of these and other construction teaching techniques with Hong Kong sixth formers. First we 'noticed' forms in text types that were critical to the project work in which we were engaged. Thus, for example, a group who were required to write an editorial for a class newspaper noted the construction, 'He drew attention to his problems' in an editorial. They would next rewrite the construction with proforms to show places where different lexis could be used. Thus they wrote: 'drew attention to something/someone'. They placed this form at the top of a substitution table such as that shown in Table 1.

**Table 1.** Making Constructions with substitution tables

| Somebody | *drew* (someone's) *attention to* | | | some/thing/one |
| --- | --- | --- | --- | --- |
| Sally | *drew attention to* | | | her dress |
| The teacher | *drew* the class's *attention to* | | | the equation |
| Somebody | drew | (...) attention | *to* | something |
| We | turned | our interest | *to* | the matter in hand |
| The chair | moved | the meeting | *on to* | the next topic |

Next, in a brainstorming session learners were invited to come up with suitable lexical items to substitute for the proform, producing such sentences as 'don't draw attention to your mistakes'. After, the learners were encouraged to decide whether the pattern was still meaningful with its new lexis. If they thought it made sense they would propose contexts in which the new version of the construction could be used.

At the end of the intervention the experimental class was asked to recognize and complete unfamiliar versions of the construction under test conditions. They showed a significantly greater ability to produce correct versions of the constructions than the control group. Though this achievement attested to the worth of examining forms in the ways discussed, the result was unsurprising because the experimental group had greater time on task. More interesting was how the experimental groups also showed a significantly greater improvement in the accuracy with which they reproduced the text types where the constructions had been spotted.

## Conclusions

In this paper I have tried to look at the CL notion of a construction from a pedagogical perspective. I have tried to do this without going deeply into some of the controversies that surround this perspective on grammatical form. I have therefore tried to emphasise how

1. Fundamentally, teaching a grammar is about teaching the rules through which a *meaning* governs form. Students need to understand that meaning and the constraints it imposes on the generalization of form.
2. Teachers should not be making decisions about whether to teach lexis or grammar so much as exploring how lexical meanings interface with grammatical ones, or teaching along the lexico-grammatical continuum.
3. Teaching along the lexico-grammatical continuum means accepting the need to approach productive forms through restricted examples whilst helping learners look for patterns and common meanings in variable types.
4. Words and their meanings should be looked at inside the constructions where they are found to occur. Teaching new lexis can be interpreted as an opportunity for looking at the constructions that typify its use.
5. Constructions need to be practised and taught not just from the perspective of what they mean but from that of the imagery through which that meaning is construed — teachers can, for example, take an embodied approach where learners experience, or at least visualize, the imagery from which we derive the form's meaning.

There is a growing body of work in Applied CL which shows that teachers can help learners when they explore forms as motivated by their meanings and the conceptualisations from which they are derived. We now need more work on how the perception of grammatical forms as constructions can help students to gain a securer compositional control of the L2. My suspicion is that this may prove particularly useful for advanced students, whose teachers often sense that there is no more grammar to teach but that what has been taught has not been satisfactorily learnt. We may be able to help such students by encouraging them to consider whether forms that they think of as 'basic' in fact possess more complicated category meanings that need to be seperated out and then subsequently related one to another through some common conceptualisation. This could also provide them with a greater understanding of forms which are traditionally seen as lexical but are in fact compositional to some degree.

## References

Altenberg, B. 1998. On the phraseology of spoken English: The evidence of recurrent word-combinations. In *Phraseology: Theory, Analysis, and Applications*, A.P. Cowie (ed.), 101–122. Oxford: Clarendon Press.
Bencini, G. & Goldberg, A.E. 2000. The contribution of argument structure constructions to sentence meaning. *Journal of Memory and Language* 43(4): 640–651.
Beréndi, M., Csábi, S. & Kövecses, Z. 2008. Using conceptual metaphors and metonymies in vocabulary teaching. In *Cognitive Linguistics Approaches to Teaching Vocabulary and Phraseology*, F. Boers & S. Lindstromberg (eds) 65–100. Berlin: Mouton de Gruyter.
Berlin, B., Breedlove, D. & Raven, P.H. 1966. Folk taxonomies and biological classification. *Science* 154: 230–275.
Bloomfield, L. 1914. *An Introduction to the Study of Language*. New York NY: Holt.
Boers, F. 1996 *Spatial Prepositions and Metaphor: A Cognitive Semantic Journey Along the Up-Down and the Front-Back Dimension*. Tübingen: Narr.

Boers, F. 2000. Enhancing metaphoric awareness in specialised reading. *English for Specific Purposes* 19(2): 137–147.

Boers F. 2001 Remembering figurative idioms by hypothesising about their origin. *Prospect* 16 (3): 35–43.

Boers, F., Demecheleer, M. & Eyckmans, J. 2004. Etymological elaboration as a strategy for learning figurative idioms. In *Vocabulary in a Second Language, Selection, Acquisition and Testing* [Language Learning and Language Teaching 10], P. Bogaards & B. Laufer (eds), 53–78. Amsterdam: John Benjamins.

*Collins Cobuild Grammar.* 1991. Cheltenham: Harper Collins.

Coventry, K.R. & Guijarro-Fuentes, P. 2008. Spatial language learning and the functional geometric framework. In *Handbook of Cognitive Linguistics and Second Language Acquisition,* P. Robinson & N.C. Ellis (eds), 114–138. London: Routledge.

Croft, W. 2001. *Radical Construction Grammar: Syntactic Theory in Typological Perspective.* Oxford: OUP.

De Knop, S. & Dirven, R. 2008. Motion and location events in German, French and English: A typological, contrastive and pedagogical approach. In *Cognitive Approaches to Pedagogical Grammar,* S. De Knop & T. De Rycker (eds), 295–324. Berlin: Mouton de Gruyter.

Dirven, R. 2001 English phrasal verbs: Theory and didactic application. In *Applied Cognitive Linguistics* 11, M. Pütz, S. Niemeier & R. Dirven (eds), 3–28. Berlin: Mouton de Gruyter.

Eeg-Olofsson, M. & Altenberg, B. 1994. Discontinuous recurrent word combinations in the London-Lund Corpus. In *Creating and Using English Language Corpora,* U. Fries, G. Tottie & P. Schneider (eds), 63–77. Amsterdam: Rodopi.

Feldman, J.A. 2006. *From Molecule to Metaphor: A Neural Theory of Language.* Cambridge MA: The MIT Press.

Fried, M. & Östman, J.-O. 2004. Construction grammar: A thumbnail sketch. In *Construction Grammar in a Cross-Language Perspective* [Constructional Approaches to Language 3], M. Fried & J.-O. Östman (eds), 10–84. Amsterdam: John Benjamins.

Goldberg, A.E. 1995. *Constructions: A Construction Grammar Approach to Argument Structure.* Chicago IL: University of Chicago Press.

Goldberg, A.E. 2006. *Constructions at Work: The Nature of Generalisation in Language.* Oxford: OUP.

Goldberg, A.E. & Casenhiser, D. 2008. Construction learning and second language acquisition. In *Handbook of Cognitive Linguistics and Second Language Acquisition,* P. Robinson & N.C. Ellis (eds), 197–215. London: Routledge.

Gries, S. & Wulf, S. 2005. Do foreign language learners have constructions? Evidence from priming, sorting and corpora. *Annual Review of Cognitive Linguistics* 3: 182–200.

Holme, R. 2009. *Cognitive Linguistics and Language Teaching.* Basingstoke: Palgrave Macmillan.

Hudson, R. 2008. Word grammar and second language learning. In *Handbook of Cognitive Linguistics and Second Language Acquisition,* P. Robinson & N.C. Ellis (eds), 89–113. London: Routledge.

Kormos, J. 2006. *Speech Production and Second Language Acquisition.* Mahwah NJ: Lawrence Erlbaum Associates.

Kurtyka, A. 2001. Teaching English phrasal verbs: a cognitive approach. In *Applied Cognitive Linguistics* 11, M. Pütz, S. Niemeier & R. Dirven (eds), 29–54. Berlin: Mouton de Gruyter.

Lakoff, G. 1987. *Women, Fire and Dangerous Things: What Categories Reveal About the Mind.* Chicago IL: University of Chicago Press.

Lakoff, G. & Johnson, M. 1980. *Metaphors We Live By.* Chicago IL: The University of Chicago Press.

Lakoff, G. & Johnson, M. 1999. *Philosophy in the Flesh.* New York NY: Basic Books.

Langacker, R.W. 1982. Space grammar, analysability, and the English passive. *Language* 58(1): 22–80.

Langacker, R.W. 1987. *Foundations of Cognitive Grammar,* Vol.1: *Theoretical Prerequisites.* Stanford CA: Stanford University Press.

Langacker, R.W. 1990. *Concept, Image, and Symbol: The Cognitive Basis of Grammar.* Berlin: Mouton de Gruyter.

Langacker, R.W. 2008. *Cognitive Grammar: A Basic Introduction.* Oxford: OUP.

Lindblom, B. 1992. Phonological units as adaptive emergents of lexical development. In *Phonological Development Models, Research, Implications,* C.A. Ferguson, L. Menn & C. Stoel-Gammon (eds), 131–163. Parkton MD: York Press.

Lindner, S. 1981. A Lexico-Semantic Analysis of English Verb Particle Constructions with Up and Out. PhD dissertation, University of California at San Diego.

Lewis, M. 1993. *The Lexical Approach: The State of ELT and the Way Forward*. Hove: Language Teaching Publications.

Lewis, M. 1997. *Implementing the Lexical Approach: Putting Theory into Practice*. Hove: Language Teaching Publications.

Lindstromberg S. & Boers, F. 2005. From movement to metaphor with manner-of-movement verbs. *Applied Linguistics* 26(2): 241–261.

Littlemore, J. 2009. *Applying Cognitive Linguistics to English Language Teaching and Learning*. Basingstoke: Palgrave Macmillan.

Littlemore, J. & Low, G.D. 2006. *Figurative Thinking and Foreign Language Learning*. Basingstoke: Palgrave Macmillan.

MacArthur, F. & Littlemore, J. 2008. A discovery approach to figurative language learning with the use of corpora. In *Cognitive Linguistics Approaches to Teaching Vocabulary and Phraseology*, F. Boers & S. Lindstromberg (eds). 159–188. Berlin: Mouton de Gruyter.

Moon, R. 1998. *Fixed Expressions and Idioms in English: A Corpus-Based Approach*. Oxford: Clarendon Press.

Nattinger, J.R. & DeCarrico, J.S. 1992. *Lexical Phrases and Language Teaching*. Oxford: OUP.

Qun, C., Guan, F.C., Chan, D. & Perfetti, C. 2009. *Read Write Integration*. Learnlab: Pittsburg Science of Learning Centre. http://www.learnlab.org/research/wiki/index.php/Perfetti_-_Read_Write_Integration, (January 18, 2010).

Rosch, E. 1978. Principles of categorisation. In *Cognition and Categorisation*, E. Rosch & B. Lloyd (eds), 27–48. Hillsdale NJ: Lawrence Erlbaum Associates.

Rudzka-Ostyn, B. 2003. *Word Power: Phrasal Verbs and Compounds: A Cognitive Approach*. Berlin: Mouton de Gruyter.

Saussure, F. 1974. *Course in General Linguistics*. London: Fontana.

Silva, R. & Clahsen, H. 2008. Morphologically complex words in L1 and L2 processing: Evidence from masked priming experiments in English. *Bilingualism: Language and Cognition* 11: 245–260.

Sinclair, J. 1991. *Corpus, Concordance, Collocation*. Oxford: OUP.

Skoufaki, S. 2008. Conceptual metaphoric meaning clues in two idiom presentation methods. In *Cognitive Linguistics Approaches to Teaching Vocabulary and Phraseology*, F. Boers & S. Lindstromberg (eds), 101–132. Berlin: Mouton de Gruyter.

Smith, A. & Ling, J. 2005. *English for Hong Kong*. Hong Kong: Marshall Cavendish Education.

Taylor, J.R. 2002. *Cognitive Grammar*. Oxford: OUP.

Tomasello, M. 2003. *Constructing a Language: A Usage Based Theory of Language Acquisition*. Cambridge MA: Harvard University Press.

Tyler, A. 2008. Cognitive linguistics and second language instruction. In *Handbook of Cognitive Linguistics and Second Language Acquisition*, P. Robinson & N.C. Ellis (eds), 456–488. London: Routledge.

Tyler, A. 2010. A construction grammar for the classroom. *IRAL* 48–4.

Tyler, A. & Evans, V. 2001. The relationship between experience, conceptual structure and meaning: Nontemporal uses of tense and language teaching. In *Applied Cognitive Linguistics*, 1: *Theory and Language Acquisition*, M. Pütz, S. Niemeier & R. Dirven (eds), 63–105. Berlin: Mouton de Gruyter.

Tyler, A. & Evans, V. 2003. *The Semantics of English Prepositions: Spatial Scenes, Embodied Meaning, and Cognition*. Cambridge: CUP.

Ullman, S. 1962. *Semantics: An Introduction to the Science of Meaning*. Oxford: Blackwell.

Ullman, M.T. 2005. A cognitive neuroscience perspective on second language acquisition. In *Adult Second Language Acquisition: Methods, Theory and Practice*, C. Sanz (ed.), 139–177. Washington DC: Georgetown University Press.

Wong Fillmore, L. 1976. *The Second Time Around: Cognitive and Social Strategies in Second Language Acquisition*. PhD dissertation, Stanford University.

*Author's address*

Department of English
Hong Kong Institute of Education
10 Lo Ping Road
Tai Po
Hong Kong

rholme@ied.edu.hk

# Metonymic inferencing and
# second language acquisition

Antonio Barcelona
University of Cordoba

The article is a reflection on the various areas of cognitive linguistic research on metonymy that are of potential relevance for SLA. Three of them are particularly relevant: (1) research on metonymy-guided inferencing; (2) research on metonymy-based lexical polysemy, and (3) research on metonymy-based grammatical constructions. Of the three main areas with which the paper is mainly concerned, area (1) is particularly relevant for research on second language comprehension, especially in utterance and discourse types heavily relying on the inferential work of the comprehender; area (2) has already proved to be very useful for research on the inferencing strategies followed by second language learners in their comprehension of new lexical senses in context; and area (3) should be helpful for research on the acquisition of grammatical constructions by these learners.

## Introduction

I am grateful to the editors of this issue of *AILA Review* for their kind invitation to contribute a paper on this topic. Like them, I am fully persuaded that research on metonymic inferencing is highly relevant for SLA, as I will show in the rest of the article, which is both a brief survey of the results of recent cognitive linguistic (CL) research on metonymy, especially research on metonymy-based inferencing, and a brief reflection on the relevance of this research for SLA. In this survey, I draw on my experience of many years as a former ESL teacher, both at high school and university level.

What is meant by "metonymy" in CL? Though there is consensus on some of its basic properties, definitions do not always coincide, and in fact, an important research area in CL is the elucidation of the nature of metonymy and its similarities, differences and interaction with other types of figurative processes, especially metaphor (see Barcelona 2002a, 2003a, in preparation b; Benczes, Barcelona & Ruiz de Mendoza, in preparation; Kövecses & Radden 1998; Panther & Thornburg 2007, among many others). The discussion of the theoretical problems involved would take us far beyond the bounds of this article. Therefore, I will simply define metonymy informally here, avoiding where possible the use of technical terminology, so that the definition will be intelligible to non-cognitive linguists while still being a clearly CL-inspired definition: "Metonymy is a cognitive process whereby one concept is used to mentally activate (i.e., to "make us think of") another concept with which it is closely related in experience." Imperfect as it is, this definition will be sufficient for the present discussion.

A few examples might illustrate the previous definition.

On the UK-based *The Telegraph* newspaper website, one can read the headline *Downing Street refuses to rule out nationalising banks over business lending*, immediately followed by the secondary

*AILA Review* 23 (2010), 134–154. DOI 10.1075/aila.23.08bar
ISSN 1461–0213 / E-ISSN 1570–5595 © John Benjamins Publishing Company

headline *Downing Street has refused to rule out the "nuclear option" of fully nationalising British banks if they fail to meet promises to lend more freely to businesses* (by James Kirkup, Political Correspondent. Published: 5:58PM GMT 21 Nov 2008).[1] It should be obvious that in this example the notion DOWNING STREET activates the concept BRITISH PRIME MINISTER and by further extension the concept BRITISH GOVERNMENT, since LOCATIONS (in this case the official location of a political institution) are closely connected in experience to the entities habitually located in them. The first paragraph of the report actually confirms this activation: "Gordon Brown, the Prime Minister and Alistair Darling, the Chancellor, let it be known that they believe the big banks are still not doing enough to make credit available to British firms, especially small businesses that depend on overdrafts to survive".

Now, in contrast, take the chorus part of Shania Twain's song "She's Not Just A Pretty Face": *She's a soldier, she is a wife / She is a surgeon / She'll save your life / She's not just a pretty face / She's got everything it takes / She's mother of the human race / She's not just a pretty face* (http://www.metrolyrics.com/shes-not-just-a-pretty-face-lyrics-shania-twain.html; accessed July 30, 2010). In the title of the song and in one of its chorus sentences, the noun phrase *just a pretty face* activates the notion "just a pretty woman", via the metonymy FACE (a body part) FOR PERSON. "Parts" of people, animals, objects or other entities are closely connected in experience to the corresponding wholes and vice-versa: A whole may often activate its relevant part. A simple example of this situation is a headline sentence like *How to fill up your car at the petrol station* (see http://www.revolutiondrivingtuition.co.uk/blog/advice-and-how-to/how-to-fill-up-your-car-using-the-petrol-station-pumps; accessed July 30, 2010). The purpose of the article with this headline is obviously not to give advice on the best way to fill up the interior of the car itself with petrol but only its gasoline tank.

Metonymy, however, is not cognitively as simple as the previous definition might suggest: as Holme (2009: 117ff.) reminds us, metonymy actually involves a combination of a number of the mental operations described by Langacker (1987) as *attention* and *salience*, both of which are, in Langacker's construction of these notions, complex and involve other simpler mental operations.

Why, in general terms, is research on conceptual metonymy relevant for SLA? Littlemore (2009: 108ff.) gives two main reasons. One of them is that this research has shown that metonymy serves "a variety of important functions in language", such as the achievement of reference, the setting up and maintenance of discourse communities, the creation of certain types of euphemisms, the expression of evaluative attitudes, humor, deliberate vagueness, and pragmatic inferencing, especially the sort of pragmatic inferencing involved in indirect speech acts. Importantly, in all of these functions metonymy guides or supports some type of inferential process, as Littlemore observes.

Metonymy is, in fact, ubiquitous (Barcelona 2002b; Barcelona, in preparation a) in cognition and language. It has been shown to be a *fundamental, ubiquitous phenomenon* motivating the emergence and extension of:

a.    numerous conceptual prototypes (Lakoff 1987)
b.    a great many metaphors (Goossens 2002, 1995; Barcelona 2000b; Radden 2000, 2002; see also next section)
c.    innumerable lexical senses (Darmesteter 1932; Goossens 1990, 1995; Stern 1931; Taylor 1995: 127ff.)
d.    numerous grammatical phenomena and constructions:
      Important recent surveys of the interaction between metonymy and grammar are Brdar (2007b), Langacker (2009), Panther, Thornburg & Barcelona (eds.) (2009), Ruiz de Mendoza & Otal Campo (2002). Among the grammatical phenomena and constructions where metonymy-driven inferencing has been found to be a motivating factor, the following should be mentioned:

- a great many instances of active zone/profile discrepancy (Langacker 2009): topic constructions, certain relational subjects or objects (like *a novel*, standing for the relation "X writes/reads a novel" in *Zelda began a novel*), syntactic 'raising', and relative-clause constructions
- various types of clausal constructions (e.g., conditional constructions)
- certain types of conversion and other types of recategorization
- other word-formation processes, including certain types of derivation and compounding
- aspectual shift and in general the tense-aspect-mood system in English
- proper names (see the brief discussion of paragons in Section 2) and noun phrases, especially generic noun phrases
- valency extension and reduction (as in the example of *reduce* given below)

e.   pragmatic inference patterns and discourse understanding (Gibbs 1994: Chapter 7; Panther & Thornburg 2003a)

f.   iconic symbols and other types of iconicity (Barcelona 2002b).

A consequence of this ubiquity is that metonymy often operates simultaneously at various analytical levels (Barcelona 2005, 2009). Language, especially its grammar, is essentially metonymic (in a broad sense; see Langacker 2009), since it tends to underspecify, i.e., to provide a blue-print, not only for intended meaning, but very often also for form. Indirectness is the rule in thought and language and one of the main devices to create indirectness is metonymy. Even the conventional association between a form and a meaning (a "sign ICM", in Kövecses & Radden's 1998 sense) is in itself a type of metonymy (WORDS STAND FOR THEIR CONVENTIONAL MEANINGS).

The other reason for the relevance of metonymy research for SLA, according to Littlemore (2009), is that the way metonymy is used varies significantly across languages (see below).

Apart from these two reasons, researchers like Boers (2004), Littlemore & MacArthur (2007), MacArthur & Littlemore (2008), Piquer-Píriz (2008a, 2008b), Kövecses & Szabó (1996), and Holme (2004, 2009), among others, have provided important evidence for the usefulness of raising the learners' (and the teacher's) awareness of the ubiquitous figurative dimension of language. As Littlemore (2009: ch 8) claims, exploiting the cognitive and conceptual motivation of language (one of CL's main tenets) constitutes a radical (and beneficial) departure from exclusively communication-oriented teaching methodologies. And the figurative motivation of language, i.e., its metaphorical and metonymic motivation is one of the most important types of linguistic motivation (Radden & Panther 2004b).

Virtually all the various areas in cognitive-linguistic research on metonymy are of potential relevance for SLA. However, three largely overlapping areas are particularly relevant: (1) research on metonymy-guided pragmatic inferencing, including non-lexicalized referential metonymies; (2) research on metonymy-based lexical polysemy and homonymy, and (3) research on metonymy-based grammatical constructions and processes.[2] Each of these areas also overlaps with research on the interaction of metonymy with cognitive-cultural models, since metonymic inferencing and metonymy-motivated semantic extension are often constrained by culture-specific cognitive models.

Most importantly, research in these three areas necessarily has to make reference to metonymy-based inferential processes (Barcelona 2009). A fundamental property of metonymy, which is not always sufficiently stressed, is that it is fundamentally a "natural inference schema" (Panther & Thornburg 2003b), operating at many different linguistic analytical levels (Barcelona 2005, 2009, in preparation a). It is usually claimed that metonymy is primarily used for referential purposes, but it may be more frequent as a guide in pragmatic inferencing in general (Barcelona 2005, in preparation a), and even when metonymy is used for referential purposes, the identification of the referent often involves some measure of inferencing anyway, since identifying a referent amounts to identifying the implicit referential intentions of others (Nerlich & Clarke 2001); this inferencing is often guided by a metonymy activating the target. When discussing what Clark (1978) called *shorthand* (which is a type of metonymy), Saeed (1997) gave examples like *It's a struggle keeping the barnacles from off the crops*, which he had heard on the radio. The speaker actually referred to the "barnacle geese": A SALIENT PART OF A FORM, i.e., the modifier used to distinguish this species of wild geese from other species of geese, activated the WHOLE FORM. As this example shows, metonymy is often involved in certain abbreviatory phenomena (Barcelona 2009; Barcelona, in preparation a). Metonymy is fundamentally a natural inference schema because of its ability to mentally activate the implicit pre-existing connection of a certain element of knowledge or experience to another. The referential function of metonymy is thus a useful (hence extremely frequent) consequence of its inference-guiding role. Of course, the output of this inferential activity may become a matter of routine (and get lexicalized), so that the referent of a metonymic noun phrase or of a metonymic nominal construction may, in the right context, be automatically accessible to the interpreter without any cognitive effort. When this metonymy-guided referential meaning is lexicalized and becomes an established sense of a grammatical construction (typically a lexeme in polysemy), this metonymy may be said to be also 'motivational'. Whether or not it has a referential role, a metonymy has a motivational role when it crucially guides the inferences leading to the development of a constructional meaning or form, whose entrenchment then leads it to acquire what Langacker calls "unit status", i.e., to be used in a largely automatic fashion (Langacker 1987).

In the ensuing discussion, I will be reflecting on the relevance of metonymic inferencing for SLA and making some suggestions on the possible exploitation of this research in language teaching. I will also pay attention to some of the crosslinguistic differences that have been pointed out in the literature I have been able to examine. With respect to this latter point, the two main types of contrasts seem to be basically the same as those I identified for metaphor (Barcelona 2001), which can be summed up as follows:

i.    existence of conceptual metonymy X in language A and absence of it in language B. As Feyaerts (1999) claims, higher-level metonymies tend to be cross-culturally valid, whereas relatively lower-level ones are more culture-specific. Littlemore (2009:119) reports on work by Woo (2008), who claims that even some high-level metonymies such as AGENT FOR ACTION and CATEGORY FOR MEMBER do not seem to be used in Chinese and that a relatively high-level metonymy like PRODUCER FOR PRODUCT does not work in that language either.

ii.   existence of the same or a similar conceptual metonymy in both languages, which may differ (a) in the conceptual elaboration or specification of source or target and/or (b) in the grammatical properties and the degree of conventionalization of the corresponding linguistic expressions of the metonymy. This is the most frequent contrast.

Due to space limitations, I will only be able to discuss at some length (in Section 2) the first of the three overlapping areas of CL-inspired metonymy research that were enumerated (a few paragraphs earlier) as particularly relevant for SLA: area (1), i.e., "research on metonymy-guided pragmatic inferencing, including non-lexicalized referential metonymies". However, before leaving the present section, two brief examples of metonymy-motivated polysemy (a topic in area (2)) are offered below for illustration; both are also relevant for area 3, i.e., "research on metonymy-based grammatical constructions and processes"). An example which sits across areas (1) and (3) is offered in Section 2 (the grammatical effects of paragon names).

The first instance of metonymy-motivated polysemy arises through metonymic chaining, which is frequent in polysemy (Hilpert 2007; Barcelona 2005, 2009, in preparation a). Part of the polysemy of the verb *reduce* (Barcelona 2009) is due to a metonymy-guided inferential chain. Its causative transitive meaning (i), described in Webster's dictionary as "to lessen in *any way*, as in size, weight, amount, value, price, etc; to diminish", is extended to its general intransitive meaning (ii) ("becoming reduced in general") via ACTION [CAUSING X TO BECOME REDUCED IN GENERAL] FOR RESULT [X BECOMING REDUCED IN GENERAL]; and (ii) leads to its specific intransitive sense (iii) (Webster's: "lose weight, as in by dieting" i.e., "becoming reduced in weight") via CATEGORY (BECOMING REDUCED IN GENERAL) FOR MEMBER (BECOMING REDUCED IN WEIGHT). Sense (i) is older than (ii), and (ii) is older than (iii) according to the OED. These inferential connections could be highlighted fruitfully in vocabulary building or comprehension activities. Interestingly, the sense shifts are accompanied in this case by a progressive reduction of the grammatical valency of the verb.

The second instance of metonymy-motivated polysemy is constituted by certain types of noun-to-verb conversion (Dirven 1999; Ruiz de Mendoza & Otal 2002). Here are a few examples taken from Dirven (1999: 275–287), with the motivating metonymies suggested by this linguist: *He was angling* (INSTRUMENT FOR ACTION) / *The plane was forced to* land *in Cairo* (GOAL FOR MOTION) / *Mary* nursed *the sick soldiers* (CLASS MEMBERSHIP FOR DESCRIPTION). In my view, the third example can be described simply as motivated by the metonymy AGENT FOR ACTION. In these cases, polysemy becomes "polysemy-based homonymy" (Barcelona 2003b), since the extended sense is at the same time the meaning of a different lexeme with the same basic form as the "parent" lexeme.

### Research on metonymy-guided inferencing

Research on metonymy-guided inferencing is particularly relevant for research on second language comprehension, especially when the second language listener/reader is confronted with discourse types relying heavily on the comprehender's quick inferential work. This area also includes non-lexicalized referential linguistic metonymies, which regularly require inferencing by the interpreter. A further illustrative example is given by Tang (2007), cited in Littlemore (2009: 107, 112): a postgraduate student from Singapore who had a part-time job at the nursery of a British university was puzzled, when she first began working at the nursery, to often hear the nursery staff use the expression "She's got a loose nappy" in connection with one of the babies. She initially interpreted this as an injunction to check that the baby's nappy was properly fitted, but the staff simply meant to point out that the baby's bowels were "loose" and that, therefore, the baby needed changing. This relatively conventional euphemistic expression is based on the metonymic connection between a baby's bowels and its nappy and may require a metonymy-based inferencing effort for its comprehension by a speaker of a different variety of English (as in this case) or by a second language learner first hearing the expression.

The role of metonymy in pragmatic inferencing and in discourse modes is generally recognized in cognitive linguistics today. As Panther (2006) suggests, metonymy provides generic prompts that are inputs for additional pragmatic inferences. As Barcelona (2005) observes, discourse-pragmatic inferencing is often guided by chains of "active" (as opposed to "dormant") metonymies, which seem to constitute the backbone of inferential chains (see also Ruiz de Mendoza & Díez 2002). One of the first scholars to recognize the role of metonymy in inferencing was Lakoff (1987: 78f.) in his brief comments on the role of metonymy in the conversational conventions of Ojibwa and English. Since then, research on metonymy and pragmatic inferencing has grown remarkably. These are some of its main sub-areas:

–    the metonymic basis of a very large number of metaphors (see references above)
–    the metonymic basis of implicatures motivating metaphorical lexical extension in grammaticalization, a famous example being the development of the future meaning of *be going to* (Hopper & Traugott 1993; Heine, Claudi & Hünnemeyer 1991; Traugott & Dasher 2002)

- the metonymic basis of indirect speech acts (Brdar-Szabó 2007; Panther & Thornburg 1998; Thornburg & Panther 1997; Panther & Thornburg 2003a)
- the metonymic basis of other types of pragmatic inferencing, including implicatures (Barcelona 2002b, 2003b, 2005, 2007a, 2007b, 2009, in preparation a; Panther & Thornburg 2003a). Barcelona (2005, 2007a, 2007b, in preparation a) has studied metonymic chaining in implicature derivation. Ruiz de Mendoza (2007) is a highly suggestive attempt at providing a unified framework for the interaction of metonymy, metaphor and pragmatic principles in implicature derivation, indirect speech act comprehension, and constructional meaning
- the role of metonymy in other aspects of discourse understanding, such as conceptual tautologies, mental reconstruction of texts, euphemisms and film, drama and artistic conventions and techniques, including literary styles (Gibbs 1994: ch 7). The use of metonymy in literary discourse has been the object of studies by Dzeren-Glówacka (2007), Kuzniak (2007), Pluciennik (2007), and Pankhurst (1999), among others
- the function of metonymy in aphasia, iconic gestures and in sign language discourse has been discussed by Ciepiela (2007), Kwiatkowska (2007) and Wilcox (2004), among others.

In addition to these sub-areas, careful research on the comprehension and linguistic expression of referential metonymies has continued in CL and outside CL after Lakoff & Johnson (1980): Fauconnier (1994, 1997, n.d.), Croft (2002), Dirven (2002), Gibbs (2007), Panther & Radden (1999), Barcelona (2000a), Fass (1997), to point out just a few.

In the rest of this section I will give some examples of some of these sub-areas and will comment on their implications for second language learning and teaching. I will first discuss examples of "purely inferential" metonymies, i.e., those simply guiding major discourse inferences (i.e., implicatures) or other cognitive operations not directly connected to an act of reference and not directly motivating a conventional grammatical construction. The distinction between purely inferential, on the one hand, and referential and motivational metonymies is not absolute, but a matter of degree (Barcelona 2009). Then I will discuss instances of inferential metonymies guiding an act of reference, including instances of anaphora. The last two topics will be, on the one hand, the role of metonymic inferencing and reasoning as a motivation for conceptual metaphor and in the understanding of metaphor by SL learners and, on the other hand, the role of metonymy in the creation of category prototypes and in reasoning in terms of these prototypes.

*Purely inferential metonymy*
The following is an example where purely inferential metonymies guide implicature derivation. This conversation is reported to have taken place in the Spanish Parliament in the 1930's:

> Opposition M.P. (referring to the Prime Minister): *But what can we expect, after all, of a man who wears silk underpants?*
> Prime Minister (rising calmly): '*Oh, I would have never thought the Right Honorable's wife could be so indiscreet!*'

In Barcelona (2003b), I carried out a detailed study of the metonymic basis of the complex pattern of pragmatic inferences invited by this exchange. I found all of them to be guided by metonymy. These are all the inferences that were analyzed:

a. meant and conveyed by the opposition M.P:
   1. The Prime Minister is a homosexual.
   2. The Prime Minister is unfit for office.
b. meant and conveyed by the Prime Minister:

3. The M.P.'s wife shares a secret with the Prime Minister.
4. She has told the M.P. the secret.
5. She knows that the secret consists in the fact that the Prime Minister always wears silk underpants.
6. She has seen the Prime Minister undress.
7. *She has had a sexual affair with the Prime Minister, and is, thus, an adulteress* (main inference).

c. *Perhaps* meant and *perhaps* conveyed by the Prime Minister.

8. The Prime Minister is, after all, despite his supposed dressing habits, not a homosexual.
9. The M.P. is a cuckolded husband.
10. The M.P. knew that he was a cuckolded husband before uttering his words.
11. Through his words, the M.P. has publicly admitted that the Prime Minister is not a homosexual.
12. Through his words, the M.P. has publicly admitted that he is a cuckolded husband.
13. Through his words, the M.P. has publicly shown himself to be an utter fool.

Attardo (1990) claims that some type of "frame adjustment" takes place in the comprehension of jokes and funny anecdotes. I found that the two types of frame adjustment operating in this case are what he calls "frame overlap" and "frame shift": the UNDERWEAR frame overlaps with the HOMOSEXUALITY frame; the latter overlaps with the DISCRETION frame, which in turn overlaps and finally shifts to the HETEROSEXUALITY and ADULTERY frames. These adjustments are motivated by the above *chained* inferences, which are in turn guided (in part) by a *chaining* of metonymies. For the sake of brevity, only the metonymic basis of inferences 3, 5, 6 and 7 is presented below:

- inference 3 is guided by RESULT (being discreet/indiscreet) FOR CONDITION (knowing a secret)
- inference 5 is guided by ENTITY (a propositional entity, namely the fact that Prime Minister uses silk underpants) FOR ONE OF ITS CONVENTIONAL PROPERTIES (being secret)
- inference 6 is guided by FACT (knowing the underwear used by someone) FOR ONE OF ITS CONVENTIONAL EXPLANATIONS (having seen that person undress)
- the first part of inference 7 is also guided by FACT (having seen someone undress) FOR ONE OF ITS CONVENTIONAL EXPLANATIONS (having had a sexual encounter with that person)
- the second part of inference 7 is guided by DEFINITION (a married woman having a sexual encounter with a man not her husband) FOR DEFINED (adultery).

This anecdote was originally created in Spain and it was "translated" into English by an educated native speaker, but was quickly and easily understood by other native English speakers. So there are no serious cross-cultural contrasts in this example, including the clear rejection today by both cultures of the unfair stereotype associated to homosexual persons that the MP was building on. As this and many other cases show (see Barcelona 2002b, 2003b, 2005, 2007a, 2007b, in preparation a), metonymy is regularly involved in discourse-pragmatic inferencing. Panther (2005) claims that conceptual metonymies occupy an intermediate level between very abstract inference-guiding principles and heuristics (like those proposed by Sperber & Wilson or Levinson) and specific ad hoc inferences employed in the derivation of particularized conversational implicatures. Therefore, it may be convenient both to raise the learner's awareness of this fact and to exercise her in metonymy-driven inferencing. As Holme (2009: 119) suggests, a good exercise to stimulate the learners' writing and conversational skills may consist in encouraging them to exploit the metonymic connections in a frame evoked by an "aptly chosen" sentence, around which students could create a coherent text (Holme actually suggests a wonderful example of such an exercise for lower level students).

But there are often cross-cultural and/or cross-linguistic contrasts where metonymy does not work in the same way in two languages. These situations should also be taken into account in SL teaching. An example is the recent expression *Aceptamos pulpo como animal de compañía* (literally 'We accept 'octopus' as a 'pet'),[3] which has gained widespread currency in Spain. It comes from a popular advertisement in the Spanish TV for the well-known indoor game *Scattergories*: in the advert, the category at stake is "animal de compañía" ('pet') and the word for a category member has to begin with "p"; the game is played at a married couple's flat and the owner of the game is a neighbour who constantly threatens to take away his game if his utterly wrong answers (such as *ship* for "sea creature") are not accepted, but the couple likes the game so much that they constantly give in and accept his answers with resignation. One of these answers is *pulpo*[4] as a type of "pet". After a moment's hesitation, the husband accepts with resignation once more. The idiomatic expression *Aceptamos pulpo como animal de compañía*, often under its shortened form *Aceptamos pulpo* ('We accept octopus'), is now commonly used to say that one is giving in to a stronger opponent, who is putting too much pressure on the reluctant speaker. The chain of metonymies that underlies the generalization of this expression could be described like this: SALIENT MEMBER (ACCEPTING THAT OCTOPUS IS A PET IN THE "SCATTERGORIES" GAME UNDER PRESSURE FROM THE GAME OWNER) FOR CATEGORY (ANY INSTANCE OF YIELDING TO OTHERS UNDER PRESSURE) + SALIENT PART OF FORM FOR WHOLE FORM (FOR THE SHORTENED FORM). Obviously, the idiom can be learnt as a unit without knowing its origin, but knowing the latter certainly reinforces its acquisition and makes it more enjoyable.

Next I present an example of research on the metonymic guidance of indirect speech acts, borrowed from Thornburg & Panther (1997), who have insightfully discussed this issue, following Gibbs's (1994) seminal observation of the metonymic basis of indirect speech acts. Thornburg & Panther assume the existence of "Speech Act Scenarios", derived from the Action Scenario, which has the following parts: the BEFORE (preconditions); the CORE (properties defining the action); its RESULT (the immediate outcome of a successful performance of the action); and the AFTER (intended or unintended consequences of the action which are not its immediate result). An example of a speech act scenario is the Scenario for Directive Speech Acts (S = Speaker, H = Hearer, A = action requested):

(i)   the BEFORE: H can do A / S wants H to do A
(ii)  the CORE:    S puts H under a (more or less strong) obligation to do A
(iii) the RESULT:  H is under an obligation to do A (H must / should / ought to do A)
(iv)  the AFTER:   H will do A

Metonymy is claimed to operate on these scenarios to yield indirect speech acts. These are just a few examples from the corpus:

(a) a BEFORE component for the whole scenario
In this example, the metonymy ABILITY TO PERFORM AN ACTION FOR A LINGUISTIC ACTION (a manifestation of the metonymy POTENTIALITY FOR ACTUALITY) motivates an indirect request: *Can you open the door?*

(b) a CORE/RESULT component for the whole scenario
The metonymy OBLIGATION TO PERFORM AN ACTION FOR A LINGUISTIC ACTION (a manifestation of EFFECT FOR CAUSE) motivates an indirect suggestion in the first example below and an indirect request in the second:

> *Julie, you're wet*. You must change.
> *Do sit down, both of you*. You must certainly play for us, *if you will, Mr…*

(c) an AFTER component for the whole scenario

The metonymy A FUTURE ACTION FOR A LINGUISTIC ACTION motivates the indirect request here: *'Oh, Rachel, don't you see, I can ask you to marry me now,' he said huskily. 'You do care for me, dearest? You will say "yes"?'*

Again the learners' awareness of the metonymic connections of the scenario element used as vehicle for the indirect speech act will help them to grasp these uses more easily and also to understand why they constitute different instances of politeness strategies (in this case, they are normally used to save the hearer's "face").

Radden & Seto (2003) have studied indirect shopping requests in English and other HAVE languages (German, Lithuanian and Croatian; we might also add Spanish), on the one hand, and Japanese and other BE languages (Chinese, Korean, Finnish, Hungarian, Polish and Hausa), on the other hand.[5] They conclude that the grammatical structure of the language constrains the type of metonymy chosen to perform an indirect shopping request by mentioning the *precondition* of the shopping scenario, i.e., the availability of the requested articles. In English and other HAVE languages the metonymy would be POSSESSION FOR AVAILABILITY (e.g., *Do you have 40-watt light bulbs?*), and in Japanese and other BE languages it would be EXISTENCE FOR AVAILABILITY (*40 watto no denkyuu (wa) ari-masu ka*) 'Are there 40-watt light bulbs?'). They also point out how the crosslinguistic differences interact with politeness factors in the choice of the scenario component as a metonymic vehicle. These constraining facts must be taken into account when stimulating the explotation of similar metonymies in the performance of indirect speech acts (see Littlemore 2009: 118).

Feyaerts (1999) discusses the metonymies involved in the German cognitive model of stupidity. Some of them are language-specific, like OUTGROUP ORIGIN FOR STUPITY, as manifested by the expression *Du bist wohl nicht von hier?* 'You aren't from here?'. This example constitutes an indirect way of asserting the interlocutor's stupidity (it would thus be both an indirect assertion and an indirect insult).[6]

Modality (especially deontic modality) is often associated with speech acts and with implicature. It is also very often indirectly expressed by means of metonymy. Take the metonymy OBLIGATION FOR DESIRE TO CARRY OUT THE DESIRED ACTION as in the volitional use of *must*: *I must speak to you, please* (Ruiz de Mendoza & Pérez Hernández 2001). There seem to be some important crosslinguistic differences in this area. Pérez Hernández (2007) shows that the metonymy OBLIGATION FOR FUTURITY, accountig for the future meaning of *Ce groupe d'experts devrait rendre ses conclusions début Février* 'This group of experts should report back their conclusions at the beginning of February', is used with fewer grammatical restrictions in French than in English, Spanish or Italian.

The construction of social paragons (Barcelona 2004, Brdar 2007a, 2007b, Pang 2006) like *Zidane* as a soccer paragon is culturally determined (cf. *Dante* as a paragon of literary writing in Italy, but perhaps not so in other cultures, like the English-speaking or the Spanish-speaking cultures, where respectively *Shakespeare* or *Cervantes* would most likely claim this status), and in them a metonymic model of the individual affected highlights some properties and ignores others. Paragon names are often re-categorized grammatically as common nouns.

Let us consider this example, downloaded from http://www.bermant.com/chaim/articles/haroldpinter.php (accessed July 30, 2010): *Harold Pinter is a man of few words, most of them silly. Yet he is one of the foremost playwrights of our time — which does not mean he is a Shakespeare or even an Ibsen, but he does have a deep insight into the quirks of human nature, and a unique ear for the ambiguities and gaps of human speech.*

The author of this article seems to be claiming that Pinter is not a play-writing genius (Shakespeare or Ibsen were to him real geniuses). I have claimed (Barcelona 2004) that the transient grammatical recategorization of paragons like *Aristotle, Shakespeare* etc. as common nouns in English and other languages depends on a conceptual process with the following elements:

1.  a stereotypical understanding of a well-known individual like Shakespeare in terms of her/his salient characteristic property, i.e., being a playwriting genius, this stereotypical understanding being due to the metonymy CHARACTERISTIC PROPERTY ('being a playwriting genius') FOR ENTITY (Shakespeare the individual)
2.  The creation of a class of *distinct* individuals connected by sharing the same characteristic property, the ideal member of which (the paragon) is Shakespeare
3.  metonymic activation of the mental class by its most outstanding member (STEREOTYPICAL MEMBER FOR CATEGORY).

This second metonymy is directly responsible for the transient grammatical re-categorization of this name as a common noun (which allows the name to take number morpheme and to be preceded by determiners, among other grammatical properties of nouns). However, the grammatical behavior of these re-categorized names exhibits some cross-linguistic differences (Barcelona 2003c).

This recategorization is sometimes permanent and enters the dictionary as an ordinary common noun (spelled even with a low-case initial): *Caco* (mythological paragon of thieves) becomes Spanish common noun *çaco* (colloquially, 'thief'). Metonymy is also involved in the emergence of the Spanish common noun *galeno* ('doctor'), from *Galen* (*Galenus* in Latin), a famous medical doctor of the Roman period, whose theories dominated Western medical science for over a millennium.

Only a few lines, given space limitation, can be devoted to some other examples of the operation of purely inferential metonymies in discourse-pragmatic inferencing, and the list is by no means exhaustive.

Vosshagen (1999) discusses the role of metonymy in irony, especially the one deriving from the exploitation of oppositeness (*You are a brave man* — meaning "You are a coward"). Colloquial tautologies like *Boys will be boys* rely on the metonymic abstraction of the "typical" behavioral properties of boys in the second NP (and according to Littlemore, 2009: 113f., a further metonymy is often involved in discourse by women, namely the use of the word 'boys' for 'grown up men'). Paralinguistic gestures are often metonymic (Barcelona 2002b; Gibbs 1994: ch 7), like most euphemistic expressions (an example was given earlier; see also Gibbs 1994: ch 7; Barcelona 2002b; Pauwels 1999). Sometimes an extended piece of discourse systematically exploits the metonymic connection of a concept to other concepts in a frame (see Holme 2009: 17ff., or Sliwa 2007). The role of metonymy in advertising has been studied, among others, by Ungerer (2000).

*Referential metonymies*
As stated earlier, referential metonymies guide the inferal of the speaker's (or the writer's) referential intention, hence they are at the same time inferential metonymies. We include in this sub-section the metonymies that lead to the identification of the referent both in non-anaphorical and in anaphorical referring expressions.

Even a simple example of a referential metonymy like *The buses* (i.e., the bus drivers) *are on strike* reveals that it involves inferencing (Warren 1999: 123) in an adequate context, probably a discourse portion in which the topics "means of transportation" and/or "strike" are currently active. This metonymy is an instance of the metonymic pattern CONTROLLED FOR CONTROLLER (Radden & Kövecses 1999) and guides inferencing to the BUS DRIVERS as the intended referent. Referential metonymies are not necessarily restricted to noun-headed noun phrases. In an example like *I am parked over there* (Radden & Kövecses 1999) the metonymy operates over the noun phrase *I*, consisting of a personal pronoun. We find here the opposite metonymic pattern, CONTROLLER FOR

CONTROLLED, which guides the inference of the speaker's CAR as the intended referent of the NP, in a conversation taking place for example in the street or at a parking place.

Apart from the other important discourse functions of metonymy mentioned in the first section, referential metonymies are instrumental in achieving *referential coherence* (i.e., they help hearers/readers to keep track of the intended referents throughout an extended piece of discourse; see, e.g., Barcelona 2005, 2007b). These metonymies guide inferencing to the intended referent. Referential metonymies are often at the same time instrumental in achieving *relational coherence* (i.e., the conceptual connections among the various sentences in a discourse: cause-effect, exemplification, condition-result, elaboration, justification, etc.).[7] Referential metonymies often serve this purpose by chaining to other non-referential metonymies (Barcelona 2005, 2007a, 2007b). An example (borrowed and adapted from Radden 2000 and analyzed in Barcelona 2005) is this conversation:

> A: *How much gas did you buy?*
> B: *I filled 'er up*

The inferences by A that B filled the *gas tank* and that (s)he filled it with the *maximum amount* that the tank could hold are guided, among other factors, by the referential metonymy CAR FOR GAS TANK (WHOLE FOR ACTIVE ZONE PART)[8] and the non-referential metonymy UP FOR MOST (an instance of VERTICALITY FOR QUANTITY). The first of these metonymies is involved in referential coherence (it applies to an anaphorical noun phrase) and also in relational coherence, since the correct identification of intended referents is often a prerequisite for achieving relational coherence, as in this case (establishing the gas tank of the car as the container that was filled up is a prerequisite for making the response coherent with the question and with A's normal expectations in terms of cooperative maxims).

SL learners could usefully be made aware of the main conceptual metonymies used referentially in the target language and they should, where possible, be provided with examples of how these are integrated in discourse.

Particular attention could be given to contrasts in the exploitation of the same metonymy by the learner's language and by the target language. Instances of these contrasts are found in Brdar & Brdar-Szabó's paper (2009) on the referential use of place names in English, German, Hungarian, and Croatian manifesting the metonymy CAPITAL FOR GOVERNMENT. These linguists claim, on the basis of corpus analysis, that this metonymy is very frequently expressed in English and German by means of referentially used place names, as in these two examples:

– Berlin *has long argued that it is unfair to eliminate safeguards such as poison pills if countries can retain multiple voting rights*
– *Ausserdem will* London *eine Liste von Staaten aufstellen, deren Rechtsordnung als "fair" gilt* ('London also wants to make a list of countries whose legal systems count as "fair"').

In Croatian and Hungarian this metonymy is less frequently expressed by means of bare noun phrases, whereas prepositional or adpositional phrases, or phrases with attributive adjectives are often used to express it. Brdar & Brdar-Szabó hold that these phrases are full-blown linguistic referential metonymies. The preference for these phrases is due to cognitive, discourse-pragmatic (to maintain topic continuity) and cultural factors.

A metonymy which can be used referentially in English and Spanish is SALIENT/CHARACTERISTIC PROPERTY FOR ENTITY, which accounts for instances such as *el botones* (Spanish) in the sentence *Que el botones de una sucursal bancaria en Águilas alcance la presidencia del Banco Central, quiere decir mucho* ('It is a highly significant fact that the bellboy of the Aguilas branch of the Central Bank was able to become the president of the Bank').[9] The reason why the noun *botones* 'buttons' designates a hotel porter is that this type of employee used to wear a uniform prominently exhibiting a set of buttons (the noun *buttons* was also used for the same purpose in English, but it is today virtually obsolete).

However SALIENT/CHARACTERISTIC PROPERTY FOR ENTITY is not exploited in exactly the same way in both languages (this seems to be the case with most of the conceptual metonymies shared cross-linguistically). In American English, a different "salient property" is used to name and refer to these employees: the fact that they used to be summoned by the hotel's front desk clerk by ringing a bell, which made them "hop", i.e., jump to attention at the desk to receive instructions; hence the American English terms *bellboy* and *bellhop* to designate this type of employees. A further example is the use of *The Continental Divide* as a phrase (actually as a name) referring to the *Rocky Mountains* (Barcelona 2009; in preparation a), as in the sentence *If you have ever driven west on Interstate 70 from Denver to the Continental Divide, you have seen Mount Bethel* (see http://hikingincolorado.org/beth.html). This use of the phrase is motivated by the metonymy: SALIENT PROPERTY OF AN ENTITY (FUNCTION AS CONTINENTAL BASIN DIVIDE) FOR THE ENTITY (THE ROCKY MOUNTAINS). This metonymy operates within the NORTH AMERICAN GEOGRAPHY FRAME. Familiarity with this frame and knowledge of the "basin divide" role of that mountain range in that frame is essential for learners of English as a second language to understand this metonymic act of reference.

Metonymy is often involved in anaphora resolution, especially in instances of what has been called "indirect anaphora" (Emmott 1997), i.e., sentences in which the real antecedent of an anaphor is not explicitly mentioned in the preceding co-text and has to be inferred on the basis of other contextual clues and background knowledge. One of the most powerful cognitive devices guiding this inferential activity is metonymy. An example already discussed above was the petrol station one, where the conceptual antecedent (the GAS TANK) of *her* was metonymically accessed from THE CAR. Let us see some more examples below.

Langacker (1999: ch 7 and 9; 2009) claims that the only real factors constraining anaphora are conceptual rather than syntactic. He discusses instances in which the intended antecedent of the anaphor is a metonymic target of a concept (which he calls a "referent point") in the mental space currently active discursively. In *He speaks excellent* French *even though he's never lived there*, the intended antecedent of the anaphorical place adverbial *there* (which in principle should be a locative noun phrase) is the metonymic target of *French* (i.e., France). The metonymy guiding the inference of that antecedent is a PART (LANGUAGE) FOR WHOLE (COUNTRY) metonymy. Metonymy is involved in other types of indirect anaphora, including "bridging inferences" (Clark 1977): *I saw a wonderful car in the street. The steering wheel was made of ivory.* The NP *the steering wheel* is definite due to its metonymic connection to the referent already introduced by *a wonderful car*. The steering wheel can only be the one of the car just mentioned; hence it is a unique referent in this context. This inference is guided by the metonymy WHOLE [CAR] FOR PART [STEERING WHEEL]. Ruiz de Mendoza & Díez Velasco (2004) have suggested some principles that explain the selection of the anaphorical pronoun (cf. *The ham sandwich left because he/\*it didn't like the ambience*), the most important of which is the "Domain Availability Principle", which stipulates that the anaphorical pronoun must be consistent with the domain currently active, i.e., the "customer ordering and eating the ham sandwich".

It would be interesting and useful to study systematically the cross-linguistic differences in the selection of anaphorical pronouns for metonymically inferred antecedents. In the previous examples of indirect anaphora, the identification of the antecedent is not really problematic for a speaker of Spanish, but it may be problematic for speakers of other languages. Cultural, contextual, or language-specific factors may hinder the inference of the intended referent. The intended referent of the anaphorical noun phrase *the conference suits* in the text fragment *If the conference suits aren't worried, there are certainly some who are. Count N.C. State's Tom O'Brien among them* will readily be understood by a British or American speaker, but perhaps not as readily by a Spanish learner of English, who might need to have the metonymic connection between the USUAL OUTWEAR and its WEARERS explicitly pointed out to them.[10]

*Metonymy as a motivation for metaphor*
On this topic, see Barcelona (2000b, in preparation b) and Radden (2000, 2002): metonymy has been claimed by these and other linguists to motivate a great many metaphors, i.e., to connect them to their experiential bases.

According to Barcelona (2000b), two major types of metonymic motivation of metaphor can be discerned:

A.   *abstraction of a common conceptual structure between metaphoric source and target*
This abstraction occurs when both the metaphoric target and the metaphoric source are conceptualized metonymically from the *same* "subdomain". In an example like *That's a loud color,* the metaphor licensing the combination of *loud* with *color* can be called DEVIANT COLORS ARE DEVIANT SOUNDS. This metaphor is possible thanks to the abstraction of a common "subdomain", namely the effect on perceivers of both deviant colors and of deviant, "loud" sounds. This effect is that of "attracting irresistibly the perceiver's attention". The abstraction of this common subdomain is due to the conceptually prior metonymic understanding of both DEVIANT COLORS and DEVIANT SOUNDS (as metonymic targets) from their typical effect, ATTRACTING THE PERCEIVER'S ATTENTION (as metonymic source).

In a near compound like *acorn cup*, the metaphoric understanding of the lower part of this fruit as a CUP is motivated by the conceptually prior metonymic understanding both of CUPS and the relevant part of ACORNS in terms of their SHAPE (see Dirven 1985).

B.   *generalization or decontextualization of a metonymy*
The well-known metaphors MORE IS UP/LESS IS DOWN (as manifested by countless examples like *The high cost of living/Skyrocketing prices/A low level of intelligence,* etc.) is in fact the result of the decontextualization of the metonymy LEVEL OF VERTICALITY FOR QUANTITY. This metonymy is in turn due to the frequent experiential association of LEVEL OF VERTICALITY with QUANTITY in POURING or HEAPING events. When LEVEL OF VERTICALITY is used to denote QUANTITY in contexts where no real verticality is involved, the metonymy has been decontextualized and becomes a metaphor. Take *A low level of intelligence*: intelligence is not a spatial object that can be measured in terms of spatial verticality.

These two types of metonymic motivation show that metonymy-guided reasoning often underlies the emergence, understanding (and often the further exploitation) of conceptual metaphors.

It may be convenient to use materials and stimuli (say images or linguistic contexts) suggesting to the students the metonymic basis of a number of basic metaphors. Indeed, it has been found by Piquer-Píriz (2008a, 2008b) that young children (even at the age of 5) who are acquiring metaphorical senses of body-part terms like *hand, mouth* or *head* often engage spontaneously in metonymic reasoning to infer the metaphorical senses in context. For example, when asked by the researcher (in the qualitative part of the study) why he had chosen the correct meaning of *the head of the stairs* in a test, a 5-year old pupil answered:

> Pupil (P) *porque es el final de la escalera.*
> Researcher (R): *y eso ¿qué tiene que ver con 'head'?*
> P: *que es el final de la escalera — está arriba del cuerpo.*[11]

This reply manifests metonymic reasoning motivating metaphor as in A above, i.e., by understanding both the metaphorical source HEAD and the metaphorical target STAIRS from a common subdomain or property (TOP POSITION IN VERTICAL PHYSICAL ENTITY).

Metonymy-based metaphors appear to be frequent in certain types of discourse, such as advertising (Ungerer 2000; Velasco-Sacristán 2005), and they seem to exhibit certain crosslinguistic contrasts (Ibarrretxe 2005, for verbs of perception).

*Reasoning in terms of metonymic category prototypes*
Lakoff (1987: ch 5) was one of the first linguists to point out that a great many category models are organized around a metonymy-based prototype. A "prototype" is a model which provides the "best example" or one of the best examples of the category, so that people understand the whole category in terms of that model; for example the naive category BIRD is understood in terms of the degree of similarity of category members to the prototypes, which in English are the robin or the sparrow, rather than the parrot or the ostrich.

There are categories which are not organized around metonymy-based prototypes, but those which are were called by Lakoff *metonymic models*. In a metonymic model, the prototype is a subcategory connected to the whole category by metonymy. The metonymies organizing these models are normally *invisible metonymies*, since in most cases they do not directly motivate specific linguistic forms; rather they motivate the whole cognitive model. Metonymic models, like all other cognitive models, govern aspects of our reasoning and our comprehension of discourse (especially in pragmatic inferencing). An example is the "social stereotype" of BACHELORS (Lakoff 1987: ch 5); this social stereotype projects metonymically the licentious behavior of a subset of all bachelors, in such expressions as *bachelor party*. A further example is Feyaerts' (1999) study, mentioned above, of the German metonymic model for STUPIDITY. For psycholinguistic studies on the role of metonymy in cognitive models, see Gibbs (1994, 1999, 2007).

These instances of reasoning in terms of metonymic prototypes are often not wholly conventional cross-culturally. Therefore, some awareness of their special metonymic nature may be convenient for second language learners.

**Conclusions: Implications of metonymy research for second language learning and teaching**
In her chapter on metonymy and SLA, Littlemore (2009: 118ff.) discusses a number of challenges presented to SL learners by metonymy and six ways to help learners with metonymy (ibid: 120–123). In the previous paragraphs, I have been suggesting some specific possible applications to SLA of this research on metonymy. It is now time to bring all of them together in a series of general suggestions, which are complementary to Littlemore's:

*Raise learners' awareness of the ubiquity of metonymy-guided inferencing*
The benefits for SLA of awareness-raising with respect to conceptual metaphor are amply documented (see references in Section 1, especially Boers 2004 and Boers & Lindstromberg 2008). Likewise, raising the learners' awareness of the role of metonymic inferencing in communication and in concept-formation may be beneficial for SLA. Learners may be made aware of these basic notions by means of very simple, brief explanations and illustrations avoiding technical language, perhaps by means of initial exercises in associative thinking (in their mother tongue) like "Why do you think we refer to someone as "a forward" (in soccer)", or why do we call certain musicians "the sax", or "the bass guitar"? Then similar questions might be asked about other simple metonymy-based referring expressions in the mother tongue the learners are already familiar with, or about simple instances of conventionalized pragmatic inferencing like routine indirect speech acts (*Could you open the window?*).

*Use adequate contexts with metonymy triggers*
When introducing new (more complex or unfamiliar) instances of metonymic inferencing, the materials used to present them must be contextually rich, so that they will contain the main conceptual,

cultural and general contextual factors triggering the metonymies guiding the inferential process. These factors I call *metonymy triggers* (Barcelona, in preparation a). As an example, take the meaning "motivated, positive-thinking civil servants, who are thus prepared to act" of the metonymic expression *'can do' civil servants* occurring in a listening comprehension exercise (Littlemore 2009: 118). If the exercise were accompanied by visual or textual support including a rich metonymy trigger such as a picture of a civil servant with the thought balloon "I want to work, I always think positive, so I *can* do my job properly", learners would be more likely to recall the meaning of this expression. This trigger explicitly presents the whole metonymic inferential pathway.

In other cases, the trigger may be more indirect. It may be enough, for instance, to show a picture of *Manolete* (a bullfighting paragon) with the legend "Manolete was one of Spain's greatest bullfighters") next to a text including the sentence like *Juanito es un nuevo Manolete* ('Juanito is a new Manolete, i.e., a great bullfighter') to activate the metonymy-based understanding of this sentence by an English learner of Spanish as a paragon use of the name *Manolete*.

*Explain language- or culture-specific barriers*
It may sometimes be necessary to explain the language-specific grammatical factors or the culture-specific cognitive models (frames, scripts) that facilitate the use of a metonymy, or a particular version of it, in one language (typically the learner's mother tongue) and block or limit its use in another language (especially the target language).

*Stimulate metonymy-guided reasoning*
As suggested above, exploiting the metonymic connections within one frame and across distant domains could be a useful approach in language teaching settings. Take the FARMING frame, with metonymic connections across such taxonomically distant domains as PEOPLE, ANIMALS, TOOLS, BUILDINGS, PLANTS, FOOD, COMBUSTION, etc. Since each of these domains constitute generic prompts (Panther 2006) for their metonymic targets (e.g., people are metonymically connected to farm animals as shepherds, owners, buyers), the exploitation of these connections might constitute an enjoyable preparatory activity (and an opportunity for vocabulary-building) before a descriptive composition on farm life by the learners.

Similarly, the ubiquity of what Langacker (e.g., 2009) calls active zones (many, though not all of them metonymic; see Peirsman & Geeraerts in preparation) might be usefully exploited to stimulate metonymic thinking. In Langacker's (1993: 33) well-known example *Zelda began a novel*, the NP *a novel* stands metonymically for its "active zone" with respect to Zelda's action of beginning the novel. That active zone is the unmentioned relationship "write/read, *etc.* a novel", that is, an activity in which the metonymized direct object is involved.[12] An amusing exercise might consist in asking students to suggest what exactly Zelda began doing with the novel depending on the job/role chosen for her from a list (writer, reader, book binder, cover designer, bookseller, printer, etc.).

*Exploit the metonymic motivation of certain basic metaphors*
This is particularly advisable when the conceptual metaphor has a different linguistic realization in the target language (which is symptomatic of a different conceptual elaboration or exploitation). This may help learners to understand those differences more easily. For instance, the metonymic basis of the synaesthetic metaphor DEVIANT COLORS ARE DEVIANT SOUNDS commented on above, can easily be pointed out by means of two contiguous images of the same person, one in which she is being affected by a strong sound (say, a drum in the same room) and the legend 'She couldn't help noticing the loud music'; and another in which she is talking to someone wearing a gaudy-colored jacket, and the legend 'She couldn't help noticing his loud jacket'.

Although there have to date been no studies of the benefits of an explicit focus on metonymy in the language classroom, it may well help learners to both understand and use creative instances of the target language. Further research is required to establish whether this is or is not the case.

## Notes

1. Source:   http://www.telegraph.co.uk/finance/newsbysector/banksandfinance/3497672/Downing-Street-refuses-to-rule-out-nationalising-banks-over-business-lending.html. Accessed July 29, 2010 at 7:26 p.m.

2. In CL, grammatical constructions are conventional pairings of form and meaning (including all sorts of meaning: strictly semantic, pragmatic and stylistic), which range from morphemes to sentences (Goldberg 2006).

3. I thank my wife, Dr Marta Manchado López, for drawing my attention to the metonymic basis of this example.

4. On uttering the word *pulpo*, the neighbour looks at the pretty wife as a *pulpo* would (in a metaphorical sense of this word in Spanish, i.e., as a male fond of touching and hugging all sorts of women, including married ones).

5. The classification derives from how the concept of possession is encoded: An English sentence such as *John has two children* would have to be rendered in Japanese as "At/To John are two children".

6. Other useful research on metonymy and indirect speech acts (apart from the references mentioned above) is Brdar & Bdrar-Szabó (2003), Bdrar-Szabó (2007, 2009), and other papers in Panther & Thornburg (2003a). Some of these papers, especially those by Brdar & Bdrar-Szabó and Bdrar-Szabó are very relevant from a crosslinguistic perspective and very relevant for SLA. Space limitation prevents me from discussing them here.

7. These connections, when not explicitly marked linguistically are often inferred (implicatures) with the help of metonymies (referential or purely inferential; see the sub-section on purely inferential metonymies). For the notions of referential and relational coherence see Dirven & Verspoor (1998: ch. 8).

8. The car is referred to metaphorically by means of (h)er.

9. Aguilas is a small town in Spain. The text is the opening sentence of the newspaper article "El botones" ('The bellboy') by Alfonso Ussia, published in the Spanish newspaper *La Razón* on May 21, 2010. Downloaded from http://www.larazon.es/noticia/1033-el-botones, accessed July 30, 2010.

10. The larger co-text might help these learners, but since this particular version of the USUAL OUTWEAR FOR WEARER metonymy is not conventionally applied to executives in Spanish, the learner will still have to be explicitly taught this metonymic use of *the suits*. The above fragment is part of this larger fragment *Both Britton Banowsky, the commissioner of Conference USA, and Nick Carperelli, the associate commissioner for football for the Big East Conference, argued that the SEC's new TV deal is a good thing for college sports. Neither said they expected their conferences to be adversely affected. (…) If the conference suits aren't worried, there are certainly some who are. Count N.C. State's Tom O'Brien among them.* (Downloaded from http://ncaabbs.com/showthread.php?tid=377310. Accessed July 30, 2010.)

11. Tranlation into English:

P: because it's the end of the staircase
R: and what's that got to do with 'head'?
P: 'cos it's the end of the stairs — it's on top of the body

12. Note that the same metonymy would also explain the propositional or relational use of the same NP in a sentence like *A novel would be an excellent idea*, in which the NP, depending of the discourse context might indistinctly refer to writing, reading, buying, binding, filming, etc. a novel.

## References

Achard, M. & Niemeier, S. (eds). 2004. *Cognitive Linguistics, Second Language Acquisition, and Foreign Language Teaching.* Berlin: Mouton de Gruyter.

Attardo, S. 1990. The violation of Grice's maxims in jokes. In *Proceedings of the 16th Annual Meeting of the Berkeley Linguistics Society,* K. Hall, J.P. Koenig, M. Meacham, S. Reinman & L.A. Sutton (eds), 355–362. Berkeley CA: Berkeley Linguistics Society.

Barcelona, A. (ed.). 2000a. *Metaphor and Metonymy at the Crossroads. A Cognitive Perspective.* Berlin: Mouton de Gruyter.

Barcelona, A. 2000b. On the plausibility of claiming a metonymic motivation for conceptual metaphor. In *Metaphor and Metonymy at the Crossroads. A Cognitive Perspective,* Barcelona, A. (ed.), 31–58. Berlin: Mouton de Gruyter.

Barcelona, A. 2001. On the systematic contrastive analysis of conceptual metaphors. Case studies and proposed methodology. In *Applied Cognitive Linguistics,* II: *Language Pedagogy,* M. Pütz, S. Niemeier & R. Dirven, R. (eds), 117–146. Berlin: Mouton de Gruyter.

Barcelona, A. 2002a. Clarifying and applying the notions of metaphor and metonymy within cognitive linguistics: An update. In *Metaphor and Metonymy in Comparison and Contrast,* R. Dirven & R. Pörings (eds), 207–277. Berlin: Mouton de Gruyter.

Barcelona, A. 2002b. On the ubiquity and multiple-level operation of metonymy. In *Cognitive Linguistics Today,* B. Lewandowska-Tomaszczyk & K. Turewicz (eds), 207–224. Frankfurt: Peter Lang.

Barcelona, A. 2003a. Metonymy in cognitive linguistics. An analysis and a few modest proposals. In *Motivation in Language: Studies in Honor of Günter Radden,* H. Cuyckens, K.-U. Panther & T. Berg (eds), 223–255. Amsterdam: John Benjamins.

Barcelona, A. 2003b. The case for a metonymic basis of pragmatic inferencing: Evidence from jokes and funny anecdotes. In *Metonymy and Pragmatic Inferencing,* K. Panther & L. Thornburg (eds), 81–102. Amsterdam: John Benjamins.

Barcelona, A. 2003c. Names: A metonymic return ticket. *Jezikoslovlje* 4(1): 11–41.

Barcelona, A. 2004. Metonymy behind grammar: The motivation of the seemingly "irregular" grammatical behavior of English paragon names. In *Motivation in Grammar,* G. Radden & K.-U. Panther (eds), 357–374. Amsterdam: John Benjamins.

Barcelona, A. 2005. The multilevel operation of metonymy in grammar and discourse with particular attention to metonymic chains. In *Cognitive Linguistics: Internal Dynamics and Interdisciplinary Interaction,* F.J. Ruiz de Mendoza Ibáñez & S. Peña Cervel (eds), 313–352. Berlin: Mouton de Gruyter.

Barcelona, A. 2007a. The multilevel role of metonymy in grammar and discourse: A case study. In *Perspectives on Metonymy,* K. Kosecki (ed.), 103–131. Berlin: Peter Lang.

Barcelona, A. 2007b. The role of metonymy in meaning at discourse level: A case study. In *Aspects of Meaning Construction,* G. Radden, K.-M. Köpcke, T. Berg & P. Siemund (eds), 51–75. Amsterdam: John Benjamins.

Barcelona, A. 2009. Metonymy in construction meaning and form: Its motivational and inferential roles. In *Metonymy and Metaphor in Grammar,* K.-U. Panther, L. Thornburg & A. Barcelona (eds), 363–401. Amsterdam: John Benjamins.

Barcelona, A. In preparation a. *On the Pervasive Role of Metonymy in Constructional Meaning and Structure in Discourse Comprehension: An Empirical Study from a Cognitive-Linguistic Perspective.* Berlin: Mouton de Gruyter.

Barcelona, A. In preparation b. Reviewing the properties of metonymy as a technical construct, with particular attention to the view of metonymy as a prototype category. In *What Is Metonymy? An Attempt at Building a Consensus View on the Delimitation of the Notion of Metonymy in Cognitive Linguistics,* R. Benczes, A. Barcelona & F. Ruiz de Mendoza (eds). (Submitted for publication).

Benczes, R., Barcelona, A. & Ruiz de Mendoza, F. (eds). In preparation. *What Is Metonymy? An Attempt at Building a Consensus View on the Delimitation of the Notion of Metonymy in Cognitive Linguistics.* (Submitted for publication).

Boers, F. 2004. Expanding learners' vocabulary through metaphor awareness: what expansion, what learners, what vocabulary? In *Cognitive Linguistics, Second Language Acquisition, and Foreign Language Teaching*, M. Achard & S. Niemeier (eds), 211–234. Berlin: Mouton de Gruyter.

Boers, F. & Lindstromberg, S. (eds). 2008. *Cognitive Linguistic Approaches to Teaching Vocabulary and Phraseology*. Berlin: Mouton de Gruyter.

Brdar, M. 2007a. When Zidane is not simply Zidane, and Bill Gates is not just Bill Gates: Some thoughts on the construction of metaphtonymic meanings. In *Aspects of Meaning Construction*, G. Radden, K.-M. Köpcke, T. Berg & P. Siemund (eds) 125–142. Amsterdam: John Benjamins.

Brdar, M. 2007b. *Metonymy in Grammar. Towards Motivating Extensions of Grammatical Categories and Constructions*. Osijek: Josip Juraj Strossmayer University.

Brdar, M. & Brdar-Szabó, R. 2003. Metonymic coding of linguistic action in English, Croatian and Hungarian. In *Metonymy and Pragmatic Inferencing*, K.-U. Panther & L. Thornburg (eds), 241–266. Amsterdam: John Benjamins.

Brdar, M. & Brdar-Szabó, R. 2009. The (non-)metonymic use of place names in English, German, Hungarian, and Croatian. In *Metonymy and Metaphor in Grammar*, K.-U. Panther, L. Thornburg & A. Barcelona (eds), 229–257. Amsterdam: John Benjamins.

Brdar-Szabó, R. 2007. The role of metonymy in motivating cross-linguistic differences in the exploitation of stand-alone conditionals as indirect directives. In *Perspectives on Metonymy*, K. Kosecki (ed.), 175–197. Berlin: Peter Lang.

Brdar-Szabó, R. 2009. Metonymy in indirect directives: Stand-alone conditionals in English, German, Hungarian, and Croatian. In *Metonymy and Metaphor in Grammar*, K.-U. Panther, L. Thornburg& A. Barcelona (eds), 323–336. Amsterdam: John Benjamins.

Ciepiela, K. 2007. Metonymy in Aphasia — In *Perspectives on Metonymy*, K. Kosecki (ed.), 199–208. Berlin: Peter Lang.

Clark, H.H. 1977. Bridging. In *Thinking: Readings in Cognitive Science*, P.N. Johnson-Laird & P.-C. Wason (eds), 411–420. Cambridge: CUP.

Clark, H.H. 1978. Inferring what is meant. In *Studies in the Perception of Language*, W.J.M. Levelt & G.B. Flores D'Arcais (eds), 295–332. Chichester: John Wyley.

Croft, W. 2002[1993]. The role of domains in the interpretation of metaphors and metonymies. In *Metaphor and Metonymy in Comparison and Contrast*, R. Dirven & R. Pörings (eds), 161–205. Berlin: Mouton de Gruyter. (Reproduced with slight changes from the paper with the same title in *Cognitive Linguistics* 4(4): 335–371).

Darmester, A. 1932. *La vie des mots étudiée dans leurs significations*. Paris: Librairie Delagrave.

Dirven, R. 1985. Metaphor as a basic means of extending the lexicon. In *The Ubiquity of Metaphor. Metaphor in Language and Thought*, W. Paprotté & R. Dirven (eds), 85–120. Amsterdam: John Benjamins.

Dirven, R. 1999. Conversion as a conceptual metonymy of event schemata. In *Metonymy in Language and Thought*, K.-U. Panther & G. Radden (eds), 275–287. Amsterdam: John Benjamins.

Dirven, R. 2002. Metonymy and metaphor: Different strategies of conceptualisation. In *Metaphor and Metonymy in Comparison and Contrast*, R. Dirven & R. Pörings (eds), 75–112. Berlin: Mouton de Gruyter.

Dirven, R. & Pörings, R. (eds). 2002. *Metaphor and Metonymy in Comparison and Contrast*. Berlin: Mouton de Gruyter.

Dirven, R. & Verspoor, M. 1998. *Cognitive Exploration of Language and Linguistics*. Amsterdam: John Benjamins.

Dzeren-Glówacka, S. 2007. Beating up intelligence: Metonymy in Terry Pratchett's novels. In *Perspectives on Metonymy*, K. Kosecki (ed.), 335–348. Berlin: Peter Lang.

Emmott, C. 1998. Embodied in a constructed world: Narrative processing, knowledge representation, and indirect anaphora. In *Discourse Studies in Cognitive Linguistics*, K. van Hoek, A. Kibrik & L. Noordman (eds), 5–29. Amsterdam: John Benjamins.

Fass, D. 1997. *Processing Metonymy and Metaphor*. Greenwich CT: Ablex.

Fauconnier, G. 1994. *Mental Spaces: Aspects of Meaning Construction in Natural Language*. Cambridge: CUP.

Fauconnier, G. 1997. *Mappings in Thought and Language*. Cambridge: CUP.

Fauconnier, G. n.d. How compression gives rise to metaphor and metonymy. A paper presented at the 9th Conference on Conceptual Structure, Discourse, and Language (CSDL9) held at Case Western Reserve University, Cleveland, Ohio, October 18–20, 2008.

Feyaerts, K. 1999. Metonymic hierarchies. The conceptualization of stupidity in German idiomatic expressions. In *Metonymy in Language and Thought*, K.-U. Panther & G. Radden (eds), 309–334. Amsterdam: John Benjamins.

Gibbs, R.W., Jr. 1994. *The Poetics of Mind. Figurative Thought, Language, and Understanding*. Cambridge: CUP.

Gibbs, R.W. Jr. 1999. Speaking and thinking with metonymy. In *Metonymy in Language and Thought*, K.-U. Panther & G. Radden (eds), 61–76. Amsterdam: John Benjamins.

Gibbs, R.W. Jr. 2007. Experiential tests of figurative meaning construction. In *Aspects of Meaning Construction*, G. Radden, K.-M. Köpcke, T. Berg & P. Siemund (eds), 19–32. Amsterdam: John Benjamins.

Goldberg, A. 2006. *Constructions at Work. The Nature of Generalization in Language*. Oxford: OUP.

Goossens, L. 2002[1990]. Metaphtonymy: The interaction of metaphor and metonymy in expressions for linguistic action. In *Metaphor and Metonymy in Comparison and Contrast*, R. Dirven & R. Pörings (eds), 349–377. Berlin: Mouton de Gruyter. (Reproduced with slight changes from the paper with the same title in *Cognitive Linguistics* 1(3): 323–340).

Goossens, L., Pauwels, P., Rudzka-Ostyn, B., Simon-Vanderbergen, A.-M. & Vanparys, J. 1995. *By Word of Mouth. Metaphor, Metonymy and Linguistic Action in a Cognitive Perspective*. Amsterdam: John Benjamins.

Heine, B., Claudi, U. & Hünnemeyer, F. 1991. *Grammaticalization. A Conceptual Framework*. Chicago IL: University of Chicago Press.

Hilpert, M. 2007. Chained metonymies in lexicon and grammar: A cross-linguistic perspective on body terms. In *Aspects of Meaning Construction*, G. Radden, K.-M. Köpcke, T. Berg & P. Siemund (eds), 77–98. Amsterdam: John Benjamins.

Holme, R. 2004. *Mind, Metaphor and Language Teaching*. Basingstoke: Palgrave Macmillan.

Holme, R. 2009. *Cognitive Linguistics and Language Teaching*. Basingstoke: Palgrave Macmillan.

Hopper P. & Closs-Traugott, E. 1993. *Grammaticalization*. Cambridge: CUP.

Ibarretxe, I. 2005. Limitations for crosslinguistic metonymies and metaphors. In *Cognitive and Discourse Approaches to Metaphor and Metonymy*, J.L. Otal Campo, I. Navarro i Ferrando & B. Bellés Fortuño (eds), 157–173. Castelló: Universitat Jaume I.

Kosecki, K. (ed.) 2007. *Perspectives on Metonymy*. Berlin: Peter Lang.

Kövecses, Z. & Szabó, P. 1996. Idioms: A view from cognitive semantics. *Applied Linguistics* 17(3): 326–355.

Kövecses, Z. & Radden, G. 1998. Metonymy: Developing a cognitive linguistic view. *Cognitive Linguistics* 9(1): 37–77.

Kuzniak, M. 2007. Part-whole relations in the selected epigrams by J. Staudynger. In *Perspectives on Metonymy*, K. Kosecki (ed.), 323–333. Berlin: Peter Lang.

Kwiatkowska, A. 2007. Pre-linguistic and non-linguistic metonymy. In *Perspectives on Metonymy*, K. Kosecki (ed.), 297–307. Berlin: Peter Lang.

Lakoff, G. & Johnson, M. 1980. *Metaphors we Live by*. Chicago IL: University of Chicago Press.

Lakoff, G. 1987. *Women, Fire and Dangerous Things. What Categories Reveal About the Mind*. Chicago IL: University of Chicago Press.

Langacker, R.W. 1987. *Foundations of Cognitive Grammar*, Vol 1: *Theoretical Prerequisites*. Stanford CA: Stanford University Press.

Langacker, R.W. 1993. Reference-point constructions, *Cognitive Linguistics* 4: 1–38.

Langacker, R.W. 1999. *Grammar and Conceptualization*. Berlin: Mouton de Gruyter.

Langacker, R W. 2009. Metonymic grammar, In *Metonymy and Metaphor in Grammar*, K.-U. Panther, L. Thornburg & A. Barcelona (eds), 45–71. Amsterdam: John Benjamins.

Littlemore, J. 2009. *Applying Cognitive Linguistics to Second Language Learning and Teaching*. Basingstoke: Palgrave Macmillan.

Littlemore, J. & MacArthur, F. 2007. What do learners need to know about the figurative extensions of target language words? A contrastive, corpus-based analysis of thread, hilar, wing and aletear. *Language, Culture and Representation* 5: 133–155.

MacArthur, F. & Littlemore, J. 2008. A discovery approach to figurative language learning with the use of corpora. In *Cognitive Linguistic Approaches to Teaching Vocabulary and Phraseology*, F. Boers& S. Lindstromberg (eds), 159–188. Berlin: Mouton de Gruyter.

Nerlich, B. & Clarke, D. 2001. Serial metonymy. A study of reference-based polysemisation. *Journal of Historical Pragmatics* 2(2): 245–272.

Otal Campo, J.L., i Ferrando, I.N. & Bellés Fortuño, B. (eds). 2004. *Cognitive and Discourse Approaches to Metaphor and Metonymy*. Castelló: Universitat Jaume I.

Pang, K.-Y. 2010. Eponymy and life-narratives: The effect of foregrounding on proper names. *Journal of Pragmatics* 42(5): 1321–1349.

Pankhurst, A. 1999. Recontextualization of metonymy in narrative and the case of Morrison's *Song of Solomon*, in *Metonymy in Language and Thought*, K.-U. Panther & G. Radden (eds), 385–399. Amsterdam: John Benjamins.

Panther, K.U. 2005. The role of metonymy in meaning construction. In *Cognitive Linguistics: Internal Dynamics and Interdisciplinary Interaction*, F. Ruiz de Mendoza & S. Peña Cervel (eds), 353–386. Berlin: Mouton de Gruyter.

Panther, K.U. 2006. Metonymy as a usage event. In *Cognitive Linguistics: Current Applications and Future Perspectives*, G. Kristiansen, M. Achard, R. Dirven & F. Ruiz de Mendoza (eds) 147–186, Berlin: Mouton de Gruyter.

Panther, K.-U. & Radden, G. (eds). 1999. *Metonymy in Language and Thought*. Amsterdam: John Benjamins.

Panther, K.-U. & Thornburg, L. 1998. A cognitive approach to inferencing in conversation. *Journal of Pragmatics* 30: 755–769.

Panther, K.-U. & Thornburg, L. (eds). 2003a. *Metonymy and Pragmatic Inferencing*. Amsterdam: John Benjamins.

Panther, K.-U. & Thornburg, L. 2003b. Introduction: On the nature of conceptual metonymy. In *Metonymy and Pragmatic Inferencing*, K.-U. Panther & L. Thornburg (eds), 1–20. Amsterdam: John Benjamins.

Panther, K.-U. & Thornburg, L. 2007. Metonymy. In *Handbook of Cognitive Linguistics*, D. Geeraerts & H. Cuyckens (eds), 236–263. Oxford: OUP.

Panther, K.-U., Thornburg, L. & Barcelona, A. (eds). 2009. *Metonymy and Metaphor in Grammar*. Amsterdam/Philadelphia: John Benjamins.

Pauwels, P. (1999) Putting metonymy in its place. In *Metonymy in Language and Thought*, K.-U. Panther & G. Radden (eds), 255–272. Amsterdam: John Benjamins.

Peirsman, Y. & Geeraerts, D. In preparation. Zones, facets and prototype-based metonymy. In R. Benczes, A. Barcelona & F. Ruiz de Mendoza (eds).

Pérez Hernández, L. 2007. High-level metonymies in the understanding of modality. In *Perspectives on Metonymy*, K. Kosecki (ed.), 133–146. Berlin: Peter Lang.

Piquer-Píriz, A.M. 2008a. Reasoning figuratively in early EFL: Some implications for the development of vocabulary. In *Cognitive Linguistic Approaches to Teaching Vocabulary and Phraseology*, F. Boers & S. Lindstromberg (eds), 219–240. Berlin: Mouton de Gruyter.

Piquer-Píriz, A.M. 2008b. Young learners' understanding of figurative language. In *Confronting Metaphor in Use: An Applied Linguistic Approach* M.S. Zanotto, L. Cameron & M.C. Calvacanti (eds), 183–198. Amsterdam: John Benjamins.

Pluciennik, J. 2007. Princess Antonomasia, individualism, and the quixotism of culture: A case of 'Tristram Shandy' by Laurence Sterne. In *Perspectives on Metonymy*, K. Kosecki (ed.), 349–366. Berlin: Peter Lang.

Radden, G. 2000. How metonymic are metaphors? In *Metaphor and Metonymy at the Crossroads. Cognitive Approaches*, A. Barcelona (ed.), 93–108. Berlin: Mouton de Gruyter.

Radden, G. 2002. How metonymic are metaphors? In *Metaphor and Metonymy in Comparison and Contrast*, R. Dirven & R. Pörings (eds), 407–434. Berlin: Mouton de Gruyter.

Radden, G. & Kövecses, Z. 1999. Towards a theory of metonymy. In *Metonymy in Language and Thought*, K.-U. Panther & G. Radden (eds), 17–59. Amsterdam: John Benjamins.

Radden, G., Köpcke, K.-M., Berg, T. & Siemund, P. (eds). 2007. *Aspects of Meaning Construction*. Amsterdam: John Benjamins.

Radden, G. & Panther, K.-U. (eds). 2004a. *Studies in Linguistic Motivation*. Berlin: Mouton de Gruyter.

Radden, G. & Panther, K.-U. 2004b. Introduction: Reflections on motivation. In *Studies in Linguistic Motivation*, G. Radden & K.-U. Panther (eds), 2–46. Berlin: Mouton de Gruyter.

Radden, G. & Seto, K. 2003. Metonymic construals of shopping requests in HAVE- and BE-languages. In *Metonymy and Pragmatic Inferencing*, K.-U. Panther & L. Thornburg (eds), 223–239. Amsterdam: John Benjamins.

Ruiz de Mendoza, F. 2007. High-level cognitive models: In search of a unified framework for inferential and grammatical behaviour. In *Perspectives on Metonymy*, K. Kosecki (ed.), 11–30. Berlin: Peter Lang.

Ruiz de Mendoza, F. & Pérez Hernández, L. (2001). Metonymy and the grammar: motivation, constraints and interaction. *Language and Communication* 21(4): 321–357.

Ruiz de Mendoza, F. & Díez Velasco, O. 2002. Patterns of conceptual interaction. In *Metaphor and Metonymy in Comparison and Contrast*, R. Dirven & R. Pörings, (eds), 489–532. Berlin: Mouton de Gruyter.

Ruiz de Mendoza, F. & Otal Campo, J.L. 2002. *Metonymy, Grammar and Communication*. Albolote: Comares.

Ruiz de Mendoza, F. & Díez Velasco, O. 2004. Metonymic motivation in anaphoric reference. In *Linguistic Motivation*, G. Radden & K..-U. Panther (eds), 293–320. Berlin: Mouton de Gruyter.

Ruiz de Mendoza, F. & Peña Cervel, S. (eds). 2005. *Cognitive Linguistics: Internal Dynamics and Interdisciplinary Interaction*. Berlin: Mouton de Gruyter.

Saeed, J.I. 1997. *Semantics*. Oxford: Blackwell.

Sliwa, D. 2007. Metonymic inferences related to the compound noun "public opinion". In *Perspectives on Metonymy*, K. Kosecki (ed.), 289–294. Berlin: Peter Lang.

Stern, G. 1931. *Meaning and Change of Meaning*. Göteborg: Eladers boktryckeri Aktiebolag.

Tang, P. 2007. Figurative Language in a Nursery Setting and a Non-native Speaker's Perspective on this Discourse Community. MA dissertation, University of Birmingham.

Taylor, J. 1995[1989]. *Linguistic Categorization. Prototypes in Linguistic Theory*. Oxford: Clarendon.

Thornburg, L. & Panther, K.-U. 1997. Speech act metonymies. In *Discourse and Perspective in Cognitive Linguistics*, W.-A. Liebert, G. Redeker & L. Waugh (eds), 205–219. Amsterdam: John Benjamins.

Traugott, E. & Dasher, R.B. 2002. *Regularity in Semantic Change*. Cambridge: CUP.

Ungerer, F. 2000. Muted metaphors and the activation of metonymies in advertising. In *Metaphor and Metonymy at the Crossroads. Cognitive Approaches*, A. Barcelona (ed.), 321–340. Berlin: Mouton de Gruyter.

Velasco Sacristán, M., Fuertes Olivera, P. & Samaniego Fernández, E. 2005. La metáforma cultural de género en el discurso publicitario: Ejemplo de proyección metafórica de origen metonímico. In *Cognitive and Discourse Approaches to Metaphor and Metonymy*, J.L. Otal Campo, I. Navarro i Ferrando & B. Bellés Fortuño (eds), 157–173. Castelló: Universitat Jaume I.

Vosshagen, C. 1999 Opposition as a metonymic principle. In *Metonymy in Language and Thought*, K.-U. Panther & G. Radden (eds), 289–308. Amsterdam: John Benjamins.

Warren, B. 1999. Aspects of referential metonymy. In *Metonymy in Language and Thought*, K.-U. Panther & G. Radden (eds), 121–135. Amsterdam: John Benjamins.

Wilcox, P.P. 2004. A cognitive key: Metonymic and metaphorical mappings in ASL. *Cognitive Linguistics* 15(2): 197–222.

Woo, H.J. 2008. Understanding Metaphor: Taiwanese Students and English Language Metaphor. MA dissertation, University of Birmingham.

*Author's address*

Department of English and German University of Córdoba
E-14071 Córdoba
Spain

antonio.barcelona@uco.es

# Metaphorical competence in EFL

Where are we and where should we be going?
A view from the language classroom

Fiona MacArthur
Universidad de Extremadura

> *And as imagination bodies forth*
> *The forms of things unknown, the poet's pen*
> *Turns them to shapes, and gives to airy nothing*
> *A local habitation and a name*
> Shakespeare, *A Midsummer Night's Dream*, 5.1.14–17

Although there exists a number of studies that have shown the benefits of applying the cognitive linguistics notion of motivation to foster comprehension and retention of conventional English metaphors, relatively little attention has been paid to EFL learners' productive use of metaphor in speech and writing. Using data gathered in a post-intermediate English language classroom, I describe and explore the metaphorical language used by undergraduate students in their writing. The data show that learners use metaphor to express their ideas on complex, abstract topics, but that the resulting metaphorical usage is not always conventional or felicitous. Since metaphor is deployed by EFL learners in response to particular communication demands, teachers need to find ways of providing appropriate feedback on learners' efforts to make use of their limited linguistic resources to express their own meanings. However, how effective feedback is to be given is not always straightforward. I discuss some of the problems involved and suggest areas that are in need of further research.

## Introduction

The late 1970s and early 1980s were marked by the publication of a number of seminal works (e.g., Lakoff & Johnson 1980; Langacker 1986, 1987; Ortony 1979; Talmy 1978) that fundamentally changed the way that many regarded language and the business of linguistics. The 'cognitive revolution' proposed a view of language that did not see it as modular or separated from cognition generally, but sought to explain the motivation of regularities and patterns in language behaviour through cognitive operations which were, to a large extent, seen as grounded or embodied in human experience (Barsalou 2008; Gibbs 2006). In this view, the study of language reveals more than itself, but rather provides a window into the way people think and the ways they construe the physical, social and cultural worlds they inhabit. Among the many important ways that language was discovered to reveal thought patterns was metaphor, in which primary experience, or physical and social interaction with the world, was seen to structure and facilitate reasoning and communication about many other concepts — many of them abstract (Lakoff & Johnson 1980; Lakoff 1987; Lakoff & Turner

*AILA Review* 23 (2010), 155–173. DOI 10.1075/aila.23.09mac
ISSN 1461–0213 / E-ISSN 1570–5595 © John Benjamins Publishing Company

1989: Reddy 1979). Metaphorical language use could thus reveal thought patterns, ideologies or the folk theories shared by communities of speakers.

Radical shifts in theory inevitably affect practice and it is not surprising that this view of language should have drawn the attention of applied linguists, some of whom, since the publication of Low's (1988) article on teaching metaphor, have been active in exploring the role of metaphor in foreign language teaching and learning. A steady stream of publications has appeared that have discussed the benefits of using the insights of cognitive linguistics and conceptual metaphor theory (CMT) to foreign language teaching, especially English (Kövecses & Szabo 1996; Kövecses 2001; Dirven 2001; MacArthur & Piquer Píriz 2007; Piquer Píriz 2008a,b; Queller 2001; Ungerer 2001; Tyler 2008, *inter alia*). However, much of this research has been concerned with how to help learners get to grips with the metaphors of the target language community, focusing attention on how best to aid comprehension and retention of conventional figurative language but saying little about how learners actually produce metaphors in their second language. For example, in the longest and most comprehensive work on metaphor and figurative thinking in foreign language teaching (FLT) to date (Littlemore & Low 2006a), the authors acknowledge that their failure to look at how learners use metaphor in their foreign language is a result of the paucity of research into this area, adding that 'foreign language learners probably need to understand metaphor more often than they need to produce it' (2006a: 46).

While acknowledging the need of learners to understand the metaphors used by native speakers, the view sustained in the present contribution is that they also need to produce them, and will do so under communicative pressure. In this regard, looking at learners' metaphoric productions and preferences may provide important insights into how the first (L1) and second language (L2) systems interact, how the privilege of access to two linguistic and conceptual systems may favour, rather than necessarily hinder, the bilingual's metaphoric production, and to what extent the resulting metaphors are felicitous in the context of inter-cultural communication. Although some initial forays have been made into this area (for example, Littlemore 2003; Chapetón Castro & Verdaguer Clavera, forthcoming), full understanding of these phenomena involves an extremely lengthy research programme, which is well beyond the scope of an article such as this. However, I hope to offer an initial exploration of some of the issues involved through examination of data I have gathered as teacher and participant-observer in an English language course I have taught for a number of years at a Spanish university. As will become clear, the data show that metaphors are used by non-native speakers (NNSs) of English, and the uses found often do not reproduce the forms and patterns observable in native speaker production (NSs). In turn, these novel or idiosyncratic metaphors require attention, if only because language teachers need to be able to give appropriate feedback on them. As will be seen, however, the necessary tools to do so are still lacking, suggesting that a great deal of work is still needed in the field of metaphor as it is used in real world communication, particularly when this communication involves people from different linguistic and cultural backgrounds.

The data used to illustrate the points raised in the course of this article, unless otherwise stated, were gathered between October 2009 and February 2010, and are reproduced with the permission of the individuals involved, all 4th Year undergraduate students enrolled in the degree of English Language and Literature at a Spanish university. These data are of three different kinds: first, students' written production in response to writing tasks set during this period; second, discussions arising from the feedback on this written production given by me as their teacher in whole class sessions and individual conversations. The aim of these feedback sessions was to aid the processes of revision of these written tasks. The third source of data is classroom interactions that I observed during this period.

## Metaphor and foreign language learning

A number of writers have stressed the importance of fostering metaphoric competence in the foreign language classroom (e.g., Low 1988; Littlemore & Low 2006 a,b; Ponterotto 1994), for, as has so often been pointed out, metaphor, metonymy and other forms of figurative language are ubiquitous, affecting numerous aspects of a language system and its use (Paprotte & Dirven 1985; Gibbs 1994; Lakoff & Johnson 1980, 1998). Likewise, a number of studies have demonstrated the benefits that accrue to raising learners' awareness of the metaphoric motivation for diverse aspects of the English language, such as phrasal verbs (Kövecses & Szabo 1996; Condon 2008), idioms (Boers 2001; Boers et al. 2004a), or single lexical items (Verspoor & Lowie 2003, MacArthur & Littlemore 2008), using techniques such as semantic (Verspoor & Lowie 2003) or etymological (Boers et al. 2004b) elaboration, pictorial support (Boers et al. 2008, 2009), total physical response (TPR) activities (Lindstromberg & Boers 2005), and so on. However, relatively little has been said about how these insights might be integrated with each other and into long-term teaching programmes and how metaphor-related activities should be distributed in time or integrated with other activities taking place in classrooms. Indeed, it is often difficult to see how teachers are to make use of the insights provided by such small-scale studies in everyday classroom situations, where learning benefits are tracked over much longer periods of time (for example, the nine or ten months of an academic year) than those usually considered in controlled experiments, where the learning that has taken place may be assessed hard on the heels of the experiment. In this regard, it is not easy to gauge what the long-term effects of the techniques assessed by such experiments will be on the learner's growing competence in the foreign language, and whether these techniques, designed to assess the benefits of a metaphor approach in relation to local issues (for example, learning the extended senses of prepositions) may or may not have positive knock-on effects in areas of language not specifically related to them. Yet this is an important issue. As a growing number of researchers have been at pains to point out (for example, de Bot et al. 2007; Ellis & Larsen-Freeman 2006; Larsen-Freeman 1997; Larsen-Freeman & Cameron 2008), language learning is complex and dynamic; an individual's progress is unlikely to be linear but may show plateaux or even regressions depending on the interaction of many factors (including the learner's social, cognitive and affective states) in the language learning process. Thus, interlanguage systems are seen to be in constant flux, and any change in one aspect of the language learning system will impact on others. When the various parts of the system are working together, new properties will be seen to emerge. As Larsen-Freeman & Cameron (2008:135) stress, ' [l]earning is not the taking in of linguistic forms by learners, but the constant adaptation of their linguistic resources in the service of meaning-making in response to the affordances that emerge in the communicative situation, which is, in turn, affected by learners' adaptability'.

The concern addressed in this contribution is how metaphor awareness may impact on learners' expressive ability in their second language. Specifically, the purpose of the present article is to describe how metaphor awareness *generally* may be added to the experience of learning English as a foreign language in an instructed setting, where it is normal to find a mix of abilities as well as a range of cognitive styles, learning strategies, attitudes and so on. It is in this particular social world that I will consider the processes by which sustained attention may be given to metaphor as part of the range of normal class activities, and how such terms as 'metaphor', 'figurative use' and 'by extension' may become part of classroom discourse and the intersubjective world of a TEFL classroom. In this approach, the specific pedagogical techniques employed (although the general approach is described later) are seen to be less significant than the general foregrounding of metaphor and the effect(s) this may have on learners' growing awareness of how metaphor permeates language (their own and the L2 to be learnt) as reflected in the growing felicity of the metaphorical language used in their written work.

Metaphor affects many different aspects of language use and may be understood and produced by learners at all ages and stages of language learning (Piquer-Piriz 2008a,b; MacArthur & Piquer-Piriz 2007). However, my focus here is on depth of vocabulary knowledge and the development of semantic competence in students' writing at a stage of a language course that could be characterised as aimed at leading learners at post-intermediate or vantage level (B2) towards advanced or C1/2 competence or in which the independent user of English progresses towards becoming a proficient user. At C2 or mastery level, semantic competence, or the awareness and control of the organisation of meaning, is described in the Council of Europe's Common European Framework of Reference for Languages (CEFR) (2001: 112) as the ability to 'exploit a comprehensive and reliable mastery of a very wide range of language to formulate thoughts precisely, give emphasis, differentiate and elimi-nate ambiguity ... [with] no signs of having to restrict what he/she wants to say'. It is my contention that developing metaphoric competence will of necessity play a significant role in learners' develop-ing ability to formulate and express their thoughts precisely, with little or no restrictions on what they wish to say in the target language, through the appropriation of target language forms and their associated metaphorical and cultural ideas. This may enable NNSs of English to use the language in a native-like way, without appearing, or wishing to appear, to be a native speaker of the language, whatever such an abstract figure might be taken to represent.

**Metaphor, language learning and dynamical systems theory**
As Ellis & Larsen-Freeman stress (2006: 559), simple cause-effect models do not adequately account for language learning:

> There are no magic bullet explanations for the phenomena of language that concern us. Each vari-able is but a small part of a complex picture. The notion of interlanguage has, from its very begin-nings ... been characterized as reflecting the interactions of many sources of different types of knowledge of the L1 and the L2.

This caveat is most important when we interpret the results of the research that has investigated the effect of promoting metaphor awareness as a means to foster learning of different aspects of the TL and consider how they may be transferred to the classroom. Results will be variable, and no one method or technique will work for all learners; initial states, cognitive styles, mood swings, the L1 of the learners, group dynamics, and a host of other variables will be working together to affect the developing system. However, the most important consideration is that the system should be devel-oping — fossilisation or stasis is the last thing we want to see in an EFL classroom. But stasis — or failure to advance in their command of English — is often perceived by learners to be a problem. Over the years, many students have remarked to me that they feel they have reached a plateau and are not advancing in their command of English. Typically this is said by learners who have reached an intermediate level of competence in English and who are halfway through a period of language learning that is designed to bring them to an advanced level in English. At this stage, they have been learning the language for many years, mostly in the classroom, though most will have had opportu-nities to travel to an English-speaking country and will take advantage of opportunities to practise and perfect their language skills outside the classroom. Part of the problem at this stage is a mixture of boredom and frustration: it takes great discipline and dedication to do the same types of class-room activities year after year unless one feels that progress is being made. These students are able to survive in an English-speaking country, it is true, but they often do not feel that their English is good enough for them to really express all that they wish to say, to join in conversations with native speakers on an equal footing, nor to read or listen to English texts and understand them fully. They wish to be able to express themselves in ways that are faithful to their individual, social and cultural identities, but have not yet found how to do this through English. Whether or not such subjective judgements are accurate, they should be taken seriously, for boredom and frustration may impact negatively on attitude and motivation in the FL classroom. Likewise, the frustration felt at not being able to express their own thoughts and feelings adequately is one that should be addressed.

In this regard, adding metaphor to the pot, as it were, of EFL classroom activities may radically alter the way that language and language learning is viewed and act to shift fossilised language behaviour as well as shifting the way EFL practitioners regard the aims of an advanced language learning programme. Metaphor as a way of thinking about language use is new for most learners and teachers; it is interesting and flexible. Unlike grammar, it has no hard and fast rules: there are no 'correct' or 'incorrect' metaphors, but rather better, communicatively more successful ones in comparison with communicatively less successful ones. It is often picturesque and imagistic, favouring the holistic learner over the analytic one (Littlemore 2001). Most important of all, with regard to the learner of English with knowledge of a relatively impoverished stock of words, metaphor helps to make meaning from many everyday, highly familiar words, for among all the forces that drive semantic extension, the most powerful is metaphor (Taylor 2003). Metaphor is thus the foreign language learners' best ally in the quest for greater expressive powers. As will be seen in the following sections, metaphor is used by learners of English, and they can be helped to use it better, but only if it is given a prominent place in classroom discussion.

### Semantic competence and vocabulary development

Vocabulary development is an important component of developing semantic competence in terms of the *breadth* of vocabulary known (or the number of lexical forms the learners master). More important, however, is the *depth* of vocabulary knowledge acquired. As has been pointed out (Haastrup & Henriksen 2000; McCarthy 2007; Meara 1996), planning for necessary vocabulary learning beyond the upper intermediate level is fraught with problems, unless there is a need for learners to acquire the vocabulary of a particular discourse community (such as in ESP or EAP contexts). Once a learner already has a stock of the most frequent words in English, the choice of lexical input from among the less frequent words will be motivated less by what it is necessary that the learner should know and more by the kind of topics and texts that are encountered by the learner inside and outside the classroom. It may be expected, then, that vocabulary growth in terms of the number of new items learnt will to a certain extent be unpredictable. However, fostering depth of vocabulary knowledge is amenable to planning, and developing knowledge about the semantic potential of the words already known — which includes, among other things, their extended meanings, collocations, or semantic prosody — will not only extend the range of topics a learner can talk about using everyday vocabulary items but also increase the accuracy with which ideas can be expressed in the foreign language. Most importantly, discovering the meaning potential of everyday words through metaphor may allow the advanced learner of English to use the language to communicate often complex abstract ideas in appropriate, though not necessarily conventional ways.

In order to appreciate how metaphor may be deployed by learners who display advanced command of English, let us consider two instances of figurative language by NNSs of English in oral and written modes. The first was produced by a non-native speaker of English (L1 Swedish) in a video-recorded oral interview used to train oral examiners for the Cambridge Proficiency in English examination in 1996.[1] Talking about the expense associated with living away from home in the UK, this learner remarked that she *"had a telephone bill that stretched all the way to Ireland"*. The second example comes from an essay written in 2004 about the war in Iraq by a learner in the 4th year of her degree in English Language and Literature at a Spanish university. She wrote: *"Anyway, the point* *of all this is that the United States and its allies seem to be the only ones interested in waging this war and taking advantage of it, while Iraq is **left behind**. Apparently in this case **it only takes one to tango**."*

Both of these learners share a capacity to use their second language figuratively: that is, they display what has been referred to as metaphoric competence. The first produces a novel linguistic utterance, which may be seen either as an instance of metaphor (an amount of money payable as a phone bill has no physical dimensions and therefore cannot literally occupy space) or hyperbole (the telephone bill, seen as something written on a piece of paper, might conceivably contain so many billed items as to be long enough to 'stretch' from one country to another). Whichever way one chooses to classify the trope, it certainly appears to be both a comprehensible and a very apt way of figuratively expressing the notion that large sums of money are required in order to keep in touch with family and friends in the home country. Furthermore, this production appears entirely novel: a search of the BNC revealed no use of the verb 'stretch' with 'bill', 'phone bill' or variants such as 'telephone bill/account' as subject of the clause. Rather, the speaker has followed what Sinclair (1991) has called the Open Choice Principle of language use, whereby a speaker can choose to fill a slot in a grammatical string with any element that does not violate the grammaticality of the clause (1991: 109). In this case, the grammatical pattern consisting of subject-predicator-locational complement serves as the frame into which the learner creatively inserts a figuratively used verb (*stretch*) and a locational complement (*all the way to Ireland*) that congruently completes the expression of the idea.

If we focus solely on the last of the figurative uses of language in the second short extract from a learner's written text, we can see that she also produces a novel linguistic utterance, this time by creatively exploiting the second of Sinclair's two principles of language production: the Idiom Principle. As Sinclair explains, the Idiom Principle is diametrically opposed to the Open Choice principle of language production, consisting in the availability of 'a large number of semi-pre-constructed phrases that constitute single choices, even though they might appear to be analysable into segments' (1991: 110). The ubiquity of such pre-fabricated utterances in discourse is well attested (for example, Erman & Warren 2000) and recent research has focused on categorising the different types of formulaic sequences (for example, Wray 2002). *It takes two to tango* (meaning that when two people are involved in a bad situation, both are responsible) is one type of pre-fabricated sequence, an idiom or conventional metaphor. Interestingly, this learner does not just reproduce the idiom but changes it in order to express the notion that the word 'war' was a misnomer for what had occurred in Iraq, and should more accurately have been termed an invasion. That is, this NNS behaves very much like a NS, unpacking a conventional metaphor in order to express a new idea, a strategy that signals a familiarity with the form and meaning of the original idiom (Moon 1998; Carter 1999). It can thus be seen that a component of both these learners' advanced command of English is related to their metaphoric competence or capacity, their ability to exploit the semantic potential of the lexicogrammar of the target language in order to express their own ideas and opinions in a way that is far removed from simple repetition or mimicking of NSs' conventional metaphors.

## The ubiquity of metaphor

As has been pointed out, metaphor is ubiquitous. It is not confined to literary or rhetorical language uses but pervades ordinary, everyday expression, although the density of metaphors may vary quite substantially depending on the the the type of text or genre examined (Cameron & Stelma 2004; Steen et al. 2010). Among the many characteristics of this ordinary use of metaphor, it has been found to play an important role in structuring our understanding of and communication about abstract concepts such as time, argument, love, anger, and so on. As Lakoff & Johnson (1980; 1998) have shown, our physical experience of the world and bodily interactions with our environment often serve to inform and structure our understanding of abstract realms, as shown in the language used to talk about them. Indeed polysemy (Lakoff 1993) has provided much of the evidence for CMT; the epistemic correspondences between concrete source domains and abstract target domains are reflected in the lexical items used to talk about these topics. One immediate consequence of this insight into language use is that polysemy is motivated, and uncovering the metaphorical motivation for polysemous uses of language forms (lexis as well as grammar) has pedagogical implications for ELT. Apart from anything else, it means that learners do not have to master a huge number of vocabulary items in order to express complex thoughts on abstract topics. Indeed, metaphorical uses of language will become increasingly necessary for FL learners as they move from talking or writing about the here-and-now and move into the realm of abstraction. Finally, and most importantly, the insight that metaphor is ubiquitous in speech and writing alerts us to the fact that the examples cited earlier of NNSs' use of figurative language are unlikely to be unusual in NNS discourse; rather we can expect to find metaphor and other types of figurative language in other NNSs' expression as well, particularly when learners are speaking or writing about abstract topics.

In order to illustrate the kind of metaphorical language that may be produced by EFL learners, let us consider the following excerpts from the writing of Spanish university students as they begin the final two years of their undergraduate degree in English Language and Literature. The texts they are taken from are all on the topic of learning a foreign language, a task set at the beginning of the academic year as a way of getting some idea of the learners' writing skills. It is important to stress that, when the learners wrote these texts, neither metaphor nor figurative language generally had been the focus of classroom activities or discussion in their English language classes, although of course some discussion of different tropes may well have been the topic of other courses at school or in their degree. The words and expressions used with a potentially metaphorical sense are set off in bold type, which reveals at a glance how all these learners felt the need to use metaphor when talking about this topic:

1. Student A: *Learning a foreign language is useful because you can travel, and travel **broadens** the mind. If you visit another country you can know other cultures and you **open** your mind. But you can only know the culture properly if you **dominate** a foreign language because language and culture are the two **faces** of the same **coin**.* (56 words/5 used metaphorically)

2. Student B: *The first two years of my university life helped me **open** my mind and **see** that English was **far away** more complex than what I expected. It represented my first experience with the culture that **surrounded** the language, a **way** to a better understanding of English, a **path** to my original aim.* (52 words/7 used metaphorically)

3. Student C: *Language, somehow, determines the **way** its speakers conceive reality. In order to express some feeling or thought, the speakers select certain words from the flexible **net** of language, that is to say, language **works** like a **filter**. So it is very curious to **observe** the relation between the linguistic choices a person **makes** and the **way** he thinks. Words are **signs** that **stand for** experience; they **show** the **door**, but it is only oneself who has the chance to **open** it and **look beyond**.* (84 words/15 used metaphorically)

4. Student D: *Language and culture are closely related and cannot be **separated**. Each language has its cultural **background** which is necessary to **fully** understand and appreciate the language. It **expands** people's **view** of the world and makes them more tolerant and respectful with each other. So, learning a foreign language is important in order to be a skilful, intellectual, **open-minded** and **receptive** person, because each foreign language **enriches** our experience.* (68 words/8 used metaphorically)

I will discuss these and other examples of students' use of figurative language more fully in the course of this article. Here it will suffice to observe that these learners all appear to be attempting to express a similar notion with regard to language and culture. For them, learning a language benefits the learner because it alerts him/her to the possibility that, just as there are different ways of talking about something, so there are different ways of thinking about it. Therefore, learning to say something in a different way enables one to think about it in a different way, and the result is a positive expansion (*broaden the mind, open one's mind, open the door, expand, enrich*) of the range of one's thought.

Two further aspects of these students' writing deserve comment. On the one hand, there is a great deal of similarity among these learners with regard to the abstract idea they attempt to express. This is largely a consequence of the task set: although not a guided task, the topic of the written essay will constrain what the learners can talk about without writing about something else entirely. Furthermore, these learners share a common background or social world: they have all chosen to major in English Language and Literature at a Spanish university, they have inhabited the same classrooms for three years and all except one are Spanish and have learnt English or other foreign languages in very similar circumstances. On the other hand, the density and felicity of their use of metaphor varies quite substantially, and one of the striking differences between them is how they deploy metaphor and what this reveals about their grasp of this aspect of language use. The metaphors they use not only vary in their effectiveness, but also range in type, going from the reproduction of conventional English metaphors (for example, *travel broadens the mind*) or calques of conventional Spanish metaphors (for example, *open one's mind*) through more novel or creative metaphors such as *expand people's view* to extended metaphors (*signs →show door→ open* (door) *→look beyond*).

That is, the similarities and differences displayed in these students' writing reflect the kind of similarities and differences in any language classroom, where individuals may be similar in some respects but vary in dimensions such as aptitude, physical and affective states, cognitive styles, and so on. The common denominator is the group in the classroom, a relatively stable physical and social environment, where language learning activities are carried out, and ways of talking about and understanding the work in hand or the aims being pursued are shared by all participants. Among the activities carried out may be a task such as this — to write a certain number of words about an abstract but familiar topic — which creates the kind of communicative pressure that pushed the learners to produce these metaphors. Furthermore, when students prepare written texts for their teachers, these are typically the subject of a feedback session, where teachers may provide students individually or collectively with comments on their written production. If this feedback is to be of any value to the learners, the metalinguistic commentary must be clear, comprehensible and congruent with the purpose(s) of the written task, and teachers usually take great pains to establish that the feedback given is coherent with the metalanguage used in the classroom generally. In the case of the figurative uses of language illustrated above, it would appear well-nigh impossible to provide useful feedback without mentioning metaphor, and yet, unlike other aspects of language and language use that teachers and learners regularly discuss, metaphor is a relative newcomer in ELT, and decisions about what metalanguage should be adopted in classroom discourse are not necessarily straightforward, as I shall discuss in the next section.

## Metaphor and metalanguage in the EFL classroom

Teachers and learners in EFL classrooms round the world employ very similar words and expressions when discussing language and language use, although the frequency with which such terms are used may vary quite substantially, depending on the approach adopted to the teaching/learning of the language. More traditional approaches may lay stress on formal aspects of the system and refer to them as 'grammar', 'phonology', 'lexis', and give their component parts names like verb, noun, vowel, consonant, and so on. Focus on discourse makes terms like 'coherence' or 'communicative function' familiar, just as learners and teachers may share words for talking about skills and sub-skills (skimming, scanning, or fluency, for example). Although some of these terms are often less than satisfactory when describing or explaining linguistic phenomena, they nevertheless provide a shared means for reflecting on language in the classroom. In the case of metaphor, teachers have a number of options to choose among when deciding how they can talk about this phenomenon, as numerous theories can furnish them with a terminology. The view adopted here, however, is that there is little to be gained and much to be lost by importing the metalanguage of metaphor scholars to the EFL classroom.

First, the adoption of a scientific metalanguage in an educational context when what is being explored is often pre-scientific or intuitive understandings of abstract concepts (the ordinary, everyday metaphors English speakers use) may encourage learners to view the object of study (the folk theories or ideologies of a community of speakers) as representing objective truths or valid constructs, which might lead to fostering understandings which may veer dangerously close to the kind of cultural imperialism which has often been signalled as a problem in the use of English as *lingua franca* for global communication, particularly when it gives rise to 'unilateral idiomaticity' (a concern expressed by Seidlhofer (2009), among others). Moreover, we still lack the kind of comprehensive account of metaphor in language or thought that would allow us to describe and explain the phenomenon fully, as unremitting scholarly discussion on metaphor over many years has shown. Among the many thorny issues that are still unresolved are how to distinguish between metaphor and metonymy, whether metaphor is located in thought or in language, whether metaphors create or draw attention to similarities between entities and processes, why metaphor is realized in so many different forms, and so on and so forth. Terms such as *target/topic/vehicle, source/target domain* or *mapping, entailment, grounds* and so on carry theoretical assumptions that are not always able to account for metaphor as actually used by people for communicative purposes, and in the EFL class-room the goal is to foster effective communication skills in a foreign language, not to train metaphor analysts. For example, the metalanguage developed to describe linguistic metaphors (*topic/target/vehicle*) works very well when describing A-is-B metaphors realized by copular constructions, but is far less successful in dealing with other manifestations, such as verbs or phrases; topics/targets may be absent in the surrounding text and identifying the scope of a vehicle term is often far from straightforward (Littlemore & Low 2006a: 11–17).

This does not mean, of course, that important insights from research into metaphor should be ignored. For example, we know that many metaphorical expressions are systematic, in that they are not simply one off instances of a metaphorical idea. However, it is unlikely that giving labels like LIFE IS A JOURNEY to these systematic manifestations will be of much use to learners. Indeed, the very formulation of a metaphorical mapping might well induce a deep misunderstanding of what is at play here, for the reification of the concepts involved (in this case, LIFE and JOURNEY) is itself a grammatical metaphor (Halliday & Matthiessen 1999), casting as static, nominal entities that which is experienced and most often realized in language by dynamic, verbal processes (for example, 'He **came up against** an insoluble problem' or 'When I **look back** on my life, I realise how fortunate I've been'). Furthermore, the same source domain may structure a great many different targets (Kövecses 2000) and vice versa, a source of potential confusion for learners rather than a helpful way of abstracting rules for metaphorical language use if confronted with such contradictory evidence as upper case VISIBLE IS OUT (for example, 'the flowers are out', 'the book came out', 'I can't make out what that says') or (possibly) INVISIBLE IS OUT (for example, 'the fire died out' or 'He snuffed out the candle'). Untangling the different mappings involved, and ensuring that learners understand the difference between them would take time that can be ill afforded in the classroom. Furthermore, recent research has challenged the view of metaphor as being located as the level of abstraction proposed by CMT, and suggests that the metaphor scenario has greater descriptive and explanatory potential than conceptual mapping (see Musolff 2006). And for language teaching purposes, we may find that scenarios account better for the many manifestations of metaphor, (for example, idioms such as *play ball* or *show someone the ropes*) that do not instantiate conceptual metaphors or metaphoric themes. Likewise, the discourse dynamics view of metaphor view adopted by Cameron et al. (2009: 67) that '[m]etaphor, whether conceptual or linguistic ... becomes processual, emergent, and open to change' is likely to be more helpful when considering learners' metaphoric productions than that which sees metaphor as some kind of fixed tool to be deployed by NNSs in interaction.

Finally, and most importantly, the adoption of a complex scientific metalanguage may well impede the development of the individual and shared understandings that are likely to emerge in classroom interactions (as will be seen below) and which may lead to those creative uses of metaphor that will enable learners to fully express their ideas. Instead, the adoption of Schön's (1993) fairly neutral but descriptively adequate way of talking about metaphor as 'seeing-as' is particularly apt in the context of language learning, for many of the activities designed to promote understanding of the metaphoric motivation of words and expressions will involve learners' 'seeing' the source domain entities and scenarios that motivate metaphors in the form of physical enactment by the various participants in the classroom, pictorial representations or verbal stimulation of appropriate mental images. Metaphor can thus be talked about as a way of 'seeing' particular entities or processes in terms of other entities or processes, and the resulting language uses can be discussed in general as 'metaphoric' or 'figurative' and the relationship between core/basic senses and figurative ones as one of 'extension', a term which also serves adequately to refer to the 'stand for' relations expressed by metonymy. Most important, perhaps, is the notion that 'seeing-as' can be readily understood as involving different perspectives on similar scenes: a shift of position or movement of the eyes can radically change the way something is experienced or viewed. For example, MacArthur (2005: 87) discusses how the different experiential perspectives adopted on horse scenarios may motivate very different metaphorical meanings, even when the same lexical items are used figuratively to talk about different topics. It is thus vital that learners grasp that viewpoints shift if they are to understand how the same or similar source domains or scenarios motivate very different metaphorical meanings — and how their own individual, socially or culturally induced ways of 'seeing-as' may be similar to or different from those of speakers of English.

### The (mis)appropriation of metaphor in EFL learner's writing

Teachers often informally refer to students' ability to produce natural-sounding, effective uses of English as revealing their 'feel' for the language, and competence in dealing with different aspects of the language as showing they 'grasp' it. These metaphors can themselves give some insight into the differing competence that learners display in their use of metaphor in English, for it is here that we may discern learners' understanding of the basic and extended senses of words and their ability to use these appropriately. For example, a learner writes:

5.    *Time went by very quickly and I saw my greatest opportunity when I **bumped into** a poster announcing the arrival of Erasmus grants.*

The awkwardness of this clause is largely a result of this learner's failure to find the best way of expressing the fact that he saw the poster by chance: *bump into* can certainly describe a chance encounter (*e.g., I bumped into John the other day*) but not between an animate subject (*I*) and an inanimate object (*a poster*) unless the writer means that he literally collided with the object. This kind of problem with target language metaphors is far from infrequent and shows that learners have not engaged with the basic sense of the words that make up this expression and which motivate its collocational patterns. This learner knows that *bump into* is a way of talking about chance encounters and in a bilingual dictionary will find that it is offered as a possible translation of *'encontrarse con'* along with *come across* or *meet* but none of these expressions are truly synonymous.

This failure to engage with the individual words that make up multi-word metaphorical expressions is more tellingly illustrated by Student A's use of *travel broadens the mind*, cited previously. Data culled from the same written assignment over a period of five years with 5 different groups of students showed that Student A's use of the expression was far from unusual. During this period, of the 165 resulting essays, 86 contained the expression *travel broadens the mind*, a not altogether surprising finding given the topic of the essay and the fact that the learners had all attended the same language classes in the previous three years (where they presumably learnt the phrase). More surprising was that, although in 74 cases (or 86%) the expression was used in the topic sentence of a paragraph, in only one of these cases did a learner later develop the idea in this paragraph in a way congruent with the metaphor (this student later referred to the mind's 'plasticity'). In all other cases, the metaphor was either abandoned (linguistically and ideationally) or 'developed' in subsequent clauses which included calques of the Spanish idiomatic equivalent *open/close one's mind* (58%), as Student A did. The following is an example of this:

6. *Travel broadens the mind and learning a foreign language is very useful if you want to go abroad. You can visit other countries and know new people, new cultures, and this can open your mind.*

That is, although many learners knew the phrase *travel broadens the mind* and were able to use it in an appropriate context, most failed to show awareness either of the metaphorical motivation of the phrase or its potential for exploitation in discourse. Although *have/keep an open/closed mind* is used in English, the metaphorical idea has been instantiated somewhat differently here. The learner has, as is possible and idiomatic in Spanish, expressed this as a dynamic process (*abrir/cerrar la mente a algo*) rather than a state. Nevertheless, the fact that *open/close your mind* is not part of an average speaker's repertoire of conventional metaphors in English does not rule it out as a possible way of formulating an idea: if this were so, no creative or novel metaphor — whether uttered by a native or a non-native speaker — would be deemed apt. Rather, the metaphor fails to work in the context in which it has been produced because of the conceptual clash between the metaphoric formulation of the first idea (*travel broadens the mind*) which 'sees' the mind as a malleable substance, and the second (*open/close the mind*) which conceptualizes the mind as a (rigid) container. Furthermore, the use of *have an open/closed mind* in this context seems to show equal lack of awareness of the metaphorical expression in the L1. Both are produced unreflectively as a way of expressing an idea in a way that must have appeared to these learners perfectly idiomatic and hence highly acceptable to their audience (an English language teacher).

The focus on fluency development through fostering the acquisition of large numbers of unanalysed chunks (advocated by Wray & Fitzpatrick 2008, among others) may have undesirable consequences for learners' productive use of conventional metaphors and idioms once they have to produce them in authentic communicative situations as opposed to producing them in guided 'fill the gap' exercises. The way that Spanish learners of English used the expression *travel broadens the mind* illustrates two aspects of use of the target language which seem irreconcilable. On the one hand, the learners who used the expression produced it accurately: no synonymous words were substituted at different points in the string, article usage was consistent with the standardized expression and none of them failed to mark the verb for third person singular, although any of these types of inaccuracies might surface in production of other utterances. These learners thus demonstrate that they have successfully learnt a formulaic expression as a chunk: they have all 'left it alone' (Wray & Fitzpatrick 2008), failing to analyze the component parts, which is often seen as an important component of fluency. However, while this may be desirable in increasing the speed of delivery and naturalness of speech, it is not necessarily advantageous in planned language production, such as writing, nor will it serve the learners' purpose of expressing their own meanings in thoughtful ways. Rather, if learners were to be encouraged to break down the meaning of component words in figurative expressions of this kind they might consider what is implied by the use of words such as *bump into*, or *broaden*. Indeed, it may well be of great benefit for learners to literally 'feel' or 'see' what these words mean in basic contexts of use, for this will remind them of what the words entail when used metaphorically.

Metaphor awareness and metaphoric competence will often involve revisiting well-known lexical items to (re)discover their concrete senses. As Lindstromberg & Boers (2005) have shown, TPR activities accompanying and supporting the learning of verbs of movement (like 'stumble') leads to understanding and retention of the metaphorical meanings of these verbs. Although their study only looked at verbs which expressed complex manner of movement, the very same techniques will be useful in fostering learners' recall and 'feel' for the basic senses of more frequent and familiar verbs such as *go, come, run, push, pull, throw*, and so on, as well as the spatial configurations associated with prepositions, because learners often appear not to possess that 'feel' for or 'grasp' of their basic senses that is necessary for using them metaphorically. Visual illustrations and physical enactment may thus be used regularly in the classroom to support the verbal explanations of how concrete scenarios may motivate metaphorical uses of words and phrases.

### Shifts in understanding in the EFL classroom

Exploration of metaphor in the EFL classroom may occur at different moments in the classroom and be sparked by seemingly unrelated tasks that learners are dealing with. An example of this from the author's data was an idle question put to the class by the teacher regarding the motivation of use of 'up' in the phrasal verbs *come up (to so. or sth.)* and the sense of 'near' during rephrasing exercise, in which learners had to replace a verb or phrase (for example, *attribute to*) with a phrasal verb (in this case, *put down to*). None of the students in the class were able to come up with any verbal explanation at all, other than that was the way it was said. However, at this point, several students were observed to be tracing an upwards movement with their hands (palms flat and facing downwards) as they thought about the question. The teacher quickly sketched on the blackboard two straight lines intersecting at a vanishing point. In the centre, between the two lines, she added small dashes decreasing in size from bottom to top, to suggest a road, and then asked the students if they recognised what the lines represented. They confirmed that it was a drawing of a road. At the teacher's request (the excuse given was that she was very bad at drawing) a volunteer then came forward to complete the drawing by adding two figures, one which was to appear nearer to the observer and one further away. Once this was done, the teacher asked the group to confirm that the distance between the observer and the two figures was adequately represented and, when they said it was, the teacher asked how they knew which figure was closer than the others. At this point, a number of students spoke at once, offering 'big', 'large' or 'size' as the explanation; others, while looking at the drawing made similar gestures moving their hands up and down with their hands held flat, palm downwards. Several students nodded and said 'ah!' One student then offered 'close up' as 'the same thing', and another asked whether 'turn up' or 'catch up' would be examples of similar uses. Rather than answering the question herself, the teacher asked the group what they thought. Although only four or five students intervened to confirm that these were indeed related senses, others were observed to be rehearsing this possibility in gestures involving their right hands, in which the flat palm facing the speaker was drawn upwards and towards the eyes from a point in the middle of the body. At this point again, several students were heard again to say 'ah', to nod and to write something down in their notebooks.

'Ah-ha' moments such as this mark shifts in understanding among members of the learner group (Larsen-Freeman & Cameron 2008: 59). The one described here is only one of many in which the understanding of how words metaphorically extend their meanings may take place in a classroom over the weeks and months that a group meets for the purpose of learning English. Littlemore & Low (2006a: 7) describe another such moment in a university classroom in Britain when one student asked about the meaning of 'skirt' used as a verb. The spontaneous use of gestures by two other students, each demonstrating a different understanding of how the physical characteristics of a skirt might motivate the meaning of the verb, led to enlightenment among these learners. Another example is given by MacArthur & Littlemore (2008: 179) in which two learners discuss their understanding of the senses of 'shoulder' and 'elbow' as verbs; one expresses his understanding that 'elbow aside' implies great rudeness, showing this understanding by making jabbing motions outwards with both elbows.

Salutary lessons may also be learnt from an approach to metaphor that does not always involve teacher-led explanation, for, as has been pointed out earlier, metaphor scholars (let alone language teachers) do not have all the answers to what motivates metaphorical uses of words. This does not mean that learners cannot discover motivations that make sense to them (even if they do not accord with the accounts given by experts in metaphor) or even make more sense than the accounts currently available. For example, in a session involving Erasmus students at the University of Birmingham (MacArthur & Littlemore, in preparation), students were asked to do a gap-fill exercise where gaps had to be filled with an appropriate denominal verb they had previously studied. One learner, when asked why he had correctly guessed that 'shoulder' was the most appropriate verb in one sentence, replied that, for him, the clue had been the subject of the clause ('he') because 'to shoulder' was a very masculine action. As he said this, he hunched his shoulders and moved his upper body backwards and forwards with alternate movements of each shoulder. The two researchers, both native speakers of English, were somewhat surprised by this reasoning, although this student's intuitions seemed perfectly plausible. In fact, a quick look at corpus lines in the BNC for 'shouldered' rapidly confirmed his reasoning, as masculine subjects were found to be overwhelmingly preferred in the recorded instances of the use of this verb. This learner's intuitive understanding of the verbal use of 'shoulder' was more insightful than his teachers'.

Thus far, I have discussed metaphor awareness in terms of the target language only. However, metaphor competence in the L1 has been found to correlate with metaphor competence in the L2 (Littlemore 2010). It will therefore be necessary for learners to be equally aware of the metaphors they employ in their L1 in order to avoid or mitigate transfer effects and avoid problems in communication. As is well known, the fundamental difference between learning a first and a second language is that in the second case, the foreign language is competing with well-developed automatic conceptual and linguistic routines in the L1. Transfer effects are evident in all aspects of language production and comprehension — and metaphor is no exception. As has been seen, students A and B both produced 'open one's mind' to express the notion of the intellectual growth associated with learning a foreign language, a perfectly idiomatic metaphor in Spanish, although not in English. A further example of a transferred metaphor in a learner's writing is when one student wrote: *My sister was really annoying me talking about my boyfriend, but I tried to hold back my nerves*. In feedback sessions, it became very clear that these learners were not aware that the expressions they were using might cause any problems of comprehension for a non-native speaker of Spanish. 'Nervios' ('nerves') is a metonym standardly used in Spanish to refer to 'temper' or 'anger', which in English might be 'restrained', 'controlled' or — metaphorically — 'curbed' or 'held in check'. Although 'nerves' is also used in English to stand for mood or temper (for example, *he really got on my nerves*), the most frequent use of the plural form is to signify nervousness in the face of a somewhat frightening event. Local discussion of such cases may often highlight the communicative inefficacy created by this type of transfer; more generally, awareness of metaphor in the L1 will need to go hand in hand with developing metaphorical competence in the L2. Consequently, activities aimed at drawing attention to how systematic metaphors may be different or similar in the two languages will also be helpful in helping learners gain greater understanding of how metaphor permeates much of their most ordinary expression in the L1 and alerting them to possible problems they may create for their interlocutors if they use certain calques.

### Metaphors in students' writing: Resources, tasks and feedback

Developing metaphoric competence in written expression in the EFL classroom will depend largely on the resources that learners have at their disposal to explore metaphor, the tasks that they carry out and the quality of feedback received on it. The resources may be of various kinds and will range from the types of written and oral texts that the learners are exposed to inside and outside the classroom to the kind of activities that may be used to promote deep engagement with aspects of metaphorically motivated uses of English, such as those which have proved valuable in controlled experiments. However, learners also use reference works, like dictionaries or electronic corpora, which teachers encourage learners to consult when planning and writing up their assignments. Of the dictionary sources, bilingual dictionaries, while perhaps the easiest form of reference to find how to express notions, are often extremely unhelpful in helping learners to develop sensitivity to metaphor. The learner who wrote that he *bumped into a poster*, or another who wrote *[m]oreover, it is considered the most important manner to put people's learning into practice facing up to different situations and problems* have found that these are translations offered of the L1 expressions they wanted to use (*encontrarse con* and *enfrentarse con*, respectively) but which do not work in the context in which they were used. Monolingual dictionaries, when used side by side with bilingual dictionaries, may offer supplementary information about how words are typically used in context which learners can benefit from. However, students can also be encouraged to use a large electronic corpus to check that their planned use of a target word seems possible and to gain familiarity with the contexts in which it is usually used (MacArthur & Littlemore 2008). In interpreting feedback, corpus data can also reveal very quickly why a teacher might query or mark as an error a learner's use of 'dominate', for example, when she wrote that *[i]n order to get a good job nowadays, it is necessary to **dominate** a foreign language*. However, although this learner might see at a glance that 'language' was not a significant collocate to the right of 'dominate' in the BNC, this will not necessarily lead to a solution to how to express this idea. A further consultation of the bilingual dictionary would reveal that that numerous possibilities are offered as translations of *dominar*: 'dominate', 'control', 'rule', 'overpower', 'check', 'bring under control', 'overcome', 'master', or 'tower over' are all possible translations of the Spanish verb offered by the Collins Spanish Dictionary (2005), but this source provides only one example of how to talk about language: ***domina cuatro idiomas*** is glossed as *he's fluent in four languages*. In order to play safe, then, the learner might have opted for this formulation and reworded her expression accordingly: *[i]n order to get a good job nowadays, it is necessary to speak a foreign language fluently*. However, in 'playing safe', an important part of the original idea would have been lost: the metaphorical construal of an abstract skill (such as speaking a foreign language) as physical control of an object. Of course, the teacher might easily have provided an appropriate formulation for the idea ('master a foreign language') but if the aim is to foster learners' growing autonomy (cf. Littlemore & Low 2006: 68–85), s/he may be very unwilling to do so. Instead, the learner was referred to a dictionary of synonyms and antonyms such as Roget's Thesaurus (1997) and invited to explore the word originally used ('dominate') or a related concept (for example, 'skill').

A thesaurus such as Roget's is a potentially very rich resource for learners as they seek to find words to explain abstract concepts which they may not have considered very deeply before and, as metaphor scholars themselves have found, provide a mine of information on the metaphors English speakers use to talk about different topics. Learning how to use thesauri can have a positive impact on learners' written production, particularly when they are provided with some guidance on how to make use of this resource (for example, how to search for appropriate entries and how to check the meaning of the new words and phrases found in a monolingual dictionary). Simply reading an entry for a particular concept (for example, 'skill') can not only provide the words and expressions the learner needs ready made, but may suggest ideas and ways of developing his/her own thoughts. So, after looking up 'skill', the learner who had used 'dominate' rewrote the idea in the following way: *[i]n order to get a good job nowadays, it is necessary to show you master a foreign language and have a flair for communicating with people from other countries. These talents are highly valued in the modern world.* 'Flair' and 'talent' are words that are included in the section of the Thesaurus devoted to the notion of 'skill', and served to expand the original clause to produce a more interesting and thoughtful proposition.

As has been pointed out, the type of writing task assigned will have an influence on the need for metaphorical language, with abstract topics in particular creating a communicative pressure (Robinson 2001) that will most likely result in increased density of metaphorical language. In order to prepare for writing assignments on abstract topics, it will be helpful if teachers prepare the ground by not only ensuring exposure to texts on similar topics (as is normal in ELT) but also by revisiting the source domain language that may inform the metaphors learners are likely to use. So for example, writing about lifestyle choices, careers, aspirations for the future, professions, or love and marriage may well require metaphors appealing to PATHS, JOURNEYS and DESTINATIONS, so revision of the language needed to talk about these experiences (through reading, teacher explanation, another writing task or other focused activity) will reactivate known language that can usefully be employed in writing about these abstract domains, and make it possible for learners to produce linguistic metaphors that — if not completely idiomatic — are comprehensible because they are congruent with the type of source domain scenarios appealed to by native speakers of English when talking about their lives. Similarly, writing about anger or conflict (whether physical, verbal, or of other types) may allow learners to explore the metaphoric potential of caused motion patterns (producing, for example, *they were hurling insults at each other* or *when my boyfriend tried to explain I just shouted him down*) or the potential of verbs describing the noises animals make to express attitude and emotions in reporting human speech (for example, *Getting no rest he howled that he only wanted to know if I knew how to set the video in order to record the football match. 'You wanted what?' I squawked* ).

Feedback on written production focuses on strong and weak points of learners' writing. However, difficulty is likely to be experienced when evaluating learners' metaphoric productions, for metaphor appreciation continues to be more art than science. So, for example, student C's extended metaphor (*Words are **signs** that **stand for** experience; they **show** the **door**, but it is only oneself who has the chance to **open** it and **look beyond***) may strike different readers in different ways. For some, this may successfully explore the notion that learning a language is like a journey into the dark; for others it might fail to convey this because it explores the metaphorical idea in too great depth and calls too great attention to itself (inviting a literal rather than a metaphorical reading). Similarly, when a student writes '*There is a Chinese proverb that states that learning is a **treasure** that will **follow** its **owner** everywhere, and one of the **treasured possessions** a person can own is a foreign language*', there appears to be a mismatch between a 'treasure' (perhaps a valuable object such as a jewel) and 'follow' (implying an animate subject). However, since it is unlikely that this mismatch would be noticed by any but the most attentive readers, it would seem unnecessary to comment on this. Likewise, the 'mixed' metaphor identified earlier (*broaden* vs *open the mind*) may appear perfectly acceptable to some readers. Until there exist more studies on the mixing of metaphor, like that of Kimmel (2010), which can fully account for this widespread phenomenon and its appropriacy in different discourse contexts, teachers will no doubt need to rely on the prevailing view on the mixing of metaphors in the educational communities to which they belong, and give students feedback accordingly. Likewise, until we have more evidence about the way that metaphor is used in cross-cultural communication, teachers have no guidelines to follow in how they may help learners to develop metaphoric competence in ways that do not simply involve teaching learners to use the conventional metaphors already available in the target language, although fostering the ability to use metaphor creatively is likely to serve advanced learners' communicative purposes better.

## Conclusion

In this article, I have tried to illustrate the uses that foreign learners of English make of metaphor in their written production, and have associated this need for metaphor with the kind of topics that advanced learners may be asked to write and speak about. Given that metaphor appears spontaneously in response to task, rather than appearing as a result of any pedagogical focus on metaphor awareness, I have suggested that ways of talking about metaphor need to be found in the EFL classroom. However, the metalanguage adopted must reflect the current state of knowledge about metaphor, which is incomplete, and at the same time be 'user-friendly'. The attention given to metaphor in the EFL classroom, just as with the attention given to any aspect of the target language, will seek to make it salient for learners, provoking changes in understanding that may emerge in learners' interlanguage, fostering shifts from established language behaviour towards new ways of understanding and using metaphor.

However, as is clear from the discussion of feedback on learners' metaphoric production, we know little about the difficulties that interlocutors may encounter when metaphor is used in cross-cultural encounters, and what the limits of comprehensibility are when L1 metaphors are calqued in the L2 or when speakers create their own novel metaphors to express abstract concepts. To what extent can NNSs of English expect to be able to appeal to their own familiar ways of expressing metaphorical ideas and still expect to be understood? Do the grounds of a metaphorical expression need to be made explicit in order for unfamiliar metaphors to be understood by speakers with different L1s? To what extent could this explicitness impact negatively on a listener's perception of the speaker/writer's verbal and conceptual fluency? These are only some of the questions that need to be explored in naturally occurring interaction between native and non-native speakers of English in order to inform classroom practice and apply the insights of metaphor theory in benign ways to ELT.

## Note
1. University of Cambridge Local Examinations Syndicate: International Examinations. CPE 1996 Standardization video.

## References

Barsalou, L.W. 2008. Grounded cognition. *Annual Review of Psychology* 59: 617–45.
Boers, F. 2001. Remembering figurative idioms by hypothesizing about their origins. *Prospect* 16(3): 35–43.
Boers, F., Demecheleer, M. & Eyckmans, J. 2004a. Cultural variation as a variable in comprehending and remembering figurative idioms. *European Journal of English Studies* 8/3: 375–388.

Boers, F., Demecheleer, M. & Eyckmans, J. 2004b. Etymological elaboration as a strategy for learning figurative idioms. In *Vocabulary in a Second Language: Selection, Acquisition and Testing* [Language Learning and Language Teaching 10], P. Bogaards & B. Laufer (eds), 53–78. Amsterdam: John Benjamins.

Boers, F., Lindstromberg, S., Littlemore, J., Stengers, H. & Eyckmans, J. 2008. Variables in the mnemonic effectiveness of pictorial elucidation. In *Cognitive Linguistic Approaches to Teaching Vocabulary and Phraseology*, F. Boers & S. Lindstromberg (eds), 189–216. Berlin: Mouton de Gruyter.

Boers, F., Piquer-Píriz, A., Stengers, H. & Eyckmans, J. 2009. Does pictorial elucidation foster recollection of idioms? *Language Teaching Research* 13: 367–382.

Cameron, L.J., Maslen, R., Todd, Z., Maule, J., Stratton, P. & Stanley, N. 2009. The discourse dynamics approach to metaphor and metaphor-led discourse analysis. *Metaphor and Symbol* 24: 63–89.

Cameron, L.J. & Stelma, J.H. 2004. Metaphor clusters in discourse. *Journal of Applied Linguistics* 1(2):7–36

Carter, R. (1999). Common language: corpus, creativity and cognition. *Language and Literature* 8(3): 195–216.

Chapetón Castro, C.M. & Verdaguer Clavera, I. Forthcoming. Researching linguistic metaphor in native, non-native and expert writing. In *Metaphor in Use: Context, Culture, and Communication*, F. MacArthur, J.L. Oncins Martínez, A. Piquer Píriz & M. Sánchez García (eds). Amsterdam: John Benjamins.

Condon, N. 2008. How cognitive linguistic motivations influence the learning of phrasal verbs. In *Cognitive Linguistic Approaches to Teaching Vocabulary and Phraseology*, F. Boers & S. Lindstromberg (eds), 133–158. Berlin: Mouton de Gruyter.

Council of Europe. 2001. *Common European Framework of Reference for Languages: Learning, Teaching, Assessment*. Cambridge: CUP.

De Bot, K., Lowie, W. & Verspoor, M. 2007. A dynamic systems theory approach to second language acquisition. *Bilingualism, Language and Cognition* 10(1): 7–21.

Dirven, R. 2001. English phrasal verbs: Theory and didactic application. In *Applied Cognitive Linguistics*, II: *Language Pedagogy*, M. Pütz, S. Niemeier & R. Dirven (eds), 3–27. Berlin: Mouton de Gruyter.

Ellis, N.C. & Larsen-Freeman, D. 2006. Language emergence: Implications for applied linguistics. Introduction to special issue. *Applied Linguistics* 27(4): 558–89.

Erman, B. & Warren, B. 2000. The idiom principle and the open choice principle. *Text* 20(1): 29–62.

Gibbs, R.W. (1994). *The Poetics of Mind: Figurative Thought, Language, and Understanding*. Cambridge: CUP

Gibbs, R.W. 2006. *Embodiment and Cognitive Science*. Cambridge: CUP.

Haastrup, K. & Henriksen, B. 2000. Vocabulary acquisition: Acquiring depth of knowledge through network building. *International Journal of Applied Linguistics* 10(2): 221–240.

Halliday, M.A.K. & Matthiessen, C.M.I.M. 1999. *Construing Experience through Meaning: A Language-Based Approach to Cognition*. London: Cassell.

Kimmel, M. 2010. Why we mix metaphors (and mix them well): Discourse coherence, conceptual metaphor, and beyond. *Journal of Pragmatics* 42: 97–115.

Kövecses, Z. 2000. The scope of metaphor. In *Metaphor and Metonymy at the Crossroads*, A. Barcelona (ed.), 79–92. Berlin: Mouton de Gruyter.

Kövecses, Z. 2001. A cognitive linguistic view of learning idioms in an FLT context. In *Applied Cognitive Linguistics*, II: *Language Pedagogy*, M. Pütz, S. Niemeier & R. Dirven (eds), 87–115. Berlin: Mouton de Gruyter.

Kövecses, Z. & Szabó, P. 1996. Idioms: A view from cognitive semantics. *Applied Linguistics* 17(3): 326–355

Lakoff, G. 1987. *Women, Fire, and Dangerous Things: What Categories Reveal about the Mind*. Chicago IL: University of Chicago Press.

Lakoff, G. 1993. The contemporary theory of metaphor. In *Metaphor and Thought*, A. Ortony (ed.), 202–251. Cambridge: CUP.

Lakoff, G. & Johnson, M. 1980. *Metaphors We Live By*. Chicago IL: University of Chicago Press.

Lakoff, G. & Johnson, M. 1999. *Philosophy in the Flesh: The Embodied Mind and its Challenge to Western Thought*. New York NY: Basic Books.

Lakoff, G. & Turner, M. 1989. *More than Cool Reason: A Field Guide to Poetic Metaphor*. Chicago IL: University of Chicago Press.

Langacker, R.W. 1986. An introduction to cognitive grammar. *Cognitive Science* 10: 1–40.

Langacker, R.W. 1987. *Foundations of Cognitive Grammar*, I: *Theoretical Prerequisites*. Stanford CA: Stanford University Press.

Larsen-Freeman, D. 1997. Chaos/complexity science and second language acquisition. *Applied Linguistics* 18(2): 141–65.

Larsen-Freeman, D. & Cameron, L. 2008. *Complex Systems and Applied Linguistics*. Oxford: OUP.

Lindstromberg, S. & Boers, F. 2005. From movement to metaphor with manner-of-movement verbs. *Applied Linguistics* 26(2): 241–261.

Littlemore, J. 2001. Metaphoric competence: A language learning strength of students with a holistic cognitive style? *TESOL Quarterly* 35(3): 459–491.

Littlemore, J. 2003. The communicative effectiveness of different types of communication strategy. *System* 31: 331–347.

Littlemore, J. 2010. Metaphoric competence in the first and second language: Similarities and differences. In *Cognitive Processing in Second Language Acquisition*, M. Pütz & L. Sicola (eds), 293–315. Amsterdam: John Benjamins.

Littlemore, J. & Low, G.D. 2006a. *Figurative Thinking and Foreign Language Learning*. Basingstoke: Palgrave Macmillan.

Littlemore, J. & Low, G.D. 2006b. Metaphoric competence and communicative language ability. *Applied Linguistics* 27(2): 268–294

Low, G.D. 1988. On teaching metaphor. *Applied Linguistics* 9(2): 125–147.

MacArthur, F. 2005. The competent horseman in a horseless world: Observations on a conventional metaphor in Spanish and English. *Metaphor and Symbol* 20(1): 71–94.

MacArthur, F. & Littlemore, J. 2008. A discovery approach to figurative language learning with the use of corpora. In *Cognitive Linguistic Approaches to Teaching Vocabulary and Phraseology*, F. Boers & S. Lindstromberg (eds), 159–188. Berlin: Mouton de Gruyter.

MacArthur, F. & Littlemore, J. In preparation. Exploring the extended senses of English denominal verbs in corpus: A Classroom Study.

MacArthur, F. & Piquer-Piriz, A. 2007. Staging the introduction of figurative extensions of familiar vocabulary items in EFL: Some preliminary considerations. *Isla de Desterro: A Journal of English Language, Literatures in English and Cultural Studies* 53:123–134.

McCarthy, M. 2007. Assessing development of advanced proficiency through learner corpora. Position Paper. http://calper.la.psu.edu/downloads/pdfs/CALPER_ALP_Corpus.pdf.

Meara, P. 1996. The dimensions of lexical competence. In *Performance and Competence in Second Language Acquisition*, G. Brown, K. Malmkjaer & J. Williams (eds), 35–53. Cambridge: CUP.

Moon, R. 1998. *Fixed Expressions and Idioms in English: A Corpus-Based Approach*. Oxford: Clarendon Press.

Musolff, A. 2006. Metaphor scenarios in public discourse. *Metaphor and Symbol* 21(1): 23–38.

Ortony, A. (ed.). 1979/1993. *Metaphor and Thought*. Cambridge: CUP.

Paprotte, W. & Dirven, R. (eds). 1985. *The Ubiquity of Metaphor*. Amsterdam: John Benjamins.

Piquer-Piriz, A. 2008a. Reasoning figuratively in early EFL: Some implications for the development of vocabulary. In *Cognitive Linguistic Approaches to Teaching Vocabulary and Phraseology*, F. Boers & S. Lindstromberg (eds), 233–257. Berlin: Mouton de Gruyter.

Piquer-Piriz, A. 2008b. Young learners' understanding of figurative language. In *Confronting Metaphor in Use: An Applied Linguistic Approach*, M.S. Zanotto, L. Cameron & M.C. Cavalcanti (eds), 183–198. Amsterdam: John Benjamins.

Ponteretto, D. 1994. Metaphors we can learn by: How insights from cognitive linguistic research can improve the teaching/learning of figurative language. *English Teaching Forum* 32 (3). http://exchanges.state.gov/englishteaching/forum/archives/1994/94-32-3.html.

Queller, K. 2001. A usage-based approach to modelling and teaching the phrasal lexicon. In *Applied Cognitive Linguistics*, II: *Language Pedagogy*, M. Pütz, S. Niemeier & R. Dirven (eds), 55–83. Berlin: Mouton de Gruyter.

Reddy, M.J. 1979. The conduit metaphor: A case of frame conflict in our language about language. In *Metaphor and Thought*, A. Ortony (ed.), 284–324. Cambridge: CUP.

Robinson, P. 2001. Task complexity, task difficulty and task production: Exploring interactions in a compo-
nential framework. *Applied Linguistics* 22(1): 27–57.

Schön, D.A. 1993. Generative metaphor: A perspective on problem-setting in social policy. In *Metaphor and
Thought*, A. Ortony (ed.), 137–163. Cambridge: CUP.

Seidlhofer, B. 2009. Accommodation and the idiom principle in English as a Lingua Franca. *Intercultural
Pragmatics* 6 (2): 195–215.

Sinclair, J. 1991. *Corpus, Concordance, Collocation*. Oxford: OUP.

Steen, G.J, Dorst, A.G., Herrmann, B. & Kaal, A.A. 2010. *A Method for Linguistic Metaphor Identification:
From Mip to Mipvu*. Amsterdam: John Benjamins.

Talmy, L. 1978. The relation of cognition to grammar: A synopsis. In *TINLAP-2* [Theoretical Issues in Natural
Language Processing 2], D. Waltz (ed.), 14–24. New York NY: Association for Computing Machinery.

Taylor, J.R. 2003. Polysemy's paradoxes. *Language Sciences* 25: 637–55.

Tyler, A. 2008. Cognitive linguistics and second language instruction. In *Handbook of Cognitive Linguistics
and Second Language Acquisition*, P. Robinson & N.C. Ellis (eds), 456–488. London: Routledge.

Ungerer, F. 2001. Basicness and conceptual hierarchies in foreign language learning: A corpus-based study. In
*Applied Cognitive Linguistics*, II: *Language Pedagogy*, M. Pütz, S. Niemeier & R. Dirven (eds), 201–222.
Berlin: Mouton de Gruyter.

Verspoor, M. & Lowie, W. 2003. Making sense of polysemous words. *Language Learning* 53(3): 547–586.

Wray, A. 2002. *Formulaic Language and the Lexicon*. Cambridge: CUP.

Wray, A. & Fitzpatrick, T. 2008. Why can't you just leave it alone? Deviations from memorised language as a
gauge of native-like competence. In *Phraseology in Foreign Language Learning and Teaching*, F. Meunier
& S. Granger (eds), 123–48. Amsterdam: John Benjamins.

*Author's address*

Fiona MacArthur
Departamento de Filología Inglesa
Facultad de Filosofía y Letras
Universidad de Extremadura, 10071 Caceres, Spain

fionamac@unex.es

# Access to online full text

ingenta *connect*

John Benjamins Publishing Company's journals are available in online full-text format as of the volume published in 2000. Some of our journals have additional (multi-media) information available that is referred to in the articles.

Access to the electronic edition of a volume is included in your subscription. We offer a pay-per-view service per article for those journals and volumes to which you did not subscribe.

Full text is provided in PDF. In order to read these documents you will need Adobe Acrobat Reader, which is freely available from **www.adobe.com/products/acrobat/readstep2.html**

You can access the electronic edition through the gateways of major subscription agents (SwetsWise, EBSCO EJS, Maruzen) or directly through IngentaConnect.

If you currently use **www.ingenta.com** or **www.ingentaselect.com** (formely, Catchword) to access your subscriptions, these rights have been carried over to **www. ingentaconnect.com**, the new, fully merged service. All bookmarked pages will also be diverted to the relevant pages on **www.ingentaconnect.com**.

If you have not yet set up access to the electronic version of the journal at IngentaConnect, please follow these instructions:

*If you are a personal subscriber:*
- Register free at **www.ingentaconnect.com**. This is a one-time process, that provides IngentaConnect with the information they need to be able to match your data with the subscription data provide by the publisher. Your registration also allows you to use the e-mail alerting services.
- Select *Personal subscriptions.*
- Select the publication title and enter your subscription number. Your subscription number can be found on the shipping label with the print journal, and on the invoice/renewal invitation.
- You will be notified by email once your online access has been activated.

*If you are an institutional subscriber:*
- Register free at **www.ingentaconnect.com** by selecting the registration link and following the link to institutional registration.
- Select *Set up subscriptions.*
- Select the publication title and enter your subscription number. Your subscription number can be found on the shipping label with the print journal, and on the invoice/renewal invitation.
- You will be notified by email once your online access has been activated.
If you purchase subscriptions via a subscription agent they will be able to set up subscriptions on IngentaConnect on your behalf – simply pass them your IngentaConnect ID, sent to you at registration.

If you would like further information or assistance with your registration, please contact **help@ingentaconnect.com**.

For information on our journals, please visit **www.benjamins.com**

## Language Use and Language Learning in CLIL Classrooms

### Edited by Christiane Dalton-Puffer, Tarja Nikula and Ute Smit

University of Vienna / University of Jyväskylä / University of Vienna

This volume explores a highly topical issue in second and foreign language education: the spreading practice in mainstream education to teach content subjects through a foreign language. CLIL has been enthusiastically embraced as a language enrichment measure in many contexts and finally research can offer principled insights into its dynamics and potentials. The editors' introductory and concluding chapters offer a synthesis of current CLIL research as well as a critical discussion of unresolved issues relating both to theoretical concerns and research practice. The individual contributions by authors from a range of European contexts report on current empirical research in this dynamic field. The focus of these chapters ranges from theoretical to empirical, from learning outcomes to classroom talk, examining both the written and spoken mode across secondary and tertiary educational contexts. This volume is a valuable resource not only for researchers and teachers but also for policy makers.

[AILA Applied Linguistics Series, 7] 2010. x, 291 pp. + index
HB 978 90 272 0523 0 EUR 95.00 / USD 143.00

## English in Europe Today

### Sociocultural and educational perspectives

### Edited by Annick De Houwer and Antje Wilton

University of Erfurt

This volume discusses several facets of English in today's multilingual Europe. It emphasizes the interdependence between cultures, languages and situations that influence its use. This interdependence is particularly relevant to European settings where English is being learned as a second language. Such learning situations constitute the core focus of the book. The volume is unique in bringing together empirical studies examining factors that promote the learning of English in Europe. Rather than assuming that English is a threat to linguistic diversity and cultural independence, these studies discuss psycholinguistic factors such as the input, and sociolinguistic factors such as the type of English that is targeted in learning. The contributing authors are well-established specialists who have worked on multilingualism, English as a Lingua Franca and second language acquisition.

The book will be of interest to applied linguists, sociolinguists and teachers of English as a foreign language.

[AILA Applied Linguistics Series, 8] 2011. ix, 166 pp. + index
HB 978 90 272 0524 7 EUR 85.00 / USD 128.00

## For full title information see *www.benjamins.com*

## Speech Act Performance

Theoretical, empirical and methodological issues

### Edited by Alicia Martínez-Flor and Esther Usó-Juan

University Jaume I, Castelló

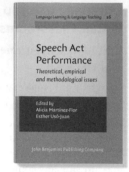

Speech acts are an important and integral part of day-to-day life in all languages. In language acquisition, the need to teach speech acts in a target language has been demonstrated in studies conducted in the field of interlanguage pragmatics which indicate that the performance of speech acts may differ considerably from culture to culture, thus creating communication difficulties in cross-cultural encounters. Considering these concerns, the aim of this volume is two-fold: to deal with those theoretical approaches that inform the process of learning speech acts in particular contextual and cultural settings; and, secondly, to present a variety of methodological proposals, grounded on research-based ideas, for the teaching of the major speech acts in second/foreign language classrooms. This volume is a valuable theoretical and practical resource not only for researchers, teachers and students interested in speech act learning/teaching but also for textbook writers wishing to have an informed opinion on the pedagogical implications derived from research on speech act performance.

[Language Learning & Language Teaching, 26]  2010.  xiv, 277 pp.

HB   978 90 272 1989 3  EUR 105.00  /  USD 158.00
PB   978 90 272 1990 9  EUR   36.00  /  USD   54.00

## Experimental Methods in Language Acquisition Research

### Edited by Elma Blom and Sharon Unsworth

University of Amsterdam / Utrecht University

*Experimental Methods in Language Acquisition Research* provides students and researchers interested in language acquisition with comprehensible and practical information on the most frequently used methods in language acquisition research. It includes contributions on first and child/adult second language learners, language-impaired children, and on the acquisition of both spoken and signed language. Part I discusses specific experimental methods, explaining the rationale behind each one, and providing an overview of potential participants, the procedure and data-analysis, as well as advantages and disadvantages and dos and don'ts. Part II focuses on comparisons across groups, addressing the theoretical, applied and methodological issues involved in such comparative work. This book will not only be of use to advanced undergraduate and postgraduate students, but also to any scholars wishing to learn more about a particular research method. It is suitable as a textbook in postgraduate programs in the fields of linguistics, education and psychology.

[Language Learning & Language Teaching, 27]  2010.  vii, 292 pp.

HB   978 90 272 1996 1  EUR 105.00  /  USD 158.00
PB   978 90 272 1997 8  EUR   36.00  /  USD   54.00

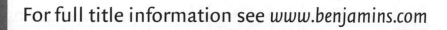

## For full title information see *www.benjamins.com*

# New in Applied Linguistics

## Appraising Research in Second Language Learning

A practical approach to critical analysis of quantitative research. **Second edition**

### Graeme Keith Porte

#### University of Granada

*Second edition*

Designed for students of applied linguistics and second language acquisition on research training courses, practising language teachers, and those in training, this combination textbook/workbook is a set or recommended textbook on more than a hundred undergraduate and postgraduate courses worldwide. Now in its **second edition**, it remains the only book to provide specific advice and support to those wishing to learn a methodical approach to the critical analysis of a research paper. It seeks to answer a current need in the literature for a set of procedures that can be applied to the independent reading of quantitative research. Innovative features of the workbook include awareness-raising reading tasks and guided exercises to help develop and practise the critical skills required to appraise papers independently. Through informed and constructive appraisal of others' work, readers themselves are shown how to become more research literate, to discover new areas for investigation, and to organise and present their own work more effectively for publication and peer evaluation. This revised second edition sees a closer integration of the text-and workbook and a number of additions to the text itself, as well as further guided and unguided research appraisal exercises.

[Language Learning & Language Teaching, 28]  2010.  xxv, 307 pp.

HB   978 90 272 1991 6  EUR 105.00  /  USD 158.00
PB   978 90 272 1995 4  EUR  33.00  /  USD  49.95

## A Dynamic Approach to Second Language Development

Methods and techniques

### Edited by Marjolijn H. Verspoor, Kees de Bot and Wander Lowie

#### University of Groningen

Dynamic systems theory, a general theory of change and development, offers a new way to study first and second language development and requires a new set of tools for analysis of empirical data. After a brief introduction to the theory, this book, co-authored by several leading scholars in the field, concentrates on tools and techniques recently developed to analyze language data from a dynamic perspective. The chapters deal with the general thoughts and reasoning behind coding data, analyzing variability, discovering interacting variables and modeling. The accompanying *How to* sections give step-by-step instructions to using macros to speed up the coding, creating a dedicated lexical profile, making min-max graphs, testing for significance in single case studies by running simulations, and modeling. Example files and data sets are available on the accompanying website. Although the focus is on second language development, the tools are applicable to a wide range of phenomena in applied linguistics.

[Language Learning & Language Teaching, 29]  2011.  vii, 207 pp. + index

HB   978 90 272 1998 5  EUR 95.00  /  USD 143.00
PB   978 90 272 1999 2  EUR 33.00  /  USD  49.95

For full title information see *www.benjamins.com*

# New in Applied Linguistics

## Poetry as Research

Exploring second language poetry writing

**David Ian Hanauer**

**Indiana University of Pennsylvania**

*Poetry as Research* develops an approach that allows poetry writing to be used as a research method for exploring questions relating to second language learners and more broadly for studies within the humanities and social sciences. The book investigates the characteristics of poetry writing and situates poetry writing as a qualitative, arts-based, research process. The book utilizes computational linguistics, qualitative, bibliographic, and philosophical methods and investigates the process of writing poetry, the textual and literary characteristics of second language poetry, poetic identity and inquiry. The developed methodology is exemplified through a poetic inquiry of the study abroad experiences of ESL students. The book provides a comprehensive, informed and innovative approach to the investigation of understandings of personal experience. This book should be of interest to the fields of applied linguistics, stylistics, literary studies, creative writing and composition as well as anyone interested in using writing as a research method.

[**Linguistic Approaches to Literature, 9**]  2010.  xiii, 164 pp.

HB   978 90 272 3341 7  EUR 99.00 / USD 149.00
PB   978 90 272 3342 4  EUR 33.00 / USD   49.95

## Society and Language Use

**Edited by Jürgen Jaspers, Jan-Ola Östman and Jef Verschueren**

**University of Antwerp / University of Helsinki**

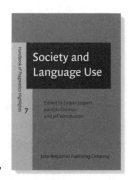

The ten volumes of *Handbook of Pragmatics Highlights* focus on the most salient topics in the field of pragmatics, thus dividing its wide interdisciplinary spectrum in a transparent and manageable way. While the other volumes select specific philosophical, cognitive, grammatical, cultural, variational, interactional, or discursive angles, this seventh volume underlines the mutually constitutive relation between society and language use. It highlights a number of the most prominent approaches of this relation and it draws attention to a selected number of topics that the study of language in its social context has characteristically brought to bear. Despite their theoretical and methodological differences, each of the chapters in this book assumes that it is necessary to look at society and language use as interdependent phenomena, and that by attending to microscopic linguistic phenomena one is also keeping a finger on the pulse of broader, macroscopic social tendencies that at the same time facilitate and constrain language use. The introduction provides a sketch of the intellectual antecedents of the volume's two 'mother disciplines', viz., linguistics and social theory before pointing at recent common ground in the rising attention for discourse and what has come to be called 'late-modernity'.

[**Handbook of Pragmatics Highlights, 7**]  2010.  xiii, 324 pp.
PB   978 90 272 0784 5  EUR 39.00 / USD 59.00

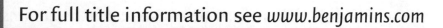

## For full title information see *www.benjamins.com*